PRAISE FOR *GOD IS GOOD*

"At the heart of the challenge of the new atheists to attack on the very character of God. In this brilliant, written book, Martin Kuhrt does a spectacular job responding to many of their common accusations. Biblically grounded, well argued, meticulously detailed, generous to his opponents, and very accessible—*God is Good* is the ideal book for Christians seeking for help responding to atheist friends, or for skeptics willing to take the trouble to discover what Christians actually believe. A timely, important book."

—Andy Bannister, Director, Solas Centre for Public Christianity

"Richard Dawkins and his followers spew out adjectives in an attempt to discredit the God made known to us in the Bible. By contrast, Martin Kuhrt here shows that when the Bible is read carefully and with attentiveness to its real content, it shows us a God who is good and worthy of worship. This is indeed good news."

—David Firth, Tutor in Old Testament, Academic Dean, Trinity College Bristol

"In their attacks on Christianity and the Bible, Richard Dawkins and his friends think they have served up a bunch of unreturnable 'aces'. But Martin Kuhrt returns them all. He is gritty, passionate, argumentative, and very readable in this book. He combines his understanding of the new atheists with his massive Bible knowledge and peppers the whole book with lots of illustrations and personal stories. If you are struggling with these issues this is a great book to read."

—Robin Gamble, Bishops' Adviser for Church Growth, Diocese of Leeds

"Martin Kuhrt has given us an outstanding resource in answering many of the genuine and difficult questions leveled at the Christian faith. This is a brilliant, pastoral, accessible, biblical, and ultimately compelling apologetic for the God who is good."

—Simon Ponsonby, Teaching Pastor, St Aldates Oxford

"This well-written and carefully researched book is a detailed, informative, and comprehensive response to the biblical criticism of the new atheists. Martin goes out of his way to help us read and understand these ancient accounts, not shying away at all from the difficult issues often raised about the Old Testament. The reader comes away with a fuller, richer, more rounded understanding of these Scriptures, better equipped to understand the wisdom, justice, and mercy of God. A book not only for reading, but for referencing when needing insight into complex biblical passages."

—DAVE HOPWOOD, author, speaker, and biblical dramatist

"Martin Kuhrt gives Christians a biblical defense to an aggressive atheistic challenge! An encouraging and positive exposition of what our God is really like. Pastors could use this material in a preaching series and all of us would benefit from a careful reading of this book."

—STEPHEN GAUKROGER, international Bible teacher, entrepreneur, and author

"I commend this book to Christians who want to face up to the undoubted challenges in the Bible about the nature of God. I hope Richard Dawkins and Dan Barker will read it too!"

—DON BREWIN, former Director of SOMA (Sharing of Ministries Abroad)

"As the leader of Flame International, which ministers God's healing to the spirits, souls, and bodies of the poorest of people made in his image, I read this book with wonder. Martin has written with an insight and revelation into biblical truth from both the Old and New Testaments that I have not come across before. I have personally been challenged and given fresh understanding of the nature of God. May I commend this book to readers who want new insights into the character of the God of the Bible. The chapter on forgiveness, for example, is truly inspiring, and I believe that as people apply what they read this book will be life changing."

—JAN RANSOM, Director of Flame International

God is Good

God is Good

Exploring the Character of the Biblical God

MARTIN G. KUHRT

foreword by Alex Jacob

RESOURCE *Publications* • Eugene, Oregon

GOD IS GOOD
Exploring the Character of the Biblical God

Copyright © 2020 Martin G. Kuhrt. All rights reserved. Except for brief quotations in critical publications or reviews, no part of this book may be reproduced in any manner without prior written permission from the publisher. Write: Permissions, Wipf and Stock Publishers, 199 W. 8th Ave., Suite 3, Eugene, OR 97401.

Unless otherwise stated, all biblical quotations are taken from the New International Version (NIV)

Resource Publications
An Imprint of Wipf and Stock Publishers
199 W. 8th Ave., Suite 3
Eugene, OR 97401

www.wipfandstock.com

PAPERBACK ISBN: 978-1-7252-6394-9
HARDCOVER ISBN: 978-1-7252-6395-6
EBOOK ISBN: 978-1-7252-6396-3

Manufactured in the U.S.A.   07/13/20

*For my older sons Ben and Harry, who study philosophy and ethics
and who think about these things, and
for Olly and Elsie, my younger two children, who are very special*

Contents

Foreword by Alex Jacob		xi
Preface		xiii
Acknowledgments		xvii
Introduction		1
Chapter 1	Jealous—and proud of it?	25
Chapter 2	Petty?	31
Chapter 3	Unjust?	41
Chapter 4	Unforgiving?	54
Chapter 5	Control Freak?	61
Chapter 6	Vindictive?	66
Chapter 7	Bloodthirsty?	70
Chapter 8	Ethnic Cleanser?	78
Chapter 9	Misogynistic?	88
Chapter 10	Homophobic?	112
Chapter 11	Racist?	137
Chapter 12	Infanticidal?	155
Chapter 13	Genocidal?	168
Chapter 14	Filicidal?	177
Chapter 15	Pestilential?	186
Chapter 16	Megalomaniacal?	194
Chapter 17	Sadomasochistic?	197
Chapter 18	Capriciously Malevolent?	201
Chapter 19	Bully?	210

Chapter 20	Pyromaniacal?	215
Chapter 21	Angry?	219
Chapter 22	Merciless?	226
Chapter 23	Curse Hurling?	229
Chapter 24	Vaccicidal?	231
Chapter 25	Aborticidal?	234
Chapter 26	Cannibalistic?	237
Chapter 27	Slavemonger?	239
Chapter 28	Jesus and the Cross	248
Chapter 29	The Integrity and Authority of Scripture	262
Chapter 30	A Final Word	278
Bibliography		283

Foreword

This book is a fine piece of Christian apologetics and is also a timely response to the atheistic agenda promoted by Richard Dawkins, Dan Barker and others.

Martin Kuhrt draws upon his deep understanding of Scripture, his pastoral gifts and his cultural insights to engage systematically with each of the nineteen "character slurs" Dawkins hurls at his perception of "God," plus eight additional slurs presented by the "Dawkins disciple," Barker.

Martin avoids the pitfalls of a selective biblical hermeneutic and deals with the whole biblical witness and strongly confirms the continuity of the Old and New Testament. He also is clearly focused upon the core Gospel realities of the atoning sacrifice of Jesus, his glorious resurrection (and ascension) and his promised return.

As I progressed through each of the chapters my appreciation for Martin's forensic approach grew, as time and time again he brings insightful analysis which helps the reader to refocus on the true revelation of God in Scripture.

I warmly commend this book and I hope it is read, discussed and studied widely. I am sure many will find this book a helpful resource in their own search for truth and understanding. I think the clear chapter layouts will mean that the book could well provide a good structure for a group study program.

This is not always a comfortable read but how can it be when one is brought face to face with subjects such as genocide, filicide, sadomasochism, and ethnic cleansing? (to name just four!) This is also not a comfortable read because above all the God Martin serves and loves is not a comfortable God, but he is good.

Rev Alex Jacob M.A, M.Phil
CEO The Church's Ministry among Jewish People (UK)

Preface

I sat listening to the radio broadcast, eyes welling up. Nadim Adnan-Laperouse, the father of a beautiful fifteen-year-old girl called Natasha, was being interviewed. He was talking about how she suffered a severe allergic reaction to the sesame seeds in a *Pret a Manger* sandwich on a holiday flight to France. Despite the frantic efforts of paramedics to save her, she died before his eyes. As a father of a precious daughter myself, I imagined the agony he went through. Nadim had never given God much thought before. A successful businessman, he felt no need to, even though his daughter had been attending church for a year before her death and had told him she wanted to be baptized. But now he was angry—angry with God.

This book is an argument for the goodness of the God revealed in the pages of the Christian Bible. The "New Atheists" are saying that the God of the Bible is not good, because of some of the things in the Bible that make it appear to them that he is not. There are very real problems regarding the goodness of God for Christian believers to wrestle with in Scripture. However, these, I believe, are no more difficult, and are probably *less* difficult, than the problem of reconciling belief in an all-powerful, all-good God with the suffering there is in the world we live in.

As an ordained Christian minister, I think of some deeply sad pastoral situations, where it seems that God has allowed something to happen that is cruel and pointless. In my local park where I walk our dogs I often go past the spot where I led prayers at a large gathering of people mourning the death of a teenage boy as a result of an accidental collision in a football match. I remember taking the funeral of a toddler whose little coffin was brought to church in a fire engine truck because he loved *Fireman Sam*. Another funeral I conducted was for a young, married woman killed in a random knife attack while out on a walk. A Christian believer, I spoke on the phone to her one morning and in the afternoon she was dead. On a wider plane there are cyclones, floods, earthquakes, pandemics, famines, wars, ethnic cleansing and genocide. How can an all-loving, good, omnipotent God permit these things?

In this book I am not going to attempt to tackle the overall problem of suffering in this world, but I do intend to reply to the angry accusations against the biblical God which some have made in recent years. I do believe there are some answers to these accusations, but these answers are not such as to remove the need for persistent faith while "we see through a glass darkly."[1]

Natasha's father went through an excruciating experience. In his grief there were no easy answers to help him feel better. But the remarkable thing is that he has gone from being disinterested in God to having a newfound faith in Jesus Christ as the Son of God, having seen angels attend to his daughter when she died. This is one of the good things he says God brought out of her tragic death. Another is that after a campaign led by the family, a regulation named "Natasha's Law" has been brought in to compel food manufacturers to clearly label pre-packaged food with its full list of ingredients so people with life-threatening allergies, or their parents, can know whether or not something is safe for them to eat.

It is my hope that this book will help those finding it hard to believe that the character of the God revealed in the Bible is consistently good and that the difficult passages will eventually be seen as part of an authentic testimony to the God who the Bible says is love, just as Nadim Adnan-Laperouse testifies that despite everything, "God is good."

The problems people have in squaring the goodness of God with events in the world today tend to be expressed in the question "why does God *allow* these things to happen?" By contrast, the problems people have with the Bible tend to be framed by the question "how can a God of love *do this* or *command that*?"

This book is an attempt to use reason to show that the God revealed in Scripture is good in a way that we can recognize, and whose every action and command is consistent with his essential nature, which is love.

I sympathize with those who read parts of the Bible and struggle to reconcile what they read with the God of love they have heard spoken of. In the New Testament, for example, Jesus warned of the reality of hell[2], and said that we cannot be his disciple unless we "hate" our nearest and dearest.[3]

---

1. First Corinthians 13:12 *KJV*

2. See just some of the many references, e.g. Matthew 10:28, 25:46; Mark 9:47–48; Luke 16:19–31

3. Luke 14:26

The apostle Paul warns of God's wrath.[4] The apostle Peter warns of a day of destruction and judgment.[5] The last book, Revelation, pictures Christ as a warrior on a white horse, dressed in a robe dipped in blood, wielding a sharp sword with which to strike down the nations and who "treads the winepress of the fury of the wrath of God Almighty."[6]

For others, and they are primarily who this book is written for, it will be the Old Testament which presents the most difficulty. In the Flood, God destroys the earth and all its human inhabitants save Noah and his family. God tests Abraham to the limit, even asking him to sacrifice his son Isaac. He allows the righteous man Job to suffer terribly through no fault of his own. There is not only war in the Bible, but God-sent war. He orders the Israelites to invade Canaan and drive out the people living there, becoming implicated in violence and slaughter. Assyria, one of the cruelest nations in history, is called the rod of God's anger. He commands the death penalty for Israelites who commit certain offences and directly strikes some down dead himself. People are devastated by plague and famine.

I decided that, in writing this book, I would face all the difficult issues and not duck any of them. It will be my argument that, despite these difficulties, God's actions and commands in the Old Testament, once seen and understood accurately for what they were in a different stage of salvation history, consistently testify to the truth that God *is* good. I have chosen to structure this book around the accusations leveled against the biblical God by Dan Barker in his book *God: The Most Unpleasant Character in all Fiction*. This is because, as far as I'm aware, this book is the most comprehensive and vitriolic attack on the God of the Bible, citing much chapter and verse (mainly from the Old Testament) in evidence, and I want to deal with the full range of moral problems people might conceivably have with the God presented in it.

I hope any failings in this book will not deter anyone from finding the true goodness of God in the faith revealed in the Holy Scriptures which are able to make us wise for salvation through Jesus Christ.[7]

4. Romans 2:5
5. Second Peter 3:7
6. Revelation 19:11–16
7. Second Timothy 3:15

Acknowledgments

I would like to thank the following people:

My father Gordon, and my two brothers Stephen and Jon, for their interest, and helpful feedback, even though we don't necessarily agree on everything! I'm particularly grateful to Dad for all his advice and his proofreading.

Alex Jacob, Jan Ransom, David French, John Watt, Sally Waugh, Dave Hopwood, Simon Ponsonby and Andrew McCausland who have been very helpful and encouraging.

Steve Burnhope, fellow minister in the Aylesbury Church Network, and Vineyard scholar, for stimulating theological discussion over lunches.

The Church of the Holy Spirit, Bedgrove, to whom it is a privilege to serve as their vicar.

Finally, my loving and patient wife Anna, to whom I underestimated the amount of time I'd take on this and who manages our home of four children, three golden retrievers, occasional puppy litters, and two guinea pigs with such skill and joy.

Introduction

THE MOST UNPLEASANT CHARACTER IN ALL FICTION?

In 2006 the first edition of Richard Dawkins's *The God Delusion* was published and in the following ten years some three million copies were sold. The book contains many lines of attack against monotheistic faith. Christian writers have defended their beliefs against the broad range of his arguments.[1] This book is mainly an attempt to tackle just one paragraph, albeit an infamous one. Dawkins wrote,

> "The God of the Old Testament is arguably the most unpleasant character in all fiction: jealous and proud of it; a petty, unjust, unforgiving control-freak; a vindictive, bloodthirsty ethnic cleanser; a misogynistic, homophobic, racist, infanticidal, genocidal, filicidal, pestilential, megalomaniacal, sadomasochistic, capriciously malevolent bully."[2]

These words inspired American preacher–turned–atheist Dan Barker to write a book seeking to justify every one of these accusations—a chapter for each one. There are nineteen in all plus another eight he has thought up himself and added for good measure. Dawkins was too kind, he says. God is also a

> ". . . pyromaniacal, angry, merciless, curse hurling, vaccicidal, aborticidal, cannibalistic slavemonger.[3]

---

1. See for example McGrath & McGrath, *The Dawkins Delusion*; Wilson, *Deluded By Dawkins*
2. Dawkins, *The God Delusion*, 51
3. Barker, *God: The Most Unpleasant Character in all Fiction*

1

Daniel Dennett, another book-writing atheist, in his afterword to the tenth anniversary edition of *The God Delusion*, referring to the criticism the Dawkins paragraph provoked, concedes that it is indeed a startling one, but says,

> "aside from deploring it, who has the temerity to go through it, point by point and dispute it? As Dawkins notes, Dan Barker has published a rollicking case for the prosecution, *God: The Most Unpleasant Character in all Fiction*, citing chapter and verse for each feature. The ball is in the critics' court but I don't expect to see a return of service."[4]

Well this book *is* a return of service. In each chapter I will respond to one of the now twenty-seven charges. The final three chapters specifically address the Jesus of the Gospels and his attitude to the Hebrew Scriptures (what Christians call the Old Testament), the general question of biblical authority and a final word on the character of God as revealed by the Old Testament.

First, I would like to make two general points. Dawkins and Barker are entitled to their opinion that the Bible is a work of fiction. However, they should at least then treat the biblical books as having literary integrity within themselves, as they would with works of fiction generally. If they did this, it would challenge some of the aspersions they cast on the character of the biblical God. So, for example, the God who tells Abraham to offer his son Isaac as a sacrifice is portrayed in the narrative of Genesis as the God who created all life and who promised Abraham that his millions of descendants would trace their line from Isaac. Isaac was the miracle child born to Sarah in her barren old age that God promised him a year earlier. So Abraham, as the writer of the New Testament book of Hebrews comments, reasoned (on the basis of God being faithful in the past and all powerful and good enough to keep his promises in the future) that God would raise Isaac to life again to fulfil what he said he would do. Thus Abraham figured God was not asking him to do anything that as an omnipotent deity he could not undo, and wanted him to simply trust in his goodness and power. (See chapter fourteen for all the problems associated with this story and the accusation that the biblical God is filicidal.)

Also, the God who commands Moses to execute a man for desecrating the Sabbath is, in the Exodus narrative, the same God who has just demonstrated his miraculous mighty power in saving the Israelites from slavery by sending supernaturally awesome plagues on the Egyptians. He had parted the Red Sea to allow them to escape from Pharaoh's chariot army, and he

---

4. Dawkins, *The God Delusion*, 424

had told the Israelites clearly that their obedience to the covenant he made with them was vital for their ongoing survival as a nation during their desert journey. (See chapter two for an exploration of the gravity of the offence of desecrating the Sabbath.)

Secondly however, the Bible is mostly not written in the style of literary fiction. Apart from some stories, the historicity of which is debated, and parables, which are short, earthly tales loaded with spiritual meaning, the Bible comprises material that purports to belong somewhere among a range of non-fiction literary genres. Historical narratives, social commentary, genealogies, inventories, songs of worship, detailed specifications for the tabernacle, laws, philosophy and poetry, prophetic oracles, apocalyptic literature, ethical exhortation, and pastoral guidance make up the vast majority of the sixty-six books.

Therefore, the picture of God which the Bible paints should be viewed differently from one created by authors who are deliberately using a fictional genre. The biblical writers explicitly claim that the God they are speaking of is not a mythical projection of human culture and values (as are the gods depicted in, for example, Babylonian and Greco-Roman literature) but the one, real, transcendent, unfathomable God who nevertheless deigns to act in human history and who remarkably calls us to respond to his revealed truth in a way that works with him in transforming the course of that history.

THE INFLUENCE OF THE BIBLE IN SHAPING OUR WORLD

The biblical God relates to the world *as it is*, not as we would like it to be, with its beauty and goodness tarnished by cruelty, injustice, pain, and misery. He is also, however, the God who *changes* things. The Bible has shaped our Western culture for so long that it is easy to fail to appreciate how different things would have been without it. It is from the Bible that we have come to believe that we can know truth, as a concept, and that the created order is rational, the product of the Word (the *Logos* of John's Gospel chapter one). Though marred by sin it still conforms to laws established by its creator and can be scientifically explored with both reason and a sense of awe and wonder. In pagan religion the world emerged from the violence, insecurity and deceit of competing gods.[5] In that worldview the priority of man was

---

5. E.g., the Babylonian creation myth, from the *Enuma Elish*...
In the beginning, there was only undifferentiated water swirling in chaos. Out of this swirl, the waters divided into sweet, fresh water, known as the god Apsu, and salty bitter water, the goddess Tiamat. Once differentiated, the union of these two entities gave

the need to appease malevolent gods or spirits, rather than rational thinking based on belief in one Almighty God, the source of all truth. Within Eastern religions, having a basis in pantheism, which denies that God is a being distinct from the universe, scientific thought fared little better. So, for example, Indian sages thought that spiritual enlightenment could be achieved getting in touch with primeval silence, senseless sound (mantra), cosmic energy and impersonal consciousness. The development of science and scholarship was therefore stunted as compared with Western culture, shaped by the Bible, because like other cultures not influenced by the Bible, Indian culture did not inspire or encourage the pursuit of rational knowledge.[6]

The Bible tells us all human beings are made in God's image and have intrinsic worth. God came in the flesh and thereby honored the lowliest of human beings. Jesus taught that whatever we do for the least of his brothers we do for him. Pagan religion didn't teach that. So it was the Bible's revelation which inspired philanthropy and care of the vulnerable.[7] The Bible

---

birth to the younger gods. These young gods, however, were extremely loud, troubling the sleep of Apsu at night and distracting him from his work by day. Upon the advice of his Vizier, Mummu, Apsu decides to kill the younger gods. Tiamat, hearing of their plan, warns her eldest son, Enki (sometimes Ea) and he puts Apsu to sleep and kills him. From Apsu's remains, Enki creates his home. Tiamat, once the supporter of the younger gods, now is enraged that they have killed her mate. She consults with the god Quingu, who advises her to make war on the younger gods. Tiamat rewards Quingu with the Tablets of Destiny, which legitimize the rule of a god and control the fates, and he wears them proudly as a breastplate. With Quingu as her champion, Tiamat summons the forces of chaos and creates eleven horrible monsters to destroy her children. Ea, Enki, and the younger gods fight against Tiamat futilely until, from among them, emerges the champion Marduk who swears he will defeat Tiamat. Marduk defeats Quingu and kills Tiamat by shooting her with an arrow which splits her in two; from her eyes flow the waters of the Tigris and Euphrates Rivers. Out of Tiamat's corpse, Marduk creates the heavens and the earth, he appoints gods to various duties and binds Tiamat's eleven creatures to his feet as trophies (to much adulation from the other gods) before setting their images in his new home. He also takes the Tablets of Destiny from Quingu, thus legitimizing his reign. After the gods have finished praising him for his great victory and the art of his creation, Marduk consults with the god Ea (the god of wisdom) and decides to create human beings from the remains of whichever of the gods instigated Tiamat to war. Quingu is charged as guilty and killed and, from his blood, Ea creates Lullu, the first man, to be a helper to the gods in their eternal task of maintaining order and keeping chaos at bay.

https://www.ancient.eu/article/225/enuma-elish—the-babylonian-epic-of-creation—fu/

Incredibly, some people claim that this myth was the inspiration for the Hebrew book of Genesis. While both speak of the bringing of some sort of "order" out of chaos, Genesis is infinitely superior in revealing the goodness, glory, and majesty of the one true God.

6. Mangalwadi, *The Book That Made Your World*, chapter six

7. Consider just some of the people in the UK inspired by a love for the biblical

teaches that all people have the potential to be used by God. Therefore biblical cultures became democratic cultures. The Bible reveals that history is linear. There was a beginning and there will be an end to this age and we are not consigned to a weary cycle of existence where our hope is only that one day we will be set free from the illusion of individual consciousness, as Hinduism and Buddhism teach. It was the Bible that inspired a vision of freedom, away from slavery and towards the Promised Land. If the speeches of Martin Luther King had been devoid of their biblical allusions, they would not have had the power they did to shape history.

The Bible has been the single most influential collection of literature in the history of the Western world, providing the philosophical underpinning for the advanced development of loving family life, community justice, human rights and respect for others, education and medical care for all, commerce and industry, banking and finance, welfare provision and political

---

God who have been influential in the area of social philanthropy at home and abroad:
  Social renewal and reform of public morals—John Wesley, George Whitefield
  Abolition of the slave trade—William Wilberforce and "The Clapham Sect"
  Prevention of exploitation of children, education, limits on working hours, mental health reform, suppression of opium trade—Anthony Ashley Cooper 7th Earl of Shaftesbury
  Care for orphans—George Muller and Dr Barnado
  Prison reform—Elizabeth Fry
  Nursing reform—Florence Nightingale
  Women's rights—Josephine Butler
  General charitable work—William & Catherine Booth (founders of *The Salvation Army*)
  Fighting infanticide and human sacrifice in West Africa—Mary Slessor
  Eradicating footbinding in China—Gladys Aylward
  Temperance and affordable holidays—Thomas Cook
  Care of the dying—Dame Cicely Saunders (founder of the modern hospice movement)
  Relief of homelessness—Rev'd. Kenneth Leech (founder of *Centrepoint*), Rev'd. Donald Soper (first chairman of *Shelter*)
  Rehabilitation from drug addiction in Hong Kong—Jackie Pullinger
  Fair trade—Richard Adams (founder of *Traidcraft* and *Tearcraft*)
  Care for those with HIV/AIDS—Dr. Patrick Dixon *(founder of Aids Care Education and Training* (ACET))
  Debt relief and budgeting advice—John Kirkby (founder of *Christians Against Poverty*)
  Care of people in town centers—Rev Les Isaac (founder of *Street Pastors*)
  Foodbanks—Carol and Paddy Henderson (founders of *The Trussell Trust*)
  Promotion of adoption and fostering—Dr Krish Kandiah (founder of *Home for Good*)
  Bringing of hope to crime-ridden urban communities—Debra Green OBE (founder of *Redeeming Our Communities*)
  Alongside these high-profile people there are innumerable others consciously inspired by the Bible who are or have been a blessing to society in the UK and beyond

emancipation, and the constructive use of time. Vishal Mangalwadi, the Indian intellectual, in *The Book That Made Your World; How the Bible Created The Soul of Western Civilization*, brilliantly outlines the Bible's impact over the years, enabling the nations most influenced by the Reformation (which promoted biblical literacy) to surge ahead in all these fields. Now, with Western intellectuals busier than ever in sawing off the branch we have all been sitting on for the last five hundred years, the decadent, postmodern West can only offer a forlorn echo of Pontius Pilate's words "What is Truth?"[8]

In *The Closing of the American Mind*, Alan Bloom wrote,

> "In the United States, practically speaking, the Bible was the only common culture, one that united the simple and the sophisticated, rich and poor, young and old and—as the very model for a vision of the whole of things, as well as the key to the rest of Western art, the greatest works of which were in some way responsive to the Bible—provided access to the seriousness of books... the very idea of such a total book is disappearing. And fathers and mothers have lost the idea that the highest aspiration they might have for their children is for them to be wise—as priests, prophets or philosophers are wise. Specialized competence and success are all they can imagine. Contrary to what is commonly thought, without the book even the idea of the whole is lost."[9]

Professor Jürgen Habermas, despite being an atheist, says this about the influence of the biblical worldview in the West.

> "Christianity has functioned for the normative self-understanding as more than a mere precursor or a catalyst. Egalitarian universalism, from which sprang the ideas of freedom and a social solidarity, of an autonomous conduct of life and emancipation, of the individual morality of conscience, human rights, and democracy, is the direct heir to the Judaic ethic of justice and the Christian ethic of love. The legacy, substantially unchanged, has been the object of continual critical appropriation and reinterpretation. To this day there is no alternative to it. And in the light of current challenges of the post-national constellation, we continue to draw on the substance of this heritage. Everything else is just idle postmodern talk."[10]

8. John 18:38

9. Mangalwadi, *The Book That Made Your World*, Quoted by J Stanley Mattson in his foreword, p xiv

10. Jürgen Habermas *Time of Transitions* (ed. and trans. Ciaran Cronin and Max

Paul Copan and Matthew Flannagan cite the research of Robert Woodberry, political scientist at the National University of Singapore, which shows how "conversionary Protestant Christians" (missionaries), preaching the Bible, produced remarkable gains in non-Western settings including "the development and spread of religious liberty, mass education, mass printing, volunteer organizations, most major colonial reforms (abolishing slavery, widow-burning, female circumcision, pre-pubescent marriage of girls, etc.), and the codification of legal protections for non-whites in the nineteenth and early twentieth centuries."[11]

> "Protestant missionaries have been the driving force behind literacy (so people could read God's word) and democracy (the result of educating all rather than just the social elites). Woodberry urges us to look at any map. Wherever Protestant missionaries established themselves, there you will find more printed books and schools per capita. And you will discover that in Africa, the Middle East and parts of Asia, most of the early nationalists who led their countries to independence graduated from Protestant mission schools. . .[These areas] . . .are on average more economically developed today, with comparatively better health, lower infant mortality, lower corruption, greater literacy, higher educational attainment (especially for women), and more robust membership in nongovernmental associations."[12]

Some attribute the emergence of democracy to the Enlightenment rediscovery of Greek ideas. However Greek "democracy" was very elitist. For example, as Copan and Flannagan point out, Plato's *Republic* emphasizes the rule of philosopher-kings; ordinary citizens are not capable of ruling. Breeding should be controlled to produce intelligent offspring. Aristotle believed that the perfect generative act would always produce male offspring (placing women in the category of genetically botched males) and that some human beings were slaves by nature. Both he and Plato considered manual labor to be undignified. Even though the writings of the Greek thinkers

---

Pensky) Cambridge: Polity, 2006, 150–1

11. Robert D. Woodberry, *The Missionary Roots of Liberal Democracy*, American Political Science Review 106, no. 2 (2012): 244–5

12. Andrea Palpant Dilley, *The Surprising Discovery about Those Colonialist, Proselytizing Missionaries,* Christianity Today, (Jan/Feb 2014), 41. An example of the benefits of Protestant missionary education is provided by the globally renowned Christian statesman and post-apartheid peacemaker Nelson Mandela. Having illiterate parents, he was a product of a Methodist mission school.

were widely read and studied in the Muslim world, these works did not bring about democratizing effects.[13]

Furthermore, the key democratic theorists of the Enlightenment were themselves shaped by the Protestant Reformation, emphasizing the reading of Scripture by laity and the consequent education and empowerment of ordinary people. The failure of the West to appreciate the Christian (and particularly Protestant Christian) roots of its democracy has led to foreign policy catastrophes. America and Britain have imposed economic sanctions, encouraged uprisings, invaded countries, and toppled dictators with the pious sounding aspiration of then facilitating freely elected governments to promote peace and justice in their nations and the wider world. But the things essential to true democracy — the shared values of everyone being subject to law; checks and balances to prevent people and institutions having too much power; religious toleration; a free press; human rights; respect for minorities, and even the concept of "secularism," have emerged over centuries from seeds planted in the soil of biblical Christianity. Hopes that you can export Western style democracy into nations dominated by Islam, for example, by simply removing distasteful regimes and holding one-off elections have proved to be wildly unrealistic.

Given that even atheists and agnostics acknowledge the Bible has had such a widespread and positive effect in the development of the West and places influenced by Western missionaries, you might have thought Dawkins would give it more respect than he does. Even Dawkins's hero Charles Darwin financially supported the Protestant Bible-based efforts of the South American Missionary Society from 1867 until his death in 1882. His annual donation was in recognition of the Society's work in transforming the lives of the Fuegian Indians, the collective name for the tribes of Tierra del Fuego.

Darwin had been shocked by the appearance, language ("scarcely deserves to be called articulate") and customs of the Fuegians, dismissing them in *A Naturalist's Voyage* in these words: "I believe in this extreme part of South America man exists in a lower state of improvement than in any other part of the world."

However, the vision of Allen Gardiner and the dedicated ministry of Bishop Waite Stirling, Thomas Bridges, and other pioneers, led to a Christian church among the Fuegians, together with schools and training in farming and useful arts. Bridges compiled a thirty-two thousand-entry dictionary of Yahgan, the main language, and was a correspondent of Darwin's.

---

13. Copan and Flannagan, *Did God Really Command Genocide?* 268–271

Sir James Sulivan, a vice-president of SAMS, was a long-time friend of the naturalist and had sailed with him as second lieutenant on the famous voyage of The Beagle. He later recalled: "Mr Darwin had often expressed to me his conviction that it was utterly useless to send missionaries to such a set of savages as the Fuegians, probably the very lowest of the human race. I had always replied that I did not believe any human beings existed too low to comprehend the simple message of the Gospel of Christ. After many years he wrote to me that recent accounts of the Mission proved to him that he had been wrong and I right in our estimates of the native character and the possibility of doing them good through missionaries." (*Life and Letters of Charles Darwin, 1887*.)

In 1870 Darwin had written to Sulivan: "The success of the Tierra del Fuego Mission is most wonderful, and charms (or shames) me, as I had always prophesied utter failure. It is a grand success. I shall feel proud if your Committee think fit to elect me an honorary member of your society."[14]

Dawkins seems to give respect to other cultural features of Christianity, such as beautiful music and architecture. Historian Tom Holland in his recent book *Dominion* argues that the heritage which shapes who we are today is "irredeemably Christian"[sic]! He points out that Dawkins's enjoyment of the sound of cathedral bells, which he favorably contrasts with the "aggressive sounding Muslim call to prayer 'Allahu Akhbar'" does not emerge by magic. Dawkins, celebrated all over the world for his anti-religious polemic "absolutely has the instincts of someone brought up in a Christian civilization."[15]

The question "what has Christianity ever done for us?" is answered by Alvin Schmidt in his book *How Christianity Changed the World*.[16] He shows that in every area, be it law, government, economics, the fine arts, science, education or health care, the Christian faith has contributed enormously to the overall well-being of mankind.

As regards health, the Greeks and Romans cared little for the sick and the dying. But the early Christians, following Jesus' example, ministered to the needs of the whole person. During the first three centuries of the church they could only care for the sick where they found them, as believers were then a persecuted people. Once the persecutions subsided, however, the institutionalization of health care began in earnest.

---

14. https://churchmissionsociety.org/our-stories/charles-darwin-i-was-wrong/

15. Holland, *Dominion*, 523

16. Schmidt, Alvin, *How Christianity Changed the World*, Grand Rapids: Zondervan, 2004

The Council of Nicaea in AD 325 directed bishops to establish hospices in every city that had a cathedral. The first hospital was built by St Basil in Caesarea in AD 369. By the Middle Ages hospitals covered all of Europe and even beyond, caring for the physically and mentally ill. Nursing also sprang from Christian concerns for the sick, and two Christians (Henry Dunant and Gustave Moynier) established the Red Cross.

Education, while important in elite Greek and Roman culture, really got going institutionally under the influence of Christianity, with the public libraries and educational institutions. Formal education arose from Christian discipleship schools. There was no bias based on gender, ethnicity or class. The concept of public education first came from the Protestant Reformers, and the rise of the modern university was largely the result of Christian educational influence.

Regarding work and economic life, the Greeks and Romans despised manual labor, and so it was the slaves and lower classes that were forced to toil with their hands. The non-slave population lived chiefly for personal pleasure. The early church changed all this. Jesus was a carpenter who said the laborer was worthy of his hire, and Paul a tent maker. Work was seen as an honorable and God-given calling. Laziness was seen as sinful.

As said above, the rise of modern science has been directly linked with the biblical understanding of the world. The many great achievements in art, literature and music also deserve mention. For example, how much poorer would the world be without the Christian artistry of da Vinci, Michelangelo, Rembrandt, Bach, Handel, Brahms, Dante, Milton, Bunyan, and countless others?

TRUTH AND SPIRITUAL INSIGHT

But Dawkins recognizes that the Bible contains serious truth claims and he is enough of a rational modernist to respond generally on the basis of his own claims to know objective truth (an idea which ironically has developed from Christian culture shaped by the Bible!) He argues that *all theistic beliefs are false*. The truth, he contends, is that we are "accidental" products of "blind" evolutionary processes. I use inverted commas to highlight the fact that even a materialist like Dawkins likes to use words and concepts borrowed from the world of value judgments. Our genes are "selfish"; nature is "pitiless"; evolutionary theory is "beautiful"; religion is "wicked"; believers are "deluded."

Dawkins and Barker are, however, tapping into post-modern ways of thinking when they argue that, irrespective of truth, the biblical God is not "nice." This approach appeals to those unwilling to take the step of believing in God unless everything he says and does in the Bible are things that they immediately understand and approve of.

It would be interesting to see how Dawkins and Barker would get on if they were to try their hands at writing a novel about a fictional God. Of course, a novel may contain insight into the disturbing reality of the human condition (William Golding's *Lord of the Flies* comes to mind.[17]) However, given our human tendency not to want to look too deeply at what lurks below the surface of our own lives, any attempt to write a comprehensive fictional or mythical account of heaven and earth is likely to produce only a narrative the author feels he can handle or which is acceptable to the readership it is aimed at.

Every human civilization and culture has to some degree recognized its spiritual alienation from the transcendent reality that is the supreme God. Hence the ancient and universal phenomenon of sacrificial worship. We must come to God as *he* is (awesome in power, holiness and purity) and we must come to him as *we* are (spiritually unclean and morally defective). Therefore any approach must be on *his* terms. Moses, during his encounter with God at the burning bush, was ordered to take off his sandals in recognition he was standing on holy ground. When he wanted to know how he was going to answer the Israelites when they asked for the name of the God he had met, *"I am who I am"* came the reply.[18]

The reason why the Bible can have a "marmite" effect on people (it is loved by some and hated by others) is that it radically challenges our paradigms. For some this is spiritual liberation—the opening of our eyes to God and the opportunity to smell the beautiful fragrance of grace and truth. For others, it is the aroma of death.[19]

In *The Times* sports section I read an amusing account of an incident at a football (soccer) match (before the days of *Video Assistant Referees*) where the referee was subjected to frustrated criticism by the home supporters for an offside decision which went against their team. Some humor and ironic cheering was brought into the situation when a fan waved his white stick around and shouted some choice words at the official. Richard Dawkins is like this partially sighted man in the stadium venting his anger and frustration at the mess the man in charge is making in running the show (who he of course claims doesn't exist). In his spiritual blindness Dawkins rails at

---

17. In Golding's famous novel, a group of boys find themselves stranded alone on an island where their common life disintegrates into tribalism and ritual murder.
18. Exodus 3:13–14
19. Second Corinthians 2:15–16

things he cannot see and does not understand, while enjoying the thrill of playing to the gallery with his rhetorical gifts. The Bible says.

> "The man without the Spirit does not accept the things that come from the Spirit of God, for they are foolishness to him, and he cannot understand them, because they are spiritually discerned."[20]

So why write this book? Why try to knock the ball back into the court of those who do not understand spiritual things? It would of course be ridiculous for me to think that God needs me to defend his Word. I heed what the great nineteenth century preacher Spurgeon said. "Defend the Bible! I'd sooner defend a lion!" What I do aim to do in this book is threefold.

1. To encourage Christians who are puzzled by aspects of the Old Testament and who might value help in knowing how to answer some of the criticisms leveled at it.
2. To reassure some people who are being drawn towards God's kingdom, but who might be daunted by the seeming weight of these accusations about the biblical God, that that God is indeed good.
3. To challenge atheists and agnostics to think again about some of the lazy misrepresentations of the biblical God that are going around.

A FALSE SOLUTION TO THE DIFFICULT TEXTS

Before going any further, it is important to identify and refute a seductive argument that seems at first to help Christians deal with all the texts which seem embarrassingly harsh. Some say that an enlightened reading of Scripture recognizes that much of what seem to be plain and factual accounts of God making real commands and performing historically real actions should be interpreted in a way that denies their actual historicity but allows for some "spiritual meaning" for the sophisticated reader.

This argument maintains that the Bible contains ideas about God which were (and still are) changing over time from those which were primitive and unworthy to those which are sophisticated and progressive. So while everything the Bible claims about God might have *some* use to us today (such as the "texts of violence" somehow pointing to the ideal of wholehearted devotion to God) much of the Old Testament distorts the truth about God. Some of these "abhorrent" texts were countermanded by certain

---

20. First Corinthians 2:14

later prophets or by Jesus. Others must be rejected in the light of modern knowledge and ethical progress within the evolving religious tradition.[21]

So it can now be understood that God didn't really command or do the problematic things the Bible says he did. The primitive tribal group called the Israelites, believing that only *they* were the "people of God" did, in their chauvinism, fear, and ignorance, mistakenly attribute to God words and deeds that we now know he could never or would never have said or done, and they wrote it all up accordingly. It is now incumbent upon us to de-construct their work, discern their errors and separate the biblical wheat from the chaff. We must be the arbiters of whether the picture given of God in each passage of Scripture is true or untrue, good or evil, worthy or belief or to be rejected.

So according to this way of reading the Bible, when Genesis 7–9 tells us that God decided to drown everyone on earth except Noah and his family and seven or two of every kind of animal, we should now see this was a mistaken, even if sincere belief, and reject it as unbearably vindictive. When the same book says "the LORD rained down burning sulfur on Sodom and Gomorrah," we should now see that this was really the Israelites giving their own attempted interpretation of a purely natural disaster (if it happened at all) affecting a people they didn't much care for.

When Genesis 22 tells us God told Abraham to sacrifice Isaac, we should read this as an example of a character in the biblical story mistakenly thinking that God told him to do something because this is the kind of thing it was believed other gods of the time wanted their followers to do. A "sophisticated" reading allows us to understand Abraham's last-minute realization that of course God would *never* have told him to do such a thing. He should have challenged what God said (or what he thought God was saying) at the outset, as he did when he appealed on behalf of Sodom and Gomorrah (chapter eighteen). This, the theory goes, was the *real* nature of the test. Thus instead of us believing that God was pleased that Abraham had the faith to trust and obey him over the life of his son, and so confirmed with an oath the covenant promise to him (as it says in Genesis 22:15–18, confirmed in the New Testament by Hebrews 11:17–20) Abraham actually

---

21. See Professor Keith Ward *Is Religion Dangerous?* for an example of this kind of thinking. On pages 113–114 Ward summarises the kind of stance I take in this book which he describes as "the conservative Christian position" but says he prefers the view that the Old Testament is a "very useful" record of a developing understanding of God which goes from a primitive and distorted one to a more just and inclusive one. My reply would be that the New Testament does not seem to see the Old Testament in that way, drawing an understanding of God's character as much from the earlier accounts of Israel's history as from the later prophetic writings. The evidence for this assertion will appear throughout this book, but see particularly chapter eleven.

failed the ethical test by obeying what he thought he heard! The idea that Abraham's willingness to sacrifice his son was an appalling spiritual failure is exactly what Barker says in his chapter charging the biblical God with being filicidal.[22]

When the Bible claims that God told the Israelites to "show no mercy" to the Canaanites in the Promised Land but drive them out with the sword, we must conclude that this was a pious mistake by the writers, or a cynical religious justification the Israelites gave for their need for living space. In truth, their action was nothing other than brutal "ethnic cleansing" or "genocide" as Dawkins and Barker contend. Surely God should not be implicated in this evil?

So, Professor Keith Ward says about God's command that the Israelites destroy all remnants of Canaanite religion,

> "I cannot believe that a God of mercy and love would command such a thing. But I can believe that people might be so devoted to one God that they think any other form of worship must be exterminated. Their belief would be false, and it arises from a perverted idea of what loyalty to God requires."[23]

When the Bible is read and studied, this approach concentrates not on what the text reveals about God and his purposes from careful exegesis of what the writer tells us he does, says or approves of, but *how the text suggests the people at the time (including the writer) saw God and what they thought his purposes were*. We are then invited to assess the adequacy of the view they had. So, in other words, what we read in the Bible says more about the people who wrote it and their understanding of God at the time of writing, than about God himself. This way of reading the Bible puts us in a position of judging the text and, apart from anything else, leads to a lack of concern for proper exegesis. If troubling or difficult problems in Scripture can be sidestepped by simply saying that the text reflects the inadequacy of the writer's theology, then there is less incentive to really understand what the text meant in the context in which it was written.[24]

Some who deny the truth of what the Scriptural writer says that God commanded or did, claim to do so on the grounds of *human reason*. Our reason, they say, tells us the picture of God these passages paint cannot be true. However, there is the question of how we can be so sure our human

---

22. Barker, *God: The Most Unpleasant Character in all Fiction*, chapter 14

23. Ward, Keith. *The Word of God? The Bible After Modern Scholarship*, (London: SPCK, 2010). 57–58

24. This is the discipline of exegesis. See chapter 29 for a discussion of exegesis and "hermeneutics," which is the wider study of biblical interpretation.

reasoning is reliable enough to make this judgment. If the New Testament is right, our ability to reason in a godly way has been damaged by human fallenness. *Our thinking has become futile and our foolish hearts darkened.*[25] Therefore, what at first *seems* unfair or too harsh to us might not be, especially if we don't even acknowledge the truth that our human reasoning has become warped by sin. What if we, in our culpable blindness to God's holiness and justice, are claiming for ourselves, in supreme arrogance, the right to judge God—to put him and his revealed Word in the dock, instead of recognizing that it is we who stand condemned as rebellious sinners before a holy God? As Clay Jones says "We don't hate sin [like God does] so we don't understand what happened to the Canaanites."[26]

Others claim a theological and spiritual basis for rejecting parts of the Old Testament. They say that the progression from the Old Testament to the New demonstrates an evolving religious tradition, from a sectarian one to a universal one, and a violent one to peace-loving one. When Jesus came as God's full and supreme revelation, we can, the argument goes, now see clearly in the light of his "gentle, loving, non-judgmental character," those parts of the Old Testament we should see as flawed and those which we can safely retain as spiritually helpful. The Holy Spirit, it is claimed, is our guide in separating the biblical dross from the biblical gold as he leads us into all truth.

There are at least four problems with this theory. First, the Old Testament does not begin with an Israelite tribal god who later evolves into the God who cares about other nations and the whole of his creation as well. Genesis reveals the God who made the whole universe and who made a covenant with Abraham *in order to bless all the nations of the earth.*[27] Yahweh was never Israel's private god and from the beginning he revealed himself as the one true God, the creator of all there is. There is much in the Old Testament about the gentleness, kindness and mercy of God and this extends to all humankind, not just Israel.

> "The LORD is good to all. He has compassion on all that he has made..."[28]

Before Joshua fought the battle of Jericho, the first Canaanite city taken on the west side of the Jordan, Joshua saw before him an angel with a drawn sword. Joshua went up to him and asked, "Are you for us or for our

---

25. Romans 1:21
26. See chapter 8
27. Genesis 12:3b
28. Psalm 145:9

enemies?" The angel replied, "Neither, but as commander of the LORD'S army I have now come." In other words, the real question for Israel was not whether God was on *their* side, but whether *they* were going to be on the LORD'S side.

The book of Deuteronomy, containing instruction from the LORD before the Israelites entered the promised land, makes it clear that if the Israelites were unfaithful to the covenant they too would eventually be driven out of the land, which of course is what in time happened. In chapter eleven, in answer to the question "Is God racist?" we will see that there was always a concern in God's heart for the non-Israelite foreigner who was willing to acknowledge him and show faith and humility, from the earliest times of the nation of Israel and throughout the times of the former prophets, not just the latter ones.

Secondly, there is a lot in the New Testament about God's wrath and judgment, and the reality of hell. Unlike the Old Testament, the New (mainly through the words of Jesus himself) emphasizes the terrible phenomenon of *eternal* judgment and is therefore even more at odds with so-called progressive ideas of what God should be like than the Old Testament is.

> "If anyone causes one of these little ones—those who believe in me—to stumble, it would be better for them to have a large millstone hung around their neck and to be drowned in the depths of the sea."[29]
>
> "In anger his master handed him over to the jailers to be tortured, until he should pay back all he owed. This is how my heavenly Father will treat each of you unless you forgive your brother or sister from your heart."[30]
>
> "The angels will come and separate the wicked from the righteous and throw them into the blazing furnace, where there will be weeping and gnashing of teeth."
>
> "But the cowardly, the unbelieving, the vile, the murderers, the sexually immoral, those who practice magic arts, the idolaters and all liars—they will be consigned to the fiery lake of burning sulfur. This is the second death."[31]
>
> "If your hand causes you to stumble, cut it off. It is better for you to enter life maimed than with two hands to go into hell, where the fire never goes out. . . if your eye causes you to sin, pluck it out and throw it away. It is better for you to enter the kingdom of God with one eye that to have two eyes and be

---

29. Matthew 18:6
30. Ibid. 18:34–35
31. Revelation 21:8

thrown into hell, where 'their worm does not die, and the fire is not quenched.'"[32]

"They will be punished with everlasting destruction and shut out from the presence of the Lord and from the glory of his might."[33]

Thirdly, as a careful reading of the New Testament shows, every book either explicitly re-iterates or assumes the authority, relevance, and trustworthiness of the Old Testament in revealing the character of the unchanging God and thus providing moral and spiritual lessons for us today. In chapters twenty-eight and twenty-nine I deal with the attitude of Jesus and the apostles to what we call the Old Testament and we will see that they saw it all as the inspired, authoritative Word of God.

Judging parts of the Old Testament as giving the false ideas of the Israelites as to the character of God undermines much of the New Testament teaching, and not just those parts which explicitly declare the God-breathed authority and reliability of all Scripture. Much of the New Testament relies for its validity on the implicit assumption that the Old Testament witness is true. So Jesus' warning in Matthew 24:37 that, "just as it was in the days of Noah, so it will be at the coming of the Son of Man" loses its credibility if we decide that we can no longer believe a God of love would bring judgment to the world in this way. Likewise, in Matthew 11:23–24 when Jesus said to the town of Capernaum "it will be more bearable for Sodom and Gomorrah on the day of judgment than for you," there is little force in what Jesus said if, in reality, God did not rain down fire and sulfur on those cities because in fact a loving God would never do such a thing.

The writer to the Hebrews says,

"If we deliberately keep on sinning after we have received the knowledge of the truth, no sacrifice for sins is left, but only a fearful expectation of judgment and of raging fire that will consume the enemies of God. Anyone who rejected the law of Moses died without mercy on the testimony of two or three witnesses. How much more severely do you think someone deserves to be punished who has trampled the Son of God underfoot, who has treated as an unholy thing the blood of the covenant that sanctified them, and who has insulted the Spirit of grace? For we know him who said, 'It is mine to avenge; I will

---

32. Mark 9:43–49
33. Second Thessalonians 1:9

repay,' and again, 'The Lord will judge his people.' It is a dreadful thing to fall into the hands of the living God."[34]

Here, the warning against turning away from the living God, revealed by the New Covenant, depends for its force on that behavior being even more serious than the consequences of rejecting the law of Moses. If the consequences of rejecting the law of Moses, as outlined in the Old Testament, were not in fact sanctioned by God but made up by the Israelites, then this robs the warning in the letter of Hebrews of its potency.

Paul says in First Corinthians 10:11,

> "These things *happened to them* as examples and were written down as warnings to us, on whom the fulfilment of the age has come."

The immediate context to this is Paul's reference to the thousands of Israelites who died after being guilty of idolatry, indulging in pagan revelry, and testing the LORD by mutinous grumbling. The LORD sent snakes and a plague and "twenty-three thousand died in one day." So if the Old Testament's accounts of God's judgment on the Israelites are not true, then the New Testament is not reliable in its teaching and warnings either.

Further, if Moses did not, as Numbers 21 says, have to lift up a bronze snake in the desert to heal those struck with the plague of God's judgment, then this undermines one of the most famous statements of the Gospel, made by the Lord Jesus himself in John 3:14–17:

> "Just as Moses lifted up the snake in the wilderness, so the Son of Man must be lifted up, that everyone who believes may have eternal life in him. For God so loved the world that he gave his one and only Son, that whoever believes in him shall not perish but have eternal life. For God did not send his Son into the world to condemn the world, but to save the world through him. Whoever believes in him is not condemned, but whoever does not believe stands condemned already because they have not believed in the name of God's one and only Son."

Fourthly, the de-constructionist approach to certain parts of the Old Testament undermines *everything* in the Old Testament. If the Scriptures contain some passages which, purporting to reveal God's commands and actions, are in fact products of "perverted ideas as to what loyalty to God requires," (as claimed by Professor Ward) then this, for example, also calls into question the very idea of loyalty to one God. Could not the Old Testament's

---

34. Hebrews 10:26–31

claim that loyalty to Yahweh *alone* was commanded by him to the Israelites be just as flawed as its claimed revelation as to what that loyalty required in their context? Should not we now recognise, in the light of modern ideas of tolerance and post-modern relativism, the belief that there is only one God should give way to a more enlightened understanding of a plurality of gods? Claiming there is only one God should perhaps now be seen as intolerant and oppressive and inimical to a progressive, multi-faith society?

To their credit, the kind of approach which denies the authenticity of the difficult biblical narratives, claims they are there simply to provide metaphors for sanitized spiritual lessons, or were abrogated by later, more humane ideas, does not cut much ice with the new atheists. Dawkins and Barker see the attempt by some Christians to disclaim responsibility for the Old Testament as if there were no continuity with the New, as a cop-out which denies what the Bible itself claims to be and makes a mockery of its reliability in revealing the character of God. And they are right. If we make a misguided attempt to save God from being implicated in politically incorrect ways of behaving, all biblical credibility is destroyed. Dawkins and Barker have more insight than some professional theologians, such as Ward, in this regard.

In his latest book *Outgrowing God*, Dawkins points out that in order to judge the Bible and discern what is "nice" and what is "nasty," you must use some criterion beyond the Bible itself. But then, he asks

> "whatever that criterion turns out to be, why don't we just use that directly? If we have some independent criterion for deciding which biblical verses are good and which are bad, why bother with the Bible at all?"[35]

A person influenced by the Christian tradition might pipe up immediately and say that the criterion is Jesus himself. But if some parts of the Old Testament are rejected as untrue in what they say about God, then the Jesus appealed to is one who is detached from some parts of the biblical revelation about his heavenly Father. The *real* Jesus however is the Torah–believing, Jewish, Jesus, not a sentimentalized Western construct whose message is allowed to go no further than what a nominally Christian liberal progressive might consider to be reasonable today.

I believe we should have a "high" view of Old Testament Scripture because Jesus did. Therefore, while I whole-heartedly agree that there is a progression in the biblical revelation, culminating in the coming of Christ, I cannot agree that anything "God-breathed" or "inspired by the Holy Spirit"

---

35. Dawkins, *Outgrowing God*, 122

(as the Hebrew scriptures are described by Paul in the New Testament) contains false, faulty or misleading revelation about the character of God or which is morally criticized or contradicted by later biblical texts or the Holy Spirit today.

As God's plan of salvation for mankind unfolds in Scripture there is fresh revelation of what God is doing, culminating in the establishment of a new and better covenant,[36] but this new revelation is not such as to render morally abhorrent previous revelation, but only misguided or unbalanced understandings of that previous revelation. Jesus' attitude to Scripture is considered in chapter twenty-eight of this book. He never taught that Old Testament scripture misrepresented God, and, like the prophets before him, criticized only wrong, superficial, hypocritical, self-serving and inadequate *interpretations* of it. Thus, for example, even though we live now in a new dispensation, under a new testament, being free from the direct observance of the biblical laws given to people living under the Old Covenant, this does not mean those laws were not God-given, good and appropriate *for then*. If we have a deeper and richer appreciation of the justice and mercy of God in the day of our Lord Jesus Christ, this does not mean God was unjust or unmerciful in his revelation of himself before Jesus came to earth. If God's character can change in one direction, it could change in another. But Malachi 3:6 says, "I the LORD do not change. Therefore, descendants of Jacob, you are not consumed."

PROTESTANT ATHEISTS AND THE MISUSE OF THE BIBLE BY CHRISTIANS

An interesting observation is that outspoken academic atheists seem to be a particular feature of cultural contexts shaped by Protestant Christianity. Why is this? One simple reason is that they are free to speak and write without restriction. If you are an atheist academic living in a Muslim-dominated country, for example, you don't give lectures or write a book rubbishing Islam or you will not live very long (and you would be taking a big risk wherever you lived). In Catholic and Orthodox countries people are more reluctant to publicly criticize Christianity because blasphemy laws are stricter and knocking the national religion is seen as unpatriotic. But as well as having full freedom to dissent, I suspect that these "culturally Protestant" atheists have subconsciously imbibed enough Reformed Christianity to have a more passionate desire to voice a protest at what they see as inconsistencies or religious humbug.

---

36. Hebrews 8:6

For it must be confessed that within Christendom the Bible has sometimes been badly misused over the centuries. It has on occasion been employed to justify self-righteousness and to reinforce prejudice. People who have claimed to be "good Christians" have quoted Bible verses in the same crooked way as the Devil can, to bolster their positions of wealth and power, and to seek to justify the plundering of the environment, the cruel transatlantic slave-trade, the oppression of women, war-mongering, apartheid racism, and lack of compassion for the poor. Biblical verses have been used with relish as sticks with which to beat others, even though the Bible nowhere encourages us to gloat when others come under the wrath of God and indeed the Old Testament explicitly warns against it.[37]

As Christians we can sometimes be selective in the parts of the Bible we notice and proclaim to others. If we're rich we might soft-pedal what Jesus and the prophets say about wealth. If we're nationalistic we might over-emphasize the significance of nation states in God's plan for mankind at the expense of a wider vision of unity in Christ. If we are judgmental, then we might happily quote verses which we think condemn the behavior of others but ignore the passages which highlight our own sinfulness. If we personally benefit from a status quo which is built on oppression, then we might ignore biblical passages about correcting injustice. The Old Testament has sometimes been read as though it did not find its fulfilment in the New Testament Christ, leading to a fortress mentality towards people who do not share our faith or who are culturally "other."

Many evils perpetrated by "Christian" nations, groups or individuals have had their biblical text, deliberately twisted or complacently misunderstood. Thus it is no wonder the severe passages of the Bible are rejected by many, because in the hands of sinful people parts of the Bible *have* indeed sometimes wrongly been claimed to justify what has been evil behavior. Because of this it is considered by many that certain passages *do* indeed support or even command religious aggression. The parts of the Bible about God's wrath and judgment are seen as buttressing the smug and vindictive attitudes of the self-righteous or even to inspire all that is cruel and oppressive. So the God of scripture is brought into disrepute. Atheists are given ammunition to use against the Faith which people like Dawkins use with passion and skilled rhetoric.

However, the fact that Christians have not always lived up to the revelation of God culminating in Christ, and have at times mishandled Scripture, does not mean the Bible itself is to blame. I will argue in this book that the unique relationship God had with Israel in the Old Testament

---

37. Proverbs 24:17

meant his commands to them, regarding war for example, cannot be taken to justify aggressive militarism today and there is nothing in the Old Testament which, *properly understood from its context*, runs counter to the New Testament example that followers of the crucified and risen Christ should be more willing to die for upholding the Gospel than kill for it.

JESUS, SIN, AND ATONEMENT

Dawkins claims (rather condescendingly) that if Jesus existed and said some of the things he is recorded as saying in the Gospels, then he is an improvement on the Old Testament. But Jesus endorsed every word of the Hebrew Scriptures.[38] Barker recognizes this in chapter twenty-eight of his book and strongly rejects Jesus as being completely compromised morally because of it. In this he is being more consistent than Dawkins, who, while echoing Bertrand Russell's rather lame complaints about Jesus cursing a fig tree, drowning a herd of pigs, and casting out demons when the problem was "obviously" mental illness, seems more reluctant to denounce Jesus. Perhaps he is intending in his polite English way to "damn him with faint praise." He thinks that the Bible portrays Jesus as generally good (even, on occasion, "progressive," for a man of his time), especially when he's contradicting "nasty Old Testament ideas" like "an eye for an eye, and a tooth for a tooth."[39]

It is, however, no mere co-incidence that those who reject the character of God, as revealed in parts of the Old Testament, also find abhorrent central tenets of New Testament theology, such as the uncompromising holiness of God, the deep rooted inter-generational nature of sin, God's severe wrath, eternal condemnation of the unrepentant, the necessity of being united with Christ and Christ alone for our salvation, and the doctrine of penal substitutionary atonement. Penal substitutionary atonement is the biblical doctrine that Jesus had to bear, in our place, the penalty we deserved, so our sins could be forgiven and we can be in a right relationship with God. Those who don't accept what the Old Testament says about God will not believe in what the New Testament teaches either. Jesus said

> "If they do not listen to Moses and the prophets, they will not be convinced even if someone rises from the dead."[40]

38. Matthew 5:17–20. And see John Wenham, *Christ and the Bible*, Baker, 1994

39. Dawkins, Outgrowing God, 116–121. See chapter 28 of this book for an understanding of what Jesus meant when he said "You have heard it was said, 'an eye for an eye and a tooth for a tooth' *but I tell you do not take revenge.*"

40. Luke 16:31

So, for example, Dawkins pours excoriating scorn on the concept of substitutionary atonement. This is because he has no time for the biblical doctrine of the holy God from whom we are alienated by sin and whose righteous and deserved wrath we are, *without atonement being made*, all under. The self-sacrifice of God in Christ on the cross is thus for Dawkins an example of gross sadomasochism. If God wants to forgive, why can't he just forgive? Why does he need to torture himself to death? Those who haven't grasped the mystical unity of Father and Son within the Triune Godhead add a further complaint; "why does he need to torture an *innocent third party*, his son, to death? Isn't this "cosmic child-abuse?"[41]

Sadly, there are some within the church, like Steve Chalke and Alan Mann, who I believe have been influenced by hostile views like Dawkins's and Barker's regarding the character of God as portrayed in the Old Testament. They therefore resist the biblical truth that the wrath of God was "propitiated" ("turned away") by the voluntary self-offering of Jesus Christ, the perfectly sinless representative of mankind, on the cross.

These people might be happy to see the cross as the finest example of inspiring martyrdom and non-retaliation (which indeed it is) or the sad but inevitable result of Jesus' humbly obedient incarnation (which it was) or the way the powers of evil were defeated by Jesus by him allowing them to do their worst before he rose in triumph (which wonderfully it was too). They might be willing to explore all sorts of theories (biblically rooted or otherwise) about why the cross was necessary and how it achieved our salvation. However, they baulk at the idea that God in Christ bore the punishment humanity deserved from God himself, according to his justice. It seems just too out of kilter with the kind of religion most people find acceptable today. But this means their theology is sub-biblical as regards God's holiness, the seriousness of sin, and the wonder of his grace. Buildings may be built tall, but if they are on shaky foundations, they can fall very quickly.

Dawkins mocks the biblical concept of sin,[42] always putting the word in inverted commas, as if it were a concept made up by Christians to make

---

41. See Chalke and Mann, *The Lost Message of Jesus*, 182

The Lost Message of Jesus presents an unfair caricature of the doctrine of penal substitutionary atonement. For me, the real "lost message of Jesus" is the Old Testament and we would do well to return to reading it, studying it and believing it in order to better understand Jesus, his atoning sacrifice and God's kingdom values. If we want a fully rounded faith then we need to wrestle with the whole Scriptural witness.

42. The meanings of the Greek and Hebrew words translated "sin" in the Bible have to do with falling short of the mark, rebellion against God, disobedience, self-centeredness, inner corruption, and spiritual captivity. Francis Spufford, in *Unapologetic: Why Despite Everything Christianity Still Makes Surprisingly Good Sense*, Faber, 2012 defines sin as "HPTFTU" (the Human Propensity to F*** Things Up). However we prefer to

people feel bad about themselves and prevent them having any fun. This is the kind of scorn that has frightened some Christians into being ashamed of the Gospel.[43] They are then tempted to reduce the Christian message to a politically correct moralism which, terrified of being thought of as foolish by the world, embraces the spirit of the age. But the apostle James said, "friendship with the world is hatred towards God."[44] Jesus warned, *"salt that loses it saltiness is thrown out and trampled underfoot."*[45]

So in responding to the twenty-seven charges against the character of God in the Old Testament, I shall also be responding to the view expressed by Dawkins (and shared by some influential church-people) that a doctrine clearly taught in the Old and New Testaments, the atoning sacrifice of Jesus on the cross by which God's wrath is turned away from those united to Christ and our sin is forgiven, is barbaric and repellent to enlightened sensibilities.

---

see it, the Bible makes clear that sin incurs God's righteous wrath and atonement is required for that wrath to be propitiated (turned away). We could not atone for ourselves, not being good enough, but God in his grace paid the cost in Christ, enabling us to be forgiven. As Cecil Frances Alexander's great hymn *There is a green hill far away* goes "*there was no other good enough to pay the price of sin, he only could unlock the gate of heaven and let us in.*"

43. Romans 1:16
44. James 4:4
45. Matthew 5:13

Chapter 1

Jealous—and proud of it?

"It was a mistake," you said. "But the cruel thing was, it felt like the mistake was mine, for trusting you."

—David Levithan, *The Lover's Dictionary*

One can see why Dawkins begins his list of accusations by saying God is "jealous and proud of it" and Dan Barker argues that he could not have begun his tirade in a stronger way. In the Old Testament God does indeed take pains to tell people he *is* a jealous God and that his very name (meaning his essential character) is *Jealous*.[1]

In the book of Exodus 20:3–5a, God says to the Israelites,

> "You shall have no other gods before me. "You shall not make for yourself a carved image, or any likeness of anything that is in heaven above, or that is in the earth beneath, or that is in the water under the earth. You shall not bow down to them or serve them, for *I the Lord your God am a jealous God. . ."*

At the same time, jealousy in human beings is spoken of throughout the Bible (Old and New) as a *bad thing*. It's what led Joseph's brothers to sell him into slavery, the Pharisees to hate Jesus, and churches to be reprimanded by the apostle Paul in his epistles. The apostle James says,

---

1. Exodus 34:14

"...where jealousy and selfish ambition exist, there will be disorder and every vile practice."[2]

In English translations of the Bible, the word "jealousy" is used interchangeably with "envy" and "covetousness" and these in Scripture are always negative things. The final commandment is "You shall not covet..."

So, it looks like the first indictment sticks. God is in the dock and already the first charge appears an open and shut case. In admitting to something he reprimands in others, we could throw in the charge of hypocrisy too. God's character is already seriously impugned and there are still another twenty-six charges to follow.

But wait a minute. The word "jealousy" is like the word "anger." Most of the time we use it, we are referring to something which is morally wrong. But that is because, due to our sinful inclinations, our strong emotions do so often lead to wrong actions. We feel angry so we gesture rudely to another motorist. We feel jealous so we bad-mouth someone to others. But, as the bible indicates, anger is a natural human reaction to many things and like other human emotions it doesn't necessarily result in wrong behavior. Paul writes to the Ephesians "In your anger do not sin"[3] and "do not let the sun go down on your anger."[4] In other words, anger itself is recognized as an inevitable part of being human in this world, but we should process our anger in a healthy, constructive way before it over-reacts or turns to bitterness. Jesus got angry but without losing his self-control, behaving badly and becoming resentful.

In the same way jealousy is an instinctive human reaction when something that is legitimately ours is threatened. Barker claims that only insecure people feel jealous, and therefore a jealous god must be an insecure god. But if someone really is taking something that is rightfully mine or threatening something I hold dear, then it is natural to feel a degree of jealousy. I could then respond in a wrong way (with intemperate rage, vindictiveness or passivity) or in a right way (with committed, or even zealous, vigilance and assertiveness).

The film *Big Eyes* tells the story of Walter and Margaret Keane. To the world of 1960s America, Walter appeared to be a successful artist, making a lot of money from the sale of his trademark paintings of people with oversized eyes. The truth was that Walter had barely any artistic talent. The person who painted the pictures was his wife Margaret. Two years into their

---

2. James 3:16 (English Standard Version)
3. Ephesians 4:26
4. Ibid

marriage, Margaret had discovered that her husband was passing off her work as his own. Rather than expose the truth, she became his artistic slave.

Walter made millions from his wife's paintings. He bought an expensive house, socialized with movie stars, and lived a life of luxury. By contrast, Margaret was shut away, forced to paint for hours on end. To stop her from leaving him and telling all, Walter threatened her with ruin and even murder. By 1970, Margaret had had enough. She left Walter and told a reporter everything. In court, the judge had them both paint a picture in the courtroom, proving Margaret's claim to be the be the true artist. Finally, the work she had done was acknowledged as her own and her husband exposed as a debauched and vicious fraud. A right kind of "jealousy" for what was rightfully hers propelled her into ending the abusive relationship and revealing the truth.

Both Dawkins and Barker copyright their books. They are the rightful owners of the works they have authored, and they are using a legal provision to protect what is theirs and prevent others from taking the credit for it. They could be said to be "jealous" for their writings. That does not make them selfish, insecure people. They have every right to be zealously vigilant for what rightfully belongs to them.

If sinful human beings can, on occasion, feel a right kind of "jealousy" then how much more can the God who the Bible claims to have created the whole universe and us as the pinnacle of his creation? He is the author of the whole show. Why shouldn't he "copyright" it? Why shouldn't he feel jealous if we as human beings do not acknowledge him as creator of everything?

And when it came to God's relationship with the people of Israel, which is what the Old Testament is about, we need to understand that that relationship was based on a solemn covenant. God promised Abraham that he would bless him with descendants who he would bring into a land of their own. The later covenant with Moses outlined the responsibilities of the Israelites to be God's people, and God's undertaking to be their God and bless them in the land he was giving them. The people were to have no truck with the gods of the heathen nations or worship idols. This would provoke the LORD to jealousy, because his people, whom he loved, would be spurning him and destroying the relationship.

Barker, in arguing that the biblical God is insecure, uses the analogy of a man who is paranoid about his girlfriend finding another man attractive. But the relationship between God and Israel was not one of boyfriend and girlfriend. It was a covenant relationship akin to marriage. Solemn vows had been made and God had invested much in the union. Why shouldn't God feel jealous if the people he lavished his affections on, rescued from slavery and brought into a land flowing with milk and honey, gave their worship and adoration to worthless idols who weren't really gods at all?

In human terms, imagine a scenario where a wife loves and feels passionately about her husband to whom she has been married for the best part of her adult life. Imagine she discovers that he is cultivating intimate feelings for another woman and pursuing this woman sexually. Feelings of anger and jealousy at his betrayal would be natural and appropriate. I suggest that the degree of her jealous feelings would likely be proportional to the extent to which, over the years, she had devoted her heart to him. In other words, the more deeply and sacrificially she had loved her husband, the more "jealous" she would feel at someone replacing her rightful place in his affections.

Of course, if she then chose to kill her husband (or even just cut up all his clothes and trash his car) that would be wrong and illegal. But if she became "zealously vigilant" in fighting for her marriage and defending her family from break-up, this would indicate passion for her husband, to whom she is bound by oaths of lifelong fidelity. If she simply shrugged her shoulders and said to herself "I'm moving on," this would either mean she was totally out of touch with her own inner emotions (and in due course heading for psychological problems) or that she was now coldly indifferent to her husband and the fate of their marriage. The position of course would be the same if the unfaithfulness were on the wife's part and it was her husband who felt jealous. This jealousy would be a normal, healthy and appropriate emotion.

In fact, the absence of any jealous feelings in these types of situations, far from being a virtue, indicates a lack of passionate love that a married person rightly desires, and might well seek elsewhere if they feel it is not forthcoming from their spouse. A husband who tells his wife that he does not feel any jealousy about her becoming emotionally and/or physically intimate with another man is telling her, in effect, that if she wants passionate love, she must indeed go elsewhere for it. I know a young couple with children who took on a male lodger. The wife found she grew close emotionally to the lodger. Instead of ending the lodging arrangement, the husband allowed a situation to develop where he was regularly going to bed alone, while his wife and the lodger stayed up into the night talking and watching television together. Unsurprisingly, in due course, his wife left him and went off with the lodger. Had the husband owned his jealous feelings earlier on, the marriage might, with help, have survived and been restored to health.

In the Old Testament book of Hosea, Israel is not only likened to an unfaithful wife but also to a child, whom God taught to walk, and lovingly looked after, but who then, ungratefully spurns him.

"When Israel was a child, I loved him, and out of Egypt I called my son. But the more they were called, the more they went away from me. They sacrificed to the Baals and they burned incense to images. It was I who taught Ephraim to walk, taking them by the arms; but they did not realize it was I who healed them. I led them with cords of human kindness, with ties of love. To them I was like one who lifts a little child to the cheek, and I bent down to feed them. Will they not return to Egypt and will not Assyria rule over them because they refuse to repent? A sword will flash in their cities; it will devour their false prophets and put an end to their plans. My people are determined to turn from me. Even though they call me God Most High, I will by no means exalt them. How can I give you up, Ephraim? How can I hand you over, Israel? . . . My heart is changed within me; all my compassion is aroused. I will not carry out my fierce anger, nor will I devastate Ephraim again. For I am God, and not a man—the Holy One among you. . ."[5]

Imagine pouring your love into a child of yours only for them to give all their appreciation for everything good in their life to someone else, who has never actually done anything good for them at all, but only harm. Would you not understandably and rightly feel jealous?

In the apostle Paul's second letter to the Corinthians, he tells the Christians in Corinth that he is "jealous for them with a godly jealousy."[6] What he means is that he is *zealously vigilant* for them, that they should not be deceived by evil forces and led astray from their pure devotion to Christ. He uses the analogy of a father who wants to present his daughter as a pure virgin to her husband (to whom she was betrothed from childhood) on their wedding day.[7] Clearly Paul, the largest contributor to the New Testament, understands there is such a thing as *godly* jealousy, which has nothing to do with having a fragile ego, but everything to do with desiring what is right and true.

In his first letter to the Corinthians, Paul tells them to "flee from idolatry."[8] How could they partake in Holy Communion and at the same time be partakers of demons by worshipping idols? He wrote, "are we trying to arouse the Lord's jealousy? Are we stronger than he?"[9]

---

5. Hosea 11:1–4
6. Second Corinthians 11:2
7. Ibid
8. First Corinthians 10:14
9. Ibid. 10:21–22

The biblical God is the God who made everything and sustains everything by the power of his love. Were he not jealous, he would be an indifferent god, emotionally unconnected to his people. Were he relaxed about us worshipping idols, given that they are false gods and their worship is inspired by demonic forces, he would not be a loving God, but a cold-hearted, unconcerned and aloof being, not caring about the resulting misery of his children. In the Bible, idol worship is always associated with cruelty, sexual depravity, slavery and spiritual death. He doesn't want that for us. Praise God that one of his names *is* Jealous.

Chapter 2

Petty?

"If I don't find myself hating sin as God hates sin, then that leaves me too secretly thinking God is petty"

—Daniel McCoy

This evidence offered by Barker for this accusation relates to laws given by the biblical God to the Israelites and to various punishments commanded or directly carried out by him. God is accused of being petty in his law-making for two reasons. First, some of the laws seem to be solely about how his people behave towards *him* rather than about their conduct towards *others*. Secondly, some of them seem bizarre, unreasonably restrictive and carry overly harsh penalties for disobedience.

VERTICAL AND HORIZONTAL COMMANDMENTS

Barker rightly notices that the first four of the "Ten Commandments" relate to the people's relationship with God. His people must have no other gods, not make idols, not "take his name in vain" and observe his Sabbath. They are what might be called "vertical" commandments. The remaining six commandments are "horizontal." They concern primarily our relationship with other human beings. Honor your parents and don't do murder, theft, adultery, slander, or covet what belongs to others. Barker claims that the first four have nothing to do with ethics or morality and are examples of a petty, insecure god who has a need to protect his own fragile ego.

If we were constructing our own, fictional god, we might well have that god give commands that are seen to relate only to our horizontal relationships with others. But remember the biblical God is the God who made everything and holds all things together. He has infused his truth, love and power into every atom in the universe. All ethics and morality find their source in him. It is only because we are made "in God's image" (as the Bible says[1]) that we have some idea of what is good and right. Sin, however, has distorted this image and it is only by submitting to the biblical God's revelation of himself that we can have saving knowledge of him.

So, it is wrong to say that the "vertical" commands have no "horizontal" consequences regarding ethics or morality. The way we respond to God has profound implications as to how we treat others. If there is only one true God who hates falsehood and deceit then those who acknowledge and worship him will learn to treat others with honesty and fairness. On the other hand, people who worship false gods who cheat and lie are going to cheat and lie themselves.

For example, the Greek pantheon of gods displayed trickery, deceit and unfaithfulness and the "heroes" who worshipped them followed their example. The most powerful figure in Greek mythology, Zeus, the "king of the gods," was always at work deceiving his wife Hera, goddess of marriage, trying to conceal his affairs. Consequently, liars are so prevalent in Greek mythology that when the ancient Greek philosopher Plato imagines his ideal city, he wants to abolish all poetry because of its association with cheating, lying and swindling. Being a hero or a god in the world of Greek myth does not mean being truthful.[2]

By contrast, followers of the biblical God, as well as learning to reject false gods and idolatry are also forbidden from using God's name wrongly by invoking God whilst not showing the integrity he desires. Using modern terminology, God does not want us to "bring his name into disrepute."

Cultures which have been influenced by the Bible over the centuries are more honest than those which have not been. Nations more shaped by the Reformation (which promoted the Bible as the supreme authority for Christians and encouraged everyone in society to read the Bible) are recognizably less corrupt than countries where biblical Christianity has not

---

1. Genesis 1:27
2. Alana Shilling https://classroom.synonym.com/famous-liars-greek-mythology-21981.html

transformed the culture.[3] Integrity and trust is vital for the development of healthy banking, finance, commercial, industrial and public service sectors.

If people worship the one true God who made human beings in his image and who deeply cares about every one of us, then this will be reflected in the way the vulnerable are treated. It is Bible-influenced people who have been at the forefront of developing care for the sick, education, and civil rights. It has often been said that the early Labor movement, seeking the welfare of ordinary working people, owed more to Methodism than to Marx. Social activists in Britain took inspiration from the God who demonstrated his care for the poor throughout the Old Testament, as well as the Christ who died who shed his blood for all, not just the rich and powerful.

If societies observe the concept of Sabbath keeping, according to the fourth commandment, then this provides a powerful corrective to the idea that life should be about relentless toil. The principle of a weekly day of rest provides enormous protection to people who would otherwise be exploited by the tendency towards materialism. Listen to the words of the prophet Amos:

> "Hear this, you who trample the needy and do away with the poor of the land, saying, 'When will the New Moon be over that we may sell grain, and the Sabbath be ended that we may market wheat?'— skimping on the measure, boosting the price and cheating with dishonest scales, buying the poor with silver and the needy for a pair of sandals, selling even the sweepings with the wheat. The LORD has sworn by himself, the Pride of Jacob: 'I will never forget anything they have done.'"[4]

The loss of Sunday in the UK as a day of rest, which was lobbied for mainly by powerful retail corporations in the 1980s and carried through by prime minister Margaret Thatcher, who, in this area, showed herself to be an ideological "neo-liberal" rather than a "conservative," has resulted in many people losing a healthy rhythm of work and rest. The country has incurred an enormous social cost. Stress, ill-health, addiction, family breakup, damage to people's quality of life, and serious weakening of the church, has followed on from the abandonment of the Sabbath idea. While the very

---

3. see The Corruption Perception Index produced by *Transparency International* https://en.wikipedia.org/wiki/Corruption_Perceptions_Index

Of the top 20 "clean" countries in 2019, 15 have been majority Protestant since the sixteenth century (or, like New Zealand and Australia, populated later by people from those countries), 3 are mainly Catholic and 1 has a large Protestant minority.

4. Amos 8:4–7

privileged can still ensure they get recreation and refreshment, ordinary people's lives are made poorer in quality.

If a society worships idols (symbols of money, sex and power, created by human beings, behind which lie demonic forces) then it will spiral down into greed, selfishness, sexual degradation and injustice. The first four commandments were given to keep the people of Israel well away from the practices of the cruel and oppressive pagan societies around them and particularly the idolatrous behavior of the Canaanites.

STRANGE LAWS AND ODD RESTRICTIONS

What about the laws that seem weird? Why did God forbid the Jewish people from eating pork or shellfish? Why do emissions of semen or a woman's menstruation or mildew in the house cause ritual uncleanness? Why no tattoos or cooking a young goat in its mother's milk? Why no mixing of fibers in clothing or blending crops in the field? Some or all of these laws could have had health, ecological or consumer benefits, but the main point of them was that they served as a daily reinforcement of the idea of "separating one thing from another" and preserving the identity of the Israelites as belonging to their covenant God and symbolically distinct from the pagan nations.

In order to understand the holiness of their God (his utter aversion to sin), every aspect of their life had to reinforce the concepts of clean and unclean, pure and impure, holy and unholy. If the pagan nations cooked young goats in their mother's milk and marked their bodies with tattoos then they must not be seen to be doing anything like that. If those who worshipped idols employed semen and menstrual blood as part of their magic rituals, then the Israelites needed to associate these things with uncleanness in the context of worship and make themselves ritually clean from them. God did not want his people wearing charm bracelets as pagan women did who engaged in sorcery. The laws would have been a constant reminder that God's people must be pure, single-minded and centered on him, not because God is petty, but because he desired the Israelites to live under his covenant blessing and, by showing the world what he is like, bring blessing to the whole of mankind in fulfilment of the promises given to Abraham.[5]

So how ethically relevant do Christians consider the Old Testament to be for us today? The starting point is that the Old Testament is considered part of the canon of Scripture and the apostle Paul says

---

5. Genesis 12:1–3, 15:1–21, 22:15–18

> "All Scripture is God-breathed and is useful for teaching, rebuking, correcting and training in righteousness, so that the servant of God may be thoroughly equipped for every good work."[6]

The scripture that Paul was referring to was what we call the Old Testament. Jesus testified

> "For truly I tell you, until heaven and earth disappear, not the smallest letter, not the least stroke of a pen, will by any means disappear from the Law until everything is accomplished."[7]

By "the Law" Jesus meant the whole Hebrew canon, as this was a common shorthand way of referring to "the Law and the Prophets." Rules and regulations form only a part of the witness to the ethical character of God in the Old Testament. We see God's values in every book— the way he shows covenant faithfulness to the Israelites, his long-term plan for the blessing of the whole world, and his just and merciful interventions into the life of his people.

However, it is a fair question to ask why Christians today do not consider themselves bound by all the commandments regarding circumcision, sacrifices, rituals, ceremonies, clothing, diet, and land use.

The answer is that it is because we are not Israelites living under the Old Covenant. God, in his wisdom, chose to save our sinful, fallen world by initially establishing a people in a land who were separated from the surrounding heathen nations by special sacrifices, rituals and ceremonies. These, the Bible teaches, were a preparation for the coming of Christ, who fulfilled all sacrifice in himself, and made all things "clean" (pure; holy) through faith in him. We do not need these ritual boundary markers today to symbolically divide what is holy and clean from what is not, because faith in the Christ who entered this world, and the moral transformation which then ensues through the impartation of the Holy Spirit (God's law written on our hearts), is now enough to show the difference between God's people and those who do not know him.

There is a sense in which no commands in the Old Testament can be read as directly addressed to Christians, the reason being that, while the Holy Spirit caused it to be written and preserved for our benefit, the commands were given to a particular people (the Israelites) in a particular context (the land of Israel, before the time of Christ). Therefore there is no basis for lifting commands, regulations, and punishments directly from the Old

---

6. Second Timothy 3:16
7. Matthew 5:18

Testament and seeking to observe or impose them in the different contexts of today.

However, because everything in the Old Testament is "God-breathed and useful," every "stroke of the pen" remains authoritative in faithfully revealing something of the character of God. So every part of Hebrew scripture has something to say that we need to hear regarding ethics. But we need to discern how the ethical heart of God manifested itself in that context and how God's eternal character might be attested to in our context today.

The main contextual difference for us today is that Christ has come, fulfilled all the sacrificial laws by his "one perfect and sufficient sacrifice, oblation and satisfaction for the sins of the whole world"[8] and abrogated the need for ritual, ceremonial, dietary and other symbolic boundary markers because the people of God are newly defined as those who are in Christ, rather than members of a culturally distinct nation state like Israel. Thus Christians can eat bacon sandwiches, blend cotton with polyester, and don't have to take a ritual bath before going to a church gathering. But we should nevertheless seek to live distinct lives from those who do not follow Christ, not just on Sundays but every day of the week, in what we think, say and do. Our penises do not need to be circumcised but our hearts still must be, which is what the LORD wanted for the Old Testament people of God.[9]

MORAL PRINCIPLES

Christians have identified laws and principles in the Old Testament which are more directly "transferable" to life today. These have to do with respect for life and family, promise-keeping, honesty, and compassion. So examples of these "moral" commands would be the commands not to steal, murder, commit adultery, lie or indulge in perverse sexual practices. God not only expected his people Israel to keep these commands and punished them when they did not, but he admonished the pagan peoples for doing these things also. For example, Leviticus chapter eighteen lists various forms of sexual behavior which God detests and he explains at the end of the chapter that it was because of these practices by the Canaanite nations that the "land vomited them out." These commands are more directly applicable to us today because the standards they reflected were universal. They were not just expected of the Israelites under the old covenant.

Until recently in Western civilization, the Ten Commandments were regarded as providing a bedrock of moral standards that all should respect.

---

8. Words used in the Anglican *Book of Common Prayer* Communion liturgy
9. Deuteronomy 10:12–17

With the widespread rejection of our Christian heritage these commandments are now little known, and even less regarded. When Stephen Fry, actor, comedian and intellectual wit, who is the foremost celebrity cheerleader for the new atheists, describes the Ten Commandments as "the hysterical believings [sic] of a group of desert tribes," he appears oblivious to the influence they have had in shaping many of the values which society today takes for granted as being the natural order of things.[10]

The Mosaic laws of social responsibility promoted a much higher standard of care for fellow citizens, particularly the vulnerable like orphans, widows, the landless poor, and foreign workers than the pagan nations had. Today, because of the historical influence of the Christian faith and the Bible, much of our law is influenced by these principles. However, Christians do not believe that all these laws and associated punishments can be directly translated from ancient Israelite society to the statute books today, both because many were time and place specific and because the people of God are not now defined by membership of a distinct political nation with a theocratic civil and criminal code. So, for example, no Christians in twenty-first-century Western liberal democracies that I am aware of would argue that today we should have the death penalty for adultery or pre-marital promiscuity. But we know God strongly disapproves of adultery and fornication because the biblical revelation of "the law and the prophets" shows that upright faithfulness, purity and self-control is intrinsic to his character and sexual immorality is offensive to him.[11]

---

10. https://www.facebook.com/SkepticusOfficial/videos/724788584390400/?v=724788584390400

In this video Fry also says "Those desert tribes have stored up more misery for mankind than any other group of people in the history of the planet and they're doing it to this day." His comments reveal the spiritual roots of anti-semitism.

11. Article VII of the Church of England's *Thirty-Nine Articles of Religion* says "Although the Law given from God by Moses, as touching Ceremonies and Rites, do not bind Christian men, nor the Civil precepts thereof ought of necessity to be received in any commonwealth; yet notwithstanding, no Christian man whatsoever is free from the obedience of the Commandments which are called Moral."

This has been criticised as suggesting too simplistic a division between ceremonial, civil, and moral law. As Chris Wright points out in *Old Testament Ethics for the People of God* God's moral character infuses all the laws in some way. However, in fairness to the Reformers who framed this article they were looking for a succinct way of saying the moral principles of God's Old Testament commands should govern our behaviour and the laws of a Christian country, while the actual laws themselves should not be directly transferred and imposed.

So, for example, a Christian politician, following Old Testament precepts, would want to uphold the sanctity of life and marriage and defend the poor and vulnerable because it is known this pleases God by reflecting his values. A Christian should not, however, feel constrained by Scripture to seek to introduce, for example, the death

GOD THAT'S NOT FAIR!

Finally, what about the seeming harshness of some of the punishments God gave for things which might seem to us to be trivial offences? Barker cites the examples of the LORD instructing Moses to stone a man for breaking the Sabbath while they were in the wilderness[12] and the LORD sending two bears to maul forty-two "children" who had mocked his prophet Elisha.[13]

When they were in the desert, a man was discovered gathering wood on the Sabbath. Some people imagine that this was a minor infringement of a law interpreted very harshly and punished cruelly by a fearful people mistakenly or cynically invoking the need to appease an offended deity. This poor fellow is going for an afternoon stroll. It's getting late and so he decides to pick up some sticks lying around to maybe make a fire for himself and his family to keep them warm and perhaps cook some food. Before he knows it, he is arrested, held in detention, and Moses, the biblical writer explicitly claims, is told by God that he must be stoned to death.

Well if this is the picture in some people's minds, then no wonder Barker sees this as useful ammunition for his case, and Christians today might refuse to believe that God did really give Moses the command to carry out the death penalty in this instance. Is the Bible's trustworthiness and credibility damaged? Is the biblical God being petty? Let us consider more carefully what was going on.

The Sabbath command was a very important law. The whole nation of Israel stopping work and collectively focusing on God in worship would have been a powerful statement of allegiance to the one true God. In providing the rhythm and structure of their corporate life it would have been essential in binding the Israelites together, especially in the early days of their wandering in the wilderness. This man was not idly collecting little sticks. Gathering wood in the desert involved planning an expedition. He would have left the camp for some time, roamed around and returned laden with timber. He didn't need wood for cooking food to avert starvation, because the Bible says that God provided his people with all their needs, even directly sending manna from heaven. The passage does not actually say what he intended to do with the wood. But that is irrelevant. He was purposefully going out to break the solemn command from the LORD. It was a

---

penalty for adultery; or a ban on eating prawns, because civil punishment codes and ritual boundary markers were given specifically for the uniquely constituted nation of Israel under the Old Covenant.

12. Numbers 15:32–36
13. Second Kings 2:23–24

combination of defiance of God and endangering the unity and collective security of thousands of people.

The Israelites were a group of ex-slaves surrounded by hostile forces and prone to ill-discipline and fragmentation. Their survival and flourishing in the desert depended on obeying God and maintaining the Covenant. Describing this man's conduct as a trivial matter is, I believe, like saying that the British subject William Joyce (popularly known as Lord Haw-Haw) who broadcast enemy propaganda from Nazi Germany to Britain during World War Two, was hanged after being captured simply for making a few harmless radio programs. He was in fact tried and executed for high treason because of his efforts to undermine British unity and discipline at a very precarious time in the nation's life.

But some might say that Jesus had a much more relaxed attitude to the Sabbath day, which shows that the Old Testament was too harsh. However, Jesus never criticized Old Testament law but always either fulfilled, confirmed or validated it. What he criticized were legalistic, pedantic, hypocritical and distorted interpretations of any law. So, with the Sabbath, the Pharisees developed lots of their own regulations to outwardly demonstrate their supposed fidelity to the Sabbath law. Jesus pointed people to the original intention of the law, which was to promote the welfare of the Israelites under God's covenant. "The Sabbath was made for man, not man for the Sabbath."[14] So, it *was* lawful to bring healing and wholeness into people's lives. The Pharisees hated to see Jesus healing people on the Sabbath, even though they would hurry to rescue their own livestock from falling into pits if they needed to on that day. Such hypocrisy and selfish cold-heartedness made Jesus angry.

What about Elisha and the she-bears? The scenario could be presented in a somewhat comic but nevertheless appalling way. Elisha the old, straight-laced and follicly-challenged prophet was on his way to do some serious God-business and gets very stroppy when some harmless kids make an innocent joke about his baldness. In a fit of pique, he demands that God does something to punish all the little squirts and so God, with intolerant and humorless over-reaction, obliges, and sends two female bears (more angry than males?) to attack them. Forty-two little cherubs—a large infant class—go home injured, bleeding and traumatized for life. Not a great public relations moment for God.

Old Testament scholar Helen Paynter thinks Elisha was behaving in a grumpy, petulant way.[15] It is certainly true that everyone used by God in

---

14. Mark 2:27
15. Paynter, *God of Violence Yesterday, God of Love Today?* 73–74

the Old Testament and New had, unlike Jesus, character flaws. The book of Jonah reveals how a prophet used by God to bring the capital of an empire to its knees in repentance, was disobedient, grumpy and vindictive. But in this story, God immediately puts Elisha's curse into effect and therefore, if Elisha was behaving badly, God is implicated in this bad behavior by aligning himself totally with it.

John Wenham paints a truer picture as to what happened.[16] Elisha was in fact a young man just starting out on his ministry which was to last a lifetime. He was not cruel and savage, as is shown by his intervention to spare the Syrian prisoners of war which were at the mercy of the king of Israel who would have quite liked to have slaughtered them. It was a perilous time in the life of Israel. Queen Jezebel was still around promoting the most cruel and debased forms of worship. Elisha was headed for Bethel, a center of this idolatry. Daunted by his task, alone and tired by his journey he is suddenly accosted by a large gang of roughs who had probably been sent to deliberately intimidate him. The NIV describes them as "youths"—a much more convincing translation of the Hebrew than the King James Version translation used by Barker which says "little children." "Go on up, you baldhead" was not a gentle tease, but scholars think it was either a jeering reference to his prophetic tonsure haircut (thus mocking his God-given vocation), or a highly offensive and intimidating insult. Elisha was faced with a nasty, threatening mob organized to put an end to his mission to restore true worship to the land of Israel.

When the Bible says that Elisha "cursed" them, it does not mean that he lost his temper or used foul language. A prophetic curse was a solemn pronouncement uttered when people needed to know the serious consequences of rejecting God. God saw fit to send a severe message that Elisha was his prophet and that those who jeered him were scorning God's man. None of the crowd were killed by the she-bears, but they learned an important lesson. We don't have any more accounts of Elisha being molested on his journeys!

A comfortable God of our own making might never say boo to a goose, but the real God will vindicate those who trust in him. In the Old Testament, vindication of God's prophets sometimes happened immediately or within their lifetime, to teach the people vital things they needed to learn. In the New Testament era, the bible teaches that vindication for God's servants is only guaranteed when Jesus returns. Either way, it comes. God will not be mocked. That is not because he is petty. It is because he is God.

---

16. Wenham, *The Enigma of Evil*, 143

Chapter 3

Unjust?

"Why do bad things happen to good people? It has only happened once and he volunteered."

—RC. Sproul Jr

Barker in his third chapter gives several reasons why he thinks the biblical God is unjust. He punishes children for the sin of their parents, and sometimes the many for the sins of the few. A single person like King Saul or King David sins and thousands then suffer God's wrath. When God's judgment comes on Israel or other nations there are lots of innocent casualties. Women are raped and children killed or enslaved, not to mention the land being devastated for years on end. As well as the innocent suffering with the guilty, God punishes some things with extreme penalties. He is particularly severe about the non-compliance with instructions about certain "holy things." At times he "hardens hearts" and still blames people for their decisions, and he even entices certain people with "lying spirits." Witches in Israel are to be put to death. He is against "inclusivity," "diversity," and "equal opportunities," penalizing disabled priests by not allowing them to offer sacrifices. Aren't these alleged examples given by Dan Barker in his third chapter enough to bring God's justice into question?

I think the first thing to say in response is that throughout the Bible there are numerous occasions where God declares his justice, commands his people to administer justice and his justice is celebrated by the prophets and psalmists and appealed to by biblical characters. To give just some examples:

> "For I, the LORD, love justice. I hate robbery and wrongdoing."[1]

> "This is what the LORD Almighty said: 'Administer true justice; show mercy and compassion to one another.'"[2]

> "He is the Rock, his works are perfect, and all his ways are just. A faithful God who does no wrong, upright and just is he."[3]

> "Righteousness and justice are the foundation of your throne."[4]

When God tells Abraham he is going to destroy Sodom and Gomorrah for its wickedness, Abraham, thinking especially of his nephew Lot and his family, worries for the fate of any righteous people who might be there. He persistently appeals to God to spare the cities if even only a few of the people are righteous. "Will not the judge of all the earth do right?" he says. What if there are fifty righteous people inside Sodom? God replies that he will not destroy it if there fifty righteous people. Abraham then says "what about forty-five?" God says he would spare the city for forty-five people who are not wicked. Abraham then tries his luck with forty good people and gets the same answer. Realizing he might be pushing things he nevertheless keeps going till he gets God to confirm that for the sake of just ten people he would spare both cities.'[5]

WHO IS GOOD?

The second thing to say is that the Bible teaches that no-one (other than Christ) is "innocent" or "good" in the absolute sense of being free from all sin. Yes, the Bible describes some as "blameless," but this carries the meaning of being not guilty of the kind of wickedness which might bring an imminent act of judgment. A "righteous" and an "upright" person is not one who never does anything morally wrong, but one who trusts in God and seeks to worship him humbly and faithfully.

1. Isaiah 61:8
2. Zechariah 7:9
3. Deuteronomy 32:4
4. Psalm 89:14
5. Genesis 18:16–33

Through the flood in the time of Noah God destroyed all humans "whose wickedness was so great, every inclination of the thoughts of his heart was only evil all the time."[6] He spared two of every kind of animal (and seven pairs of certain "clean" animals) and the family of Noah, who the Bible says was "righteous" and "blameless" among the people of his time, and "walked with God." But even though God re-started the race of mankind with a *comparatively* good man in Noah, he still lamented that "every inclination of man's heart is evil from childhood."[7]

The psalmist laments...

> "The LORD looks down from heaven on the sons of men to see if there are any who understand, any who seek God. All have turned aside, they have together become corrupt."[8]

A man of wealth and influence once approached Jesus with the words "Good Teacher, what must I do to inherit eternal life." Jesus replied,

> "why do you call me *good*? No-one is *good* except God alone."[9]

THE DEPRAVITY AND PERVASIVENESS OF SIN

Thirdly, it is impossible to appreciate the justice of God unless we begin to understand the seriousness of sin. Sin in the Bible, even when spoken of in the singular rather than the plural, is seen as not so much a transgressive act which may be viewed in isolation, but an infectious disease which spreads corruption and wickedness throughout humanity. The Bible teaches the "original goodness" of humanity, but also the pervasiveness of evil once sin came into the world. The biblical doctrine of "original sin" recognizes that every baby born into the world, no matter how cute, carries the "sin virus." Dawkins says this is a monstrous doctrine, but it reflects reality. Every human does bad things and we can't just blame it on others as if we came into the world undefiled and it's only our environment that has let us down. Many like to operate with a simplistic paradigm of "goodies and baddies," but the spiritually mature know that there is evil in every human heart which only God can defeat and eradicate. If God's justice seems too severe it is because we lack a sense of the utter sinfulness of sin.

---

6. Genesis 6:5
7. Genesis 8:21
8. Psalm 14:3a
9. Luke 18:18–19

THE SINS OF THE FATHERS

Well, let's look at some of the examples Barker gives to support Dawkins's case that the biblical God is unjust. We'll start with the words of the second commandment forbidding idol worship.

> "You shall not bow down to them or worship them; for I, the LORD your God, am a jealous God, *punishing the children for the sin of the fathers to the third and fourth generation of those who hate me*, but showing love to a thousand generations of those who love me and keep my commandments."[10]

Is it just to punish a man's children, grandchildren, great grandchildren and even great, great grandchildren for that man's sins? We could depersonalize the punishment of God by saying he created a universe of cause and effect. We are all affected by the actions of others, especially our parents. Sins of idolatry seem to take a particular hold over families down the generations. In biblical times, extended families lived together, sometimes to four generations. Sinful practices and attitudes by the head of the household will likely corrupt every member of the house.

However, God is not simply stating what would be obvious—that the family reaps the consequences of evil decisions made by its patriarch. He is saying he actively punishes the children for the sin of the fathers to the third and fourth generations. The implication seems to be that this is *because the sin itself is transmitted down the generations*. We may wish things were different, but we know enough about the world to realize that evil behavioral traits tend to get passed down the family line. Nevertheless, a person of faith will believe that God can break what would otherwise be a chain of despair. God, being a God of justice and hope, punishes this inherited sin (the Bible uses the word iniquity to describe generational sin) with a view to bringing reformation of character and breaking this chain. If the members of an extended household experienced no collective sanction for the idols brought into the family by their patriarch, they would likely continue the tradition of idolatry. The Bible says that God punishes those he loves.[11] His punishment of sin down to the third and fourth generation was intended to be both just and reformative.

There is no contradiction here between the words of the second commandment and Ezekiel 18, where the prophet, who lived hundreds of years later, is speaking about sons not *dying* for the sins of their fathers. This chapter is a good example of a biblical prophet speaking against a faulty

---

10. Exodus 20:4
11. Hebrews 12:6

understanding of what God had said earlier in Scripture, rather than contradicting it. The people of Ezekiel's time, languishing as they were in exile in Babylon, were quoting a proverb "the fathers eat sour grapes and the children's teeth are set on edge." They were either denying their own complicity in the sins of their fathers or suggesting that there was no hope for them as the children of rebels (or perhaps both). Ezekiel says that on the contrary, spiritual death is not inevitable. The children will, through God's grace, be able to choose righteousness and are not doomed to follow the way of their fathers.

> "The soul who sins is the one who will die. The son will not share the guilt of the father, nor will the father share the guilt of the son. The righteousness of the righteous man will be credited to him, and the wickedness of the wicked will be charged against him."[12]

Those descendants, disciplined by God in exile in Babylon because of the failings of their forefathers and their own inherited sin, can repent and find life. So for example, the prophet Daniel, a few years later, living under the dominant Persians, seeing himself implicated in the sins of those forefathers, confessed them representationally. His prayer was honored by God and he received a heavenly visit from the Archangel Gabriel, who said he was "highly esteemed" and gave him a messianic prophecy.[13] And to all those who love him, like Daniel, Exodus 20:4 says he continues to bless their descendants to a "thousand generations." His generational *punishments* are therefore relatively temporary. His generational *blessings*, by contrast, go on and on into eternity.

The Old Testament is clear that if a man had a wicked father but he himself lived righteously, his soul would live (he would experience God's salvation).[14] Also, God's law in Deuteronomy had specifically prohibited the practice of the death penalty being applied to the children of people convicted of serious offences.[15] This was in contrast to some heathen nations where, for example, if a man negligently constructed a building which killed someone else's son, then the negligent builder's son was to be killed in retribution.[16]

---

12. Ezekiel 18:20
13. Daniel 9:1–27
14. Ezekiel 18:20
15. Deuteronomy 24:16
16. Law Code of Hammurabi c1780 BC [code 230] http://mcadams.posc.mu.edu/txt/ah/Assyria/Hammurabi.html

The Jews, right up to Jesus time, tended to see various misfortunes as a direct consequence of one's own sin or the sin of one's forebears (despite parts of their wisdom literature, such as the Psalms and Job, which should have challenged this simplistic view). Jesus corrected this assumption,[17] but he never said anything to deny the generational effects of idolatry.

COLLECTIVE PUNISHMENT

What about the idea of wider collective punishment? The story of King David counting the fighting men of Israel (told in two slightly differing accounts in Second Samuel 24 and First Chronicles 21) is cited by Barker as evidence of God's injustice. David is guilty of a sin by taking a census of the fighting men of Israel in the wrong way and with the wrong motive. Under the law of Moses any census had to be held in a prescribed way, involving the payment of a "ransom" or "atonement offering" for the life of each person counted. The amount was a half-shekel for each adult whether they were rich or poor. (Contrary to Barker, this does not indicate God was unfair to the poor, but that each person had equal value to God). If this atonement money wasn't paid God warned that a plague would come on the people.

David's irregular census showed that he was neglecting the need for atonement for sin. It also implied that he saw the people of Israel as belonging to him rather than God, and indicated he was choosing to put his trust in his military strength rather than the LORD. Through the prophet Gad, God offered him three options as punishment for what he did. He was to think it over. Either there would be three years of famine, three months of military defeats or three days of plague.

Interestingly, a conscience-stricken David chooses the plague option. The other options would have involved putting Israel at the mercy of the other nations—either for food relief to avert starvation or quarter after surrender in battle. He would rather have the more direct sanction of God warned in the law of Moses—the plague. God might, after all, be merciful and cut short the punishment. After seventy thousand people died across the land, God did indeed withdraw the angel of death as he came to Jerusalem. David himself asked God to punish him and his family rather than the people anymore. After David had sacrificed a burnt offering of oxen on the threshing floor where God had halted the destroying angel, (land which he paid for in full himself and which was to be the site of the future Temple), the plague was finally ended.

17. John 9:1–3

There appear to be at least two problems in this story regarding God's justice. First, God is described in the Second Samuel account as being angry with Israel for something unspecified. It could perhaps have been the continuing fallout from the rebellion of David's son Absalom. Most translations of that account then say God "incited" David against the Israelites. The First Chronicles twenty-one account says it was "the adversary" (mostly translated as "Satan" but it could also have been someone who had a malign influence at court) who rose up against Israel and incited David to take the census. This apparent discrepancy could be due to the difficulty in translating the Hebrew in Second Samuel twenty-four where there is no subject for the verb "incited." It might have been God or God's anger doing the inciting, or it might have been David's own sinful inclination, or it might have been Satan or "an adversary," as in the Chronicles version. But even if the usual Second Samuel translation is correct, the apparent discrepancy can be explained by the fact that God in his sovereign power can use Satan or wicked people to accomplish his purposes, even though they act with evil motives.

Sometimes in Scripture, God punishes people by "hardening their hearts" or "giving them over" to what their foolish desires want to do, rather than fortifying them with the sense to avoid trouble. This is not unjust. We are only able to exist and make right choices by the grace of God and God has every right to withdraw his grace leaving us to the consequences of our own sinful folly. And he only does this in order to bring about some good purpose. For example, Pharaoh's heart was hardened by God against letting the Israelites go temporarily to worship God in the desert. This is another way of saying that God chose not to enable Pharaoh's stubborn will to have wise discernment in the face of devastating plagues, in order that he might carry out the permanent and complete deliverance of his people from Egypt. This was entirely compatible with Pharaoh bearing full responsibility for his cruelty and obstinacy. And if God is described as using Satan to incite someone he wishes to punish to some self-defeating action then it is the same as saying that God himself incited them. It is not unjust but a case of a guilty person being left to foolishly reap the harvest of their guilt.

Secondly, why does God punish the nation when it seemed to be only David who sinned in calling the census? David actually asks this question of God himself after he sees the plague taking its toll on the people. It could have been that God was angry with the people because although David had been the one to give the order, it was the rebellious ways of the Israelites that had pressured David into checking out how many fighting men he should have been able to count on. It could have been a reciprocal example of the representative principle in which the sin of the people caused David to incur guilt himself as their head through a foolish decision and, as head of the nation, his sin in turn brought punishment upon Israel.

International law today recognizes the validity of war or economic sanctions being carried out against countries, the leaders of which have ordered their army to undertake an illegal invasion or who are threatening world peace by commanding their scientists and engineers to develop nuclear weapons contrary to resolutions of the United Nations. The people in these countries reap the consequences of the way they are led by their leaders. If nations today recognize the principle of corporate responsibility then how much more does God have the right to bring judgment upon nations for the direction their leaders pursue?

THE HOLY THINGS

In his chapter about God's apparent injustice, Barker makes a lot of the punishments inflicted by God in relation to an object declared most holy by God—the Ark of the Covenant. The Ark was a gold-plated wooden box into which the Israelites were commanded to put the two stone tablets with the Ten Commandments engraved on them along with Aaron's staff and a gold jar of manna. These artefacts all spoke of God's divine power. The Bible says God engraved the Commandments himself. Aaron's staff, unlike the staffs of the other tribes of Israel had budded, blossomed and produce almonds overnight in a miraculous confirmation that the priesthood was vested in him and his descendants and the other tribes should stop grumbling and accept that fact.[18] The manna was the 'bread from heaven' which fed the Israelites in their desert wanderings. When the Tabernacle was built and later the Temple in Jerusalem, the Ark was kept in the curtained-off "Holy of Holies," where only the High Priest could go once a year after the appropriate sacrifices.

Of course, Barker denies there was anything miraculous in the Ark at all. He says it was all a hoax. To stop people looking into the Ark and seeing that there was nothing miraculous in it, people were instructed to keep well away. If they came near, or looked inside, they were killed by the authorities, who then claimed it was divine power that caused their deaths, in order to instill fear and compliance among the gullible people.

This is therefore, to his mind, further evidence for him saying that the "fictional," biblical God is unjust. The two specific occasions he refers to are in First and Second Samuel. In First Samuel chapters four to six the story is this. The Israelites are defeated in battle by the Philistines and four

18. Numbers 17

thousand[19] are killed. The Israelites, instead of weeping, fasting and praying and seeking the LORD as to why they were defeated, decide that they should take the Ark of the Covenant from the Tabernacle, now based at Shiloh, and carry it into battle with them. The Israelites were, in effect, making a "good luck charm" out of the Ark, seeking to use it superstitiously to give them power over their enemies. God, however, would not allow the Israelites to mis-treat a sacred object which had been given to them to remind them of his divine power and holiness.

Almighty God cannot be manipulated or controlled or domesticated to serve the interests of one group of people, even the people of Israel, his chosen ones. The Israelites were so pumped up when the Ark came into their camp that the ground shook with their shouting. But this, under God's sovereign plan, only served to put the Philistines on their mettle and they again beat the Israelites, killing thirty thousand[20] of them.

The Ark was captured and put in the Temple of the Philistine god Dagon in Ashdod, where Dagon's statue fell over and broke overnight as a result! Then God inflicted tumors on the people of Ashdod, so they passed the Ark on to the city of Gath where the same thing happened, causing mass panic. So the Philistine leaders then thought they would try Ekron, but the people there understandably would not hear of it. After seven months in Philistine territory, the priests and diviners came up with a plan to try to get the Ark safely and respectfully back to Israel, making a guilt offering to the LORD of five gold tumors and five gold rats, one for each of the Philistine rulers. They put it on a cart driven by cows that were separated from their penned up calves and which had never been yoked, along with the gold offering and watched to whether it would miraculously head straight for Beth Shemesh, the nearest town of Israel. If it did, they would conclude that it was indeed God who had been punishing them and that he wanted the Ark back in Israel.

Well the cart did go straight along the road to Beth Shemesh. The people of the town chopped up the wood of the cart and offered the cows as a sacrifice and got some Levites to put the Ark on a large rock. Only the Levites were to carry the Ark according to God's instructions. But seventy of

19. The Hebrew word translated "thousand" is *'eleph*, which sometimes means "clan" or "family unit." Often large numbers given in English translations of the Old Testament seem, on other evidence, to be too large. There is no agreement as yet on how *'eleph* should be translated in many situations and the subject is controversial. I would argue that these problems could be resolved with research and patience without resorting to the idea that the biblical writers were mistaken or made wildly exaggerated claims. See J.W. Wenham *The Large Numbers of the Old Testament*, Tyndale bulletin, 18, 1967.

20. Ibid.

the people of the town looked into the Ark and were struck down by God. Unlike the Philistines, who had learned to respect the divine name represented by the Ark, these people were taking liberties with the Almighty with extreme recklessness. They still had not learned about the holiness of God.

In the film *Raiders of the Lost Ark,* the year is 1936 and Indiana Jones is trying to find the lost Ark before the Nazi archaeologists do. The Nazis want it because they believe it will give them increased power. They should have read the book of First Samuel. When they do find it and open the cover a vortex of flame forms above the Ark and shoots bolts of fiery energy into the gathered Nazi soldiers, killing them all. Heads shrivel up or explode and faces are melted. Flames then engulf the remains of the doomed assembly, save for Jones and his girl Marion, who are tied up but have wisely averted their eyes, and the pillar of fire rises into the sky. The Ark's lid is blasted high into the air before dropping back down onto the Ark and sealing it. The film was enormously successful. As far as I know no-one has criticized the climax for being unfair to the Nazis!

In Second Samuel chapter six David decides to bring the Ark to Jerusalem. With thirty thousand[21] chosen men, he goes to the house of Abinadab, where the Ark is, on a hill. Abinadab's sons were guiding the oxen driven cart. There were enthusiastic celebrations. The oxen stumbled. Uzzah reached out and took hold of the Ark. Verse 7 says,

> "the LORD'S anger burned against Uzzah because of his irreverent act; therefore God struck him down and he died there beside the Ark of the Lord."

Wasn't poor Uzzah simply trying to be helpful? It was extremely harsh and unjust we might think. David certainly did. He was angry at first but then afraid. He appears to have reflected on the incident and repented of the careless disregard for God's commands which led to this tragedy. The next time he moved the Ark he did it much more reverently, sacrificing a bull and a fattened calf after the Ark had been carried only six paces.

God had after all given Moses and Aaron specific instructions about the movement of the Ark of the Covenant. It was to be borne upon men's shoulders, and carried by Levites only, and specifically those of the family of Kohath, using the poles prescribed.[22] "*After Aaron and his sons have finished covering the holy furnishings and all the holy articles, and when the camp is ready to move, the Kohathites are to come to do the carrying. But they must*

---

21. Ibid.
22. Numbers 7:9

not touch the holy things or they will die."[23] Touching the ark was in direct violation of God's law and he warned it would result in death.

Failure to follow God's precise instructions indicated a disobedient, rebellious heart. The Ark had been staying in his father's house. Perhaps Uzzah succumbed to pride or felt it was his job to "look after" God. Familiarity sometimes breeds contempt. Barker claims Uzzah was a righteous and helpful man who had made a harmless mistake and was mercilessly cut down as a result. But the Bible describes his conduct as *irreverent*.

The Office for Nuclear Regulation makes rules for the transport of radioactive material. If these rules were shown to be disregarded and such material transported in a slipshod manner, there would be a public outcry due to the danger to public health. We should have even more respect for the living God than we do for radioactive material. Only a fool treats God with irreverence. If the Israelites had lost sight of the awesome holiness of God, they would have quickly disintegrated as a nation. Jesus taught us to pray "our Father in heaven, *holy* is your name."

WITCHES, THE DEATH SENTENCE AND EXCLUSIVITY OF THE PRIESTHOOD

Two other "injustices" claimed by Barker include the command to execute witches[24] and the requirement that priests who come to the altar to present sacrifices must not have physical defects.[25]

In our Western culture today the term *witch* conjures up a variety of images. What the Bible meant by a witch or a sorcerer was not a mother-earth type who likes to experiment with herbal medicine. Witchcraft involved the manipulation of spiritual power in rebellion against God. In countries where animism (the worship of spirits) is entrenched the witchdoctor is a powerful and feared figure. He or she will pronounce curses on enemies for the payment of money and concoct spells and magic rituals for the relief of sickness, infertility and crop failure. Witchdoctors in Africa have been known to advise men with HIV/AIDS to seduce or rape a virgin (even a child) in order to be cured.

Toleration of this sort of witchcraft would have been disastrous for the healthy emergence of God's people in the Promised Land, prone as they were anyway to the influence of debased forms of worship. However, it is important to repeat that commands given to Israel by God in the Old

23. Ibid. 4:15
24. Exodus 22:18
25. Leviticus 21:16–23

Testament cannot or should not necessarily be directly translated into modern day situations. There have been times when witch-hunts were organized in Christendom. The problem with them was that they tended to whip up public hysteria, rumors, unjust accusation and people blaming everyone's problems on some unfortunate woman who was probably just a harmless eccentric who owned a cat. On the other hand, some things associated with witchcraft, such as physical and sexual abuse, threatening language, and the administration of noxious substances have always rightly been serious criminal offences.

There were offences in Old Testament law which carried the death penalty. Some might say this of itself shows the biblical God was unjust. However long-term imprisonment for serious wrongdoing was not an option then (even if desirable). Capital offences were all highly serious ones that tended to destroy the community through which God intended to reveal himself to the nations—for example murder, adultery, sexual perversion, cursing parents. Theft was not an offence carrying the death penalty (unless you stole a person by kidnapping them). The penal code was nothing like as harsh as the eighteenth century English one where you could be hung for pickpocketing goods worth a shilling. (£30 in today's money).[26] You do not have to advocate the death penalty today to see that capital punishment could have been appropriate for some deeds then.

What about the banning of disabled people from the priesthood? I live near Stoke Mandeville Hospital, where Dr. Ludwig Guttmann's pioneering work with people with spinal injuries led to it becoming the birthplace of the modern Paralympics. In 2012, on the same night as the opening ceremony of the Paralympic Games in London, I organized a community festival in the Stoke Mandeville Stadium. There was a live big screen link to London, and an opportunity for people to take part in Paralympic sports as well as many other games and attractions. Of course, every effort was made to make the event inclusive, with disabled tracks on the grass, multi-sensory zones, and hundreds of volunteers from churches making sure people felt welcome and had a good time—and all for free (including the barbeque food!) Today, we rightly make greater effort than ever before in history to afford opportunities for disabled people to fulfil their potential. So, wasn't it unfair and rather mean of God to say that priests could not offer sacrifices before him if they were disfigured or handicapped?

Again, we must be careful to understand what the role of a priest was in Old Testament times. People commonly use the word "priest" today to describe someone ordained in the Anglican church, such as myself. This

---

26. https://www.nationaljusticemuseum.org.uk/what-was-the-bloody-code/

is somewhat unfortunate because a pastor, vicar, minister or clergy person is not the same thing as an Old Testament priest. Apart from prayer and teaching, one of the main jobs of an Old Testament priest was to offer animal sacrifices on an altar to God on behalf of the people. A priest was to be a visual, symbolic mediator between God and Man, set apart as holy, in the same way that the Tabernacle or Temple was set apart as a "holy area." An essential part of the symbolism of the whole sacrificial system was that selected perfect animals had to be offered in a physically perfect, closed off space by specially set apart, physically perfect, human beings. The whole set-up was a visual lesson in how God's holiness meant that he was perfect, without sin and completely separate and distinct from sinful, morally disfigured humans. Sacrificial worship had to be conducted in a way that faithfully observed the God-given symbols relating to sin and holiness.

Of course, someone who was otherwise qualified to be a priest, but who was a dwarf or hunch-back, or had been castrated or had lost an arm or a leg was not by reason of their disability *morally* inferior to a priest who appeared to be a perfect specimen of manhood. But he was *symbolically* inferior. And a priest had to symbolize wholeness and perfection. The barriers of course did not just include disability. To offer sacrifices on behalf of the Jewish people you had to be a male, a descendant of Aaron and ritually clean at the time. When the Temple was built in Jerusalem, the wonder of the ancient world, you had to be a Jew to get further than the outer court, the "Court of the Gentiles." You had to be male to get past the "Court of Women." You had to be a priest to get into the "Holy Place," and you had to be a high priest to get into the "Holy of Holies" and that was only possible once a year after a special sacrifice.

When Jesus was crucified as the fulfilment of all sacrifices, the curtain separating the Holy Place from the Most Holy Place was torn from top to bottom, symbolizing new access to God by all who have faith in him. Barriers of caste, gender, national identity and disability were removed. The Temple was replaced by Jesus as the way to encounter God and God allowed a Roman army to demolish it a few years later, in 70AD, when the Jews rebelled.

The God of the Bible is at times a severe God. However, he is never unjust. Even when it comes to forgiving, God does not compromise his justice, which is why the cross was necessary for our forgiveness.

Chapter 4

Unforgiving?

"God will forgive. That's his job."
—Henrich Heine

A commodities trader emailed a man who owed him ten thousand pounds, reminding him to transfer the amount to his bank account straight away by the agreed deadline. The debtor emailed back to say that things were very difficult for him and his family just then and could he please be given a bit more time to forward the money. The trader replied that he was entitled to the money and wanted it straight away for a sunshine break in the Bahamas with his wife and kids. If it wasn't forthcoming when due he would take legal action, he threatened. The two men both happened to work for the same firm in the City of London. The next day the trader was called in to see his boss. His boss told him he'd heard about how he had threatened his colleague and he was therefore firing him for gross misconduct. He called security to come and escort him from the premises.

Why did the boss take this action? Why should the trader have let the debtor off or agreed to wait patiently for an unknown length of time for the debt to be repaid? He had the right, according to their agreement, to get his money returned by a certain date, otherwise he would be out of pocket and his family would miss out on something they were looking forward to. It was no more than he was due and he was entitled to legal redress. They'd made an agreement fair and square. So, what was going on?

The reason why the boss did this was that there was a background to the story. Just the week before, he had personally let off this very same trader a much bigger debt. For various reasons the man had accrued a debt to his boss of well over a million pounds. He had come to the office in tears to say that there was no way he could pay by the deadline, as he was facing all sorts of pressures and could he please have more time. The boss had felt sorry for him and told him not to worry about it, generously cancelling the debt and bearing the full loss himself from his own resources. Now he had heard that the man to whom he'd shown mercy had, within a few days, chosen to show no mercy at all to another man employed by the firm who owed *him* money. He was livid.

Jesus told the original story in Matthew's Gospel chapter eighteen. In Jesus' version the unforgiving servant had owed his boss, the king, the equivalent of billions of pounds, a ridiculously large amount that he had no chance of ever paying back and he had, amazingly, been forgiven the whole debt by the king. The amount owed to him by his fellow servant was a hundred days wages. It would have been in some contexts considered a significant amount but it was tiny in comparison with what he'd owed the king.

The concept of forgiveness is such a central one in Christianity that cultures shaped by the Bible tend to take the idea for granted. But why should God forgive? Why should we be let off our nasty little deeds, let alone our great crimes? Why should God not make us pay for our greed, selfishness, cruelty, lust, spite, lies, unfaithfulness and general wickedness? Shouldn't we be called to account in full for our actions? Where is the justice otherwise? If we injure others, doesn't fairness require that we in turn suffer an equal amount? Doesn't the Hindu law of karma provide something morally sharper than Christianity with its talk of sins forgiven and the guilty going free without condemnation?

Why should God show "amazing grace" to save wretches who don't deserve it or write off the moral debts of filthy rotten sinners? The only person who is entitled to expect somebody to forgive a third party is someone who has previously forgiven that somebody a greater debt, like the king in the parable Jesus told. We cannot consider God obliged to forgive because it's not as if God has been forgiven any debt *he* owed to anyone. Furthermore, what about *justice*? Barker in his third chapter charges God with being unjust. He implies that it should be his job to uphold justice as a just judge would. Well surely it is *unjust* for a judge to find a defendant liable for injuring someone in a civil suit but then decline to make them pay compensation to the plaintiff commensurate to the harm done? Or how is it just for a judge to find someone guilty of a crime in a criminal case but then let them off the appropriate sentence? Barker seems to want it both ways. He wants to accuse God of not being just in one chapter and then in the very next chapter he accuses him of being unforgiving because he is willing to sometimes carry out a just sanction. Needless to say, he gives no explanation of how justice and forgiveness could be combined.

The only way that God can be both just *and* forgiving is if he somehow both satisfies the demands of his own sense of justice (from whom all justice proceeds) *and* provides a means by which the cost of this (the moral debt) is borne by himself rather than by us. To forgive the servant, the king had to be willing to absorb the loss of the vast amount he was owed. This of course is what God has done through the cross of Christ. God paid the cost of our sin himself. More of this later in the book. But why should God *want* to be forgiving as well as just? Why doesn't he just settle for being just and fair, which nobody could rightly blame him for? It is because, contrary to Dawkins and Barker, he *is* a forgiving God. He delights in showing mercy (i.e., not giving people what they deserve but withholding judgment to allow time for repentance and then forgiving them.)

> "Do I take any pleasure in the death of the wicked? declares the Sovereign Lord: Rather, am I not pleased when they turn from their ways and live?"[1]
>
> "The Lord is compassionate and gracious, slow to anger, abounding in love. He will not always accuse, nor will he harbor his anger forever; he does not treat us as our sins deserve or repay us according to our iniquities. For as high as the heavens are above the earth, so great is his love for those who fear him; as far as the east is from the west, so far has he removed our transgressions from us."[2]

The Old Testament, according to Christian belief, is one long build-up to the coming of Christ. God was under no obligation to forgive mankind's sin or the people of Israel's sin. But even before time he had purposed to send his one and only son into the world to provide the necessary atoning sacrifice for our sins. But before this happened, the people of Israel needed to understand that God's forgiveness came at a cost and required deep repentance. The sacrifice of unblemished livestock prefigured the one perfect sacrifice to come and taught the Israelites that there was no forgiveness without the shedding of blood.[3] Why is this so? Because to be forgiven, we have "to die to ourselves" by humbly admitting that sin brings spiritual death (alienation from God) and that we can only be reconciled to him

1. Ezekiel 18:23
2. Psalm 103:8–12
3. Hebrews 9:16–28

by being given, in a mysterious way (later to be revealed as being through Christ) "new life."

It is a spiritual law that sin brings death. Mankind was warned about this by God when Adam and Eve were in the Garden of Eden.[4] But there is also a spiritual mystery that a perfectly innocent representative man can vicariously taste death for mankind, defeat it through God's resurrection power and enable spiritually dead people to receive new life. God was willing to shed the blood of his son, incarnate as man, to provide cleansing or "expiation" for our sins. In the Old Testament the Bible uses anthropomorphic language when it says that when God smelled the pleasant aroma of a burnt offering, he was no longer angry with the people.[5] If they were truly repentant, his wrath was turned away as he anticipated the one perfect sacrifice which would deal with sins once and for all planned before the creation of the world. If they were not truly repentant and remained hostile to God he warned that he would refuse to take delight in any aromas from sacrifices and his wrath would come upon them and *not* be propitiated.[6]

Forgiveness by God does require a truly repentant heart on our part. That is why there are several passages, including the ones cited by Barker, where God says he will *not* forgive (in the sense that he will not overlook) the actions of unrepentant, hard hearted people. This shows his commitment to justice. But in punishing sin more leniently than people deserved under the Old Covenant, he reveals his grace and forgiving nature. He showed the people of Israel time and time again that he was willing to forgive when they turned back to him in godly sorrow for their sins.

An example of the amazingly forgiving nature of God in Scripture is the story of King Manasseh told in Second Chronicles chapter thirty-three. He is described as "doing evil in the eyes of the LORD, following the detestable practices of the nations the LORD had driven out before the Israelites." He rebuilt high places for idol worship, erected altars to the Baals and made Asherah poles (Asherah was Baal's mother and mistress and it was held that their incestuous union brought fertility to the land. Worship of them involved degraded ritual sex.) Manasseh worshipped the stars and even built altars to them in the Temple courts. He sacrificed his sons in the Valley of Ben Himmon (the place which came to symbolize hell), practiced sorcery, divination and witchcraft, and consulted mediums and spiritualists. Manasseh led the people into doing more evil than the Canaanites had

---

4. Genesis 2:17

5. The soothing aroma of sacrificial offerings is spoken about throughout Leviticus. Leviticus 4:31 explicitly links this to atonement.

6. Leviticus 26:27–31

done before them. The LORD spoke a warning to Manasseh but he paid no attention.

Just as he had driven the Canaanites out of the land, the LORD brought the army commanders of the King of Assyria against Manasseh. They captured him and took him prisoner, put a hook in his nose, bound him with bronze shackles and took him as a prize to Babylon.

In distress, he finally turned to the LORD and humbled himself and prayed to God for mercy. Despite all the evil he had done and led others to do the Bible says "the LORD was moved by his entreaty and listened to his plea; so he brought him back to Jerusalem and to his kingdom. Then Manasseh knew that the LORD is God."[7]

Nor is God's forgiving nature in the Old Testament confined to the Israelites. Of all the nations spoken of in the Bible, Assyria was perhaps the most cruel. But God desired even the Assyrians to repent and find life. He commanded the reluctant prophet Jonah to go to its capital city Nineveh and warn them of his imminent judgment. After a roundabout route involving submarine transport, Jonah finally got there. The king and the people took Jonah seriously, fasting from food and drink (and including even their animals in this), putting on sackcloth, calling out to the LORD and repenting of their violence and evil ways. Jonah 3:10 says,

> "When God saw what they did and how they turned from their evil ways, he relented and did not bring on them the destruction he had threatened."

Jonah was angry that God chose to forgive these heathen people who were a threat to Israel and complained that his prophecy of doom would not now come about.

> "Isn't this what I said, LORD, when I was still at home? That is what I tried to forestall by fleeing to Tarshish. I knew that you are a gracious and compassionate God, slow to anger and abounding in love, a God who relents from sending calamity."[8]

After giving him some practical teaching about grace using a vine to shelter Jonah from the heat, God replied to Jonah that Nineveh "had one hundred and twenty thousand who could not tell their right hand from their left," which probably meant they lacked the moral discernment that

---

7. Second Chronicles 33:12–13
8. Jonah 4:2

the Israelites had because they did not have the covenant relationship and the Law that Israel had. "Should I not be concerned about that great city?"[9]

Sceptics doubt the historicity of the story because of the miraculous provision of the whale to save Jonah from drowning (although the same Jonah, son of Amittai, is mentioned in the historical narrative Second Kings 14:25) but the point here is that the God known to the Israelites was understood by them to care even for their greatest enemies. This is remarkable in that within the same century (quite possibly before the book of Jonah was written down) the Assyrians un-repented and invaded Israel, deported its people and re-populated the area with other groups from around its empire.

In the New Testament, Saul tried to destroy the Christian church, cruelly dragging off men and women to prison and breathing out murderous threats. Yet all his sins were forgiven when he turned to Christ and was baptized.[10] This is the God who Dawkins and Barker charge with being unforgiving!

On 7th December 2000 I was excited as it was the day of my wedding rehearsal. The following day I was going to be getting married to Anna in the cathedral church of St. Michael, Coventry. What I didn't plan for was the belated discovery of an unexploded second world war bomb in the grounds. Police cordoned the area off. Fortunately, the situation was safely resolved and our nuptials went ahead without any problems. After the service, we walked to the reception through the neighboring ruins of the old fourteenth century Gothic cathedral, destroyed by German bombers on the night of 14th November 1940, and preserved to this day as a memorial alongside the new Cathedral consecrated in 1956.

The morning after the night of the bombing, the people of Coventry walked among the ruins of their cathedral church. The Provost (cathedral worship leader) got a piece of chalk and scribbled on one of the still standing sections of wall, "Father forgive." He didn't write "Father forgive *them*" because he was conscious that everyone needs God's forgiveness.

In 2005, my late father-in-law, Colin Bennetts, the then Bishop of Coventry, and a linguist, preached in German at the re-consecration of the new Frauenkirche in Dresden, the city obliterated by the British raid on February 13th 1945. The golden orb and cross for the rebuilt church came as a gift from the Dresden Trust, set up by a former canon at Coventry Cathedral. The leader of the team of silversmiths in London which made it, the appropriately named Alan Smith, was the son of Frank Smith, the pilot of one of the 796 Lancaster bombers that eviscerated the city and its beloved

9. Ibid. 4:11
10. Acts 9:1–19

Baroque church in the resulting firestorm caused by the bombing and who suffered PTSD as a result.

After the war, Coventry became a center for reconciliation with global peace-making figures like Andrew White and Justin Welby, who became Archbishop of Canterbury, joining the Cross of Nails community at the time my father-in-law was there. The place is a highly symbolic testimony to the power of forgiveness in the name of Jesus. and the reconciliation brought about between God and us by the cross of Christ.

Today is the era of God's forgiveness and grace to all because Christ provided full atonement for all who are willing to be united to him in faith, but there will come a time when forgiveness is no longer available and the opportunity to repent (turn away from sin) will be over. Old Testament warnings of judgment prefigure the New Testament's warning that God's patience will one day come to an end with those who continually reject his offer of salvation.

Chapter 5

Control Freak?

Then God said, "Let us make man in our image, in our likeness, and let them rule over the fish of the sea and the birds of the air, over the livestock, over all the earth, and over all the creatures that move along the ground."

—Genesis 1:26

The book of Genesis chapter one reveals that from the outset God delegated authority to mankind to rule over the earth and steward its resources. In chapter two we see that God brought the animals and birds to Adam to see how he would name and classify them. There was a curiosity in the heart of God to see mankind observe and study the natural world.[1] In chapter three we see that Adam and Eve heard the sound of the LORD walking in the garden "in the cool of the day." This suggests that God appeared only at certain times and was not always breathing down the neck of Adam and Eve but giving them space to enjoy his creation and look after it. So in each of the first three chapters of the Bible we have evidence that refutes the notion of God as a control freak.

The second Old Testament book of Exodus contains the story of Israel's deliverance from slavery in Egypt. It also includes the Ten Commandments and other laws given to the people by God. But there is also a lot of detailed

---

1. Dawkins really should reflect on the number of great scientists both living and dead who are counted among the ranks of Bible-believing Christians. See https://en.wikipedia.org/wiki/List_of_Christians_in_science_and_technology

instruction about the construction and furnishing of the Tabernacle, which was basically a moveable Temple, designed to be taken with the Israelites during their desert journeys and set up when they made camp. When the pillar of cloud and fire moved from over the Tabernacle the Israelites broke camp and followed until it stopped somewhere else.[2]

Barker claims that these detailed specifications regarding the Tabernacle show the God of the Bible's controlling nature. He accuses him of being very picky with the minutiae of how he was worshipped, obsessing about the layout, dimensions, materials, color scheme and furniture and sacrificial implements. By way of contrast to this, Barker makes the startling and nonsensical claim at the beginning of chapter five of *God: the Most Unpleasant Character in all Fiction* that there are very few moral principles in the Old Testament—very little guidance toward leading mature ethical lives.

Well excuse me! The Old Testament provides a wealth of moral wisdom that has been enormously influential in the development of ethics and jurisprudence throughout the world. The books of Exodus, Leviticus and Deuteronomy contain the foundational principles of community justice, individual rights and responsibilities, environmental sustainability, care for the vulnerable, sexual purity, rest and recreation. As someone with a law degree, I find the laws relating to health and safety, personal injury, bonded servitude, protection of property, redistribution of wealth and social concern, fascinating and often reflected in the best of our laws today. And the Old Testament prophets have a great deal to say about ethical norms and standards.

> "For if you truly amend your ways and your doings, if you truly execute justice one with another, if you do not oppress the alien, the fatherless or the widow, or shed innocent blood . . . then I will let you dwell in this place, in the land that I gave of old to your fathers forever."[3]
>
> Because you trample upon the poor and take from him exactions of wheat, you have built houses of hewn stone, but you shall not dwell in them. . . ..
>
> "For I know how many are your transgressions, and how great are your sins—you who afflict the righteous, who take a bribe, and turn aside the needy in the gate."[4]

Barker argues that all God's laws relating to worship, ceremony sacrifices, ritual purity indicate a micro-managing, OCD personality more

2. Numbers 9:17
3. Jeremiah 7:5
4. Amos 5:11–12

concerned with his own ascetic pleasure than giving helpful guidelines for practical living.

For all his chapter and verse quoting, he shows no understanding of the nature of God's relationship with the people of Israel. The only thing that held this people together was the covenant bond God had made with them. When worship of the one true God ceased, the people quickly fragmented and got into all sorts of trouble. God's plan of how to structure the camp, with the Tabernacle in the middle with the Levites responsible for it, and the other tribes encamped around, was thoroughly helpful and practical. An architect's job is to produce a blueprint of his visionary creation so the builders and craftsmen can get on and do the job. The New Testament tells us that the design of the Tabernacle somehow reflected spiritual realities in Heaven so of course it was important for God to give precise instructions. God is the creator of dimension, form, proportion, color, material beauty and splendor. Physical things he made are good and can be wonderful symbols of spiritual truths. Even hard-bitten atheists seem to find something awe inspiring when they visit great cathedrals when so much modern architecture built by atheists is soul-less. Was Sir Christopher Wren being a control freak when he designed the blueprint for St Paul's cathedral?

The Tabernacle would have been a beautiful focal point for the worship of the one true God, who had chosen in love to reveal himself to a people in time and space, in order to bless mankind for all time. Of course, there were lots of detailed rules as to how their worship was to be carried out. This was for two reasons. The first was that it would have been very easy for the Israelites to have otherwise developed debased and immoral forms of worship, as did the heathen nations around them. Like these pagans, they were prone to arrogance, lust, impurity, hypocrisy, a desire to manipulate God, and a rebellious spirit. The rules God gave them helped them to know how to steer clear of these attitudes. But of course they did often choose to disobey, which always led to disaster. God's punishments for unauthorized religious practices, which often seemed very severe, were actually merciful interventions to prevent the Israelites destroying themselves.

The second reason there were detailed specifications is that God had a long-term plan for the salvation of the world through Christ. The laws of sacrifice and the elements of Tabernacle (and later Temple) worship foreshadow what he was going to do to defeat sin and reconcile sinful mankind to him.[5] The boundary fence around the Tabernacle and the divisions within it symbolized the distinction between a holy God and unholy, sinful mankind. However, the entrance at the front was wide, symbolizing God's

---

5. Hebrews 9

merciful invitation to enter his court. Jesus would later say "I am the gate."[6] The large altar, ablaze for burned offerings, symbolized his nature as a consuming fire,[7] burning away all impurity. The laver filled with water in which the priests washed their hands and feet symbolized the willingness of God to cleanse us and our duty to be cleansed. Jesus cleansed Peter's feet despite his objection and said that he must allow him to cleanse us for us to be one with Christ.[8]

The golden lampstand in the Holy Place of the Tent of Meeting speaks of God, the light of the world (a title of course claimed by Jesus[9]). The table of twelve loaves of showbread represented the God who is "the bread of life" (another title claimed by Jesus[10]) and the twelve tribes ever present before God. The golden altar of incense speaks of the prayers offered by God's people being like a "sweet smelling aroma" to him.[11]

Inside the curtained-off Holy of Holies, the lid on the Ark of the Covenant, covered by the golden cherubim, known as the "Mercy Seat" was where God appeared, enthroned in glory, symbolism all taken up in Revelation, the last book of the New Testament. Inside the Ark was Aaron's budded staff[12], which had miraculously "come to life" symbolizing resurrection power, the jar of manna representing God's supernatural provision of "the bread of life"[13] and Ten Commandments engraved on tablets, one day to be written on our hearts and not just tablets of stone.[14] Jesus fulfilled all this symbolism, being "The Resurrection," "The Bread of Life," and the one in whom God's law finds perfect expression.[15]

The high priest wore an ephod, which was a kind of apron, made, like the Tabernacle curtains, of blue, scarlet and purple yarn, with finely twisted linen, interwoven with gold, a material particularly symbolizing God's splendor. Blue speaks of heaven, purple of kingship and scarlet of rarity. Twelve precious stones representing the twelve tribes of Israel were set on a perfectly square breastplate attached to the ephod. Each stone had the name

---

6. John 10:7
7. Deuteronomy 4:24, Hebrews 12:29
8. John 13:8
9. Ibid. 8:12
10. Ibid. 6:35
11. Revelation 8:3–4
12. Numbers 17
13. Exodus 16:1–36, John 6:35
14. Jeremiah 31:33
15. Matthew 5:17

of one of the tribes engraved on it. God's people are engraved on his heart—a wonderful picture of his heavenly love for us.

The Tabernacle was no symbol of divine control freakery, but the loving gift of the one who brought his glorious presence into the midst of a people chosen as part of a plan to rescue the whole world from sin and death.

Chapter 6

Vindictive?

"Vindicate me in your righteousness, O LORD my God."
—Psalm 35:24

As someone named after Martin Luther, I was intrigued to find that according to Barker, this German Protestant Reformer had a precursor in the biblical character called Korah. Apparently, Korah, just like Luther three thousand years later, was a man who nobly challenged the concept of elevated human beings who had special access to God and was vindictively treated by the biblical God as a consequence. The popes and cardinals who raged against Luther were actually following biblical precedent!

The story of Korah's rebellion is told in Numbers 16. Moses had been called by God to the colossal task of leading the people of Israel out of slavery in Egypt to freedom in the Promised Land. Like all great leaders, he combined visionary commitment with deep personal humility.[1] When called by God he didn't feel up to the task, but he gradually learned that God didn't need a cocksure alpha male but someone who would trust and obey him. The LORD had a very close relationship with Moses. He talked with him "face to face like a man talks with his friend."[2] He gave instructions for Aaron, Moses' brother to become high priest. This wasn't nepotism, it was

---

1. Numbers 12:3 For interesting research into what makes great leaders see Jim Collins *Good to Great*, New York: Collins, 2001
2. Exodus 33:11

God's idea. Leading the people through the desert was no easy job. It was made harder by their constant grumbling and negativity. Korah and two hundred and fifty Israelite leaders are described as *insolent* in Numbers 16:1 and they rose in rebellion. Like all rebellions, mutinies or revolts, there had to be a rallying cry. Theirs was that Moses and Aaron had set themselves up as more holy than the other Israelites.

But this was untrue. It was *God* who had called them to a leading prophetic and priestly role. They were simply being obedient to God in his instructions regarding the Tent of Meeting and the regulations for worship. Also, Korah and company were not making an honest critique of corrupt religion. They were not asking Moses to refer back to commandments of God which had been departed from. They were people with a rebellious spirit, contemptuous of authority and arrogant in assuming they could do things better than God's appointed leaders. They were speaking a half-truth when they said the whole community was holy. Yes, God had called the Israelites to be set apart from the other nations, but within the nation itself there was, under the Aaronic Covenant, a hierarchy of symbolic holiness. Only the Levites (of which tribe they were members) could administer the holy things and only the specific descendants of Aaron the Levite could make the priestly sacrifices and incense offerings. God himself would not allow others to approach him like Moses and Aaron. Not content with being Levites, they wanted the priesthood too.

The New Testament book of Jude likens those who will reap the consequences of their immoral godlessness and contempt for spiritual authority to those destroyed in Korah's rebellion.[3]

Fast forward from the Exodus to the fifteenth century AD. For nearly one thousand five hundred years the church has had the Old and New Testaments together as the authentic revelation of God's saving truth. The Roman Catholic Church though has usurped the authority of the Bible with its own authority and become corrupt. The Pope said that if people gave him money he could reduce their time in purgatory (which itself was an un-biblical doctrine of an intermediate place between heaven and hell). This was the primary cause of Luther's protest. The Reformation encouraged the translation of the Bible into the vernacular, general biblical literacy and the concept of the "priesthood of all believers." It also provided the theological underpinning for eventual universal education and democracy. This was because it enabled people to understand that since Jesus died, rose and ascended, and the Holy Spirit was poured out on all believers, the Old Testament institution of a separate priestly caste performing sacrifices and mediating

---

3. Jude 11

between God and the people was no longer appropriate. Ordinary people had access to both the Word of God and the Holy Spirit. This provided a slow burning, but far reaching, godly revolution.

Luther was not an arrogant troublemaker who had a general contempt for authority. He was very aware that sinful society needed to have order and strong government and that God calls people into leadership. The Reformation was not rebellion against God but rediscovery of the Word of God. The Reformers set up new or significantly reformed churches because they were driven out of the Roman Catholic church which rejected the core Reformation principles.

Barker claims that the Roman Catholic church was being "biblical" when it sought to crush the Reformation and burn Protestants at the stake, because that was the kind of vindictiveness with which Korah and his supporters were treated by God in the Old Testament when he opposed hierarchical religion. The ground swallowed up the ringleaders and their families and fire burned up the two hundred and fifty other Levites who were approaching the Tent of Meeting to make offerings of incense. In response to this there was a more general rebellion among the other tribes, and 14,700 died before Moses and Aaron made atonement for the people, turning aside God's wrath. This though was a very different scenario to the protests against Roman Catholic practice and teaching by Luther and others. In God's eyes rebellion against lawful authority is "like the sin of divination."[4] It is profoundly anti-God. However, when leaders command things clearly against God's law, then we should refuse to comply, like the apostles in the book of Acts[5] and the Protestant Reformers.

THE VENGEANCE OF GOD

As part of his case that the biblical God is vindictive, Barker lists many verses which speak of God's vengeance. God is undoubtedly a self-declared God of vengeance. The problem with the word "vengeance", is that, like the word "jealous," we associate it with sinful human tendencies. So, a "vengeful" person is pictured as intemperately angry, unforgiving and unnecessarily violent. However, God's vengeance is simply his commitment to justice. God's vengeance is not arbitrary, dependent on irrational mood swings, unfair and out of control. He will only do things that are right. If he punishes, it is because it is deserved and just. If he did not avenge wrongs, there

---

4. First Samuel 15:23
5. Acts 5:29

would be no hope for ultimate justice and we would find ourselves living in a nightmare world.

When we feel we are wronged we, like the psalmist, long for vindication and hope that one day God will give us that vindication. This is not necessarily because we want God to be vindictive. It could be because we have a yearning for justice.

The wonder is not that God is a God of vengeance, which with all the wickedness in this world he certainly should be, but that he so often *withholds* his vengeance. And his wrath is no longer on those who look to the cross, who have been justified by Christ's blood.[6] Even for those who don't have faith in him and who disobey his commands, he nevertheless waits patiently to allow them time to repent.[7] But throughout history, as attested to in Scripture, he has allowed his wrath to break in at times as a warning of the ultimate reality facing those who do not bow the knee to him.

---

6. Romans 5:9
7. Second Peter 3:9

Chapter 7

Bloodthirsty?

"...without the shedding of blood there is no forgiveness."
—Hebrews 9:22

Barker says that compared with God, Dracula was a teetotaler. There is certainly a lot of bloodshed in the Old Testament, but that's because the world *is* so violent. When people study history, they study wars and battles, revolutions and power struggles. Blood features a lot in the New Testament too, but here it is mostly in connection with Jesus' death on the cross and the benefits that flow to us accordingly. The early Christians were accused by their Roman persecutors of drinking human blood when they partook of holy communion and Barker shows a similar level of sophistication in understanding the place of blood in biblical theology.

When the Bible talks about blood, a substance so obviously necessary for human and animal life, it is nearly always in the context of death. When blood is mentioned on its own, it carries the implication that death has occurred, because the blood is no longer coursing through the arteries and veins of a living being, but is being poured out on the land or sprinkled on sacred objects as a purifier.

Why is there so much about blood? For the same reason that death figures so much. Right at the beginning of Genesis, God warns Adam that the day he ate of the tree of the knowledge of good and evil he would die. All who have lived since that fateful day have experienced something that was not part of God's desired will. God created human beings for life with him, not death. Adam did not immediately die physically, but he did die an immediate *spiritual* death. Adam's spirit was no longer vibrant with healthy contact with God. Accordingly, his soul and body began to suffer the long slow approach of death. Physical sickness, pain and premature death through violence or disease came upon humanity from that moment onwards.

Why did God require so many blood sacrifices in the Old Testament? Well, let's think about the first murder.[1] Cain, angry with God and with his brother, and unable or unwilling to process his feelings constructively, murdered his brother Abel. Abel's blood soaked into the earth and it cried out to God from the ground. In the world God made the cry of the innocent is that murder cannot go unavenged. Yet God allowed Cain to live and even put a mark of protection on him, so that he would not be killed as he wandered the earth. Why didn't the Lord strike down Cain as he deserved? Well we know that the Lord "desires not the death of a sinner but that he should turn from his wickedness and live."[2] We also know that "there is no forgiveness without the shedding of blood."[3] In order to enjoy a new relationship with God, the old relationship, destroyed by sin, has to die so that the new one can emerge. This spiritual truth was confirmed by the cross of Christ, who provided forgiveness to all by the shedding of his blood so that, united with him, we die to sin and live a new Spirit-filled life by sharing in the hope of the resurrection.[4]

But as a precursor to the blood shed by Christ, planned since before the creation of the world,[5] God instituted a sacrificial system which involved the shedding of the blood of animals, in order to teach and reinforce the spiritual truth that sin brought death and that, mysteriously, his people's participation in the death of an appropriate substitute could make atonement for sin thus enabling a living relationship with their holy God. How did this work? It was clearly propitiatory. When God saw the blood, he foresaw the blood of his son, shed on the cross and his righteous wrath on sin was turned away. God's wrath is a concept caricatured by atheists and some liberal theologians as a humanly constructed projection onto God of our tendency to lash out at people we don't like. But God's wrath, unlike human wrath is a just and measured antipathy to sin and a righteous refusal to

1. Genesis 4
2. Ezekiel 18:23
3. Hebrews 9:22
4. Romans 6:1–14
5. Revelation 13:8

allow evil to win. Somehow the blood of a carefully prescribed animal sacrifice connected (in the spiritual realm) with the sacrifice of Christ (planned from eternity) so that some benefits of the saving work of Christ were felt by people of faith hundreds of years before he came.

Even before the sacrificial system was introduced, Abel, a righteous (though not sinless) man, understood the necessity of blood sacrifice and brought fat portions from the firstborn of his livestock in offering to God. The irony is that it was this first blood sacrifice offered by man, accepted by God, but the cause of angry resentment in Cain, which linked in with the chain of blood sacrifices leading up to Christ, allowing for forgiveness even for people who have committed murder.

Why is it that there is no forgiveness without the shedding of blood? If God is God, why can't he just forgive without the need for any atonement, any sacrifice, any blood? All I can say is that it must have something to do with the spiritual principles that are part of the mystery of God's character and which infuse God's creation. The response to the cry for justice can be delayed, but it cannot be ignored. All sin is rebellion. Rebelling against the God of life itself deserves death. Therefore, death must ensue. That is the way things are and as human beings we should have the humility to accept it. Praise God we can all participate in the saving death of Christ by faith and receive new life, free from death forever!

But what about all the smiting of Israel's enemies in battle? Surely God is implicated in too much bloodshed according to the Old Testament? Barker lists many examples. He also lists the crimes which attracted the death penalty and time and again quotes the biblical phrase "their blood will be on their own heads."

Well we need to come back the question—how exactly should a good God engage with the world *as it is*? God's salvation plan involved choosing a man of faith from the fertile crescent area four thousand years ago and from his descendants creating a people who would reject idols and worship him. They would be a witness to the other nations of God's holiness, justice and compassion in the way they ordered their society under him. In time the Messiah, the one who was the prefect expression of his character would come from this people to be their savior and the whole world's.

Nation building in a sinful world meant God had to be involved in the painful realities of life and death. His people's identity was forged in the fires of suffering in Egypt. They were rescued only because he struck down the firstborn of Egypt and drowned Pharaoh's charioteers. On their journey to the Promised Land they encountered hostile peoples who wanted to exterminate them and could only survive when they got there by driving out a number of other people groups from Canaan, so they could live in peace.

When superpowers emerged and began to tyrannize Israel and other nations, how could God stop this without raising up Israel or another nation to defeat them in bloody battle?

But in all this God was not unjust. He only punished nations with bloody defeat that were utterly depraved (like the Canaanites) or cruelly attacked Israel without cause (like the Amalekites and Midianites). He kept the Israelites in Egypt for four hundred years before driving out the Canaanites because he said that their evil ways had not yet reached a point where they deserved total expulsion from the land and destruction of their political and religious identity. We need to understand that their depravity included institutionalized child sacrifice, bestiality, incest and prostitution in worship of gods who were believed to approve of these practices. So, the shedding of the blood of those who resisted the Israelites when they entered the land needs to be seen in this context.

The Canaanites had the option of fleeing or totally aligning themselves to Israel and the one true God (like Rahab from Jericho and other people from all sorts of backgrounds). The biblical emphasis is on God driving out the Canaanites rather than the Israelites killing them, and the evidence is that most Canaanites would have fled, as all the people in the country "melted in fear."[6] The words used in connection with the commands regarding the Canaanites, such as "destruction" and "annihilation," should be understood as referring to the religious identity and politico-religious apparatus of Canaanite society.

After the Rwandan genocide, the government took the decision to remove all designation of "Tutsi" and "Hutu" on official documents. The aim was the annihilation, not of people, but of the identities which had been such a factor in the violent history of Rwanda.

However, those Canaanites who chose to resist the God of Israel were destroyed along with their idols and altars. This wasn't because God was unfairly partisan towards the Israelites. When *they* fell into evil ways and refused to repent, they too suffered bloody defeat and exile from the land. We'll consider the accusation of ethnic cleansing in the next chapter and the accusation of genocide in chapter thirteen.

ARE PACIFISTS MORE MORAL THAN GOD?

All killing is a reminder of the fact that we live in a fallen, sinful world. God wishes life not death. However, the Old Testament does teach that there is killing which is morally justified in the sight of God. Judicial execution and

---

6. Joshua 2:9 and Exodus 23:27. See next chapter.

killing in war is not necessarily sinful per se. Otherwise God would have been implicated in sin. But the prophet Isaiah looks forward to a time when

> "He will judge between the nations and will settle disputes for many peoples. They will beat their swords into ploughshares and their spears into pruning hooks. Nation will not take up sword against nation, nor will they train for war anymore."[7]

But did Jesus teach pacifism? He certainly said "turn the other cheek"[8] and "love your enemies"[9] but these commands seem to be about how we personally interact with others—not returning insult for insult and showing respect and compassion even to those who seek to persecute us— rather than abrogating the right of a lawful authority to use military force or an individual to defend himself or another under physical attack. It is true that in the garden of Gethsemane, when faced with the detachment sent to arrest him, Jesus told Peter to put away his sword and said "all who live by the sword die by the sword." Also he went willingly to his death rather than calling for legions to angels to descend with shock and awe on his enemies. But Jesus' non-resistance could simply have been because he was obeying his Father's will to lay down his life for the sins of the world, rather than out of a pacifist commitment.[10] His words to Peter sound like a warning not to embrace a violent way of life.

Neither Jesus, nor John the Baptist, nor any New Testament apostle tells soldiers that they should leave their regiments (although John told them not to extort money from people or frame the innocent and to be content with their pay[11]). Jesus told his disciples that, once he was gone, they should carry a sword and if they didn't have one to sell their cloak to buy one.[12] The context makes it clear he didn't want the disciples to accumulate weapons to prevent his arrest or lead a revolt. Presumably, he just wanted them to be able to protect themselves from bandits on their travels between towns and villages in the future.

This is not to say there have not been honorable and brave pacifists who have witnessed powerfully to the ethic of non-violence. The 2016 movie "Hacksaw Ridge" is about the American Seventh Day Adventist Christian Desmond Doss, who served as a battlefield medic and was the first

---

7. Isaiah 2:4
8. Matthew 5:39
9. Ibid 5:44
10. Ibid 26:52–54
11. Luke 3:14
12. Ibid. 22:36

conscientious objector to receive the Medal of Honor in the US forces for his heroics in the battle of Okinawa in World War Two. Certainly, Gandhi and Martin Luther-King have shown that great things can be achieved by employing non-violent resistance in certain situations, particularly when an appeal can be made to the conscience of the oppressors.[13]

However, an example from some time I spent in South Sudan in 2019 with the organization *Flame International* helps explain why I cannot embrace absolute pacifism. In the course of ministry with the military chaplains in the government forces, I met a Christian pastor who was called away from parish ministry during an outbreak of civil war three years earlier in the capital Juba. Tribal tensions had resulted in some government soldiers seeking revenge for past atrocities. He was initially reluctant to re-enlist but then was given the job by his old commanding officer of seeking to prevent such attacks on civilians. He found one group of women and children caught and about to be killed by a detachment of government soldiers from another tribe, some of whose own civilians had been massacred a few years previously elsewhere in the country by soldiers from the same tribe as these women and children. He told the government unit he was from the same tribe as them and he too had had relatives murdered during the massacre. He had chosen to forgive. He ordered them to disperse or his troops would open fire on them. He was not bluffing. They backed down. To me his actions could not be criticized in any way, but were brave and right. Peace in South Sudan depends on forgiveness and reconciliation, but also the re-establishment of godly authority, law, and order to keep people safe and end communal violence and corruption.

DOES GOD "SEND" WAR AND SUFFERING?

God's omnipotence means the distinction between God "allowing" something and "sending" it is a matter of semantics to someone of faith who is suffering. That is why the psalmist says "in faithfulness you have afflicted me" whereas he could have said "in faithfulness you have allowed me to be afflicted."[14] The latter way of putting things feels more acceptable in today's Western culture, probably because we are more anxious to avoid implicating

---

13. In India, the USA, and South Africa, non-violent civil rights movements have had a powerful impact but I would contend that this is because the Christian consciences of the authorities who were acting oppressively (and fearfully) were sufficiently awoken. Pacifist resistance did not, however, change the hearts of Hitler, Stalin and Genghis Khan.

14. Psalm 119:75

God too directly in anything that feels unpleasant than we are to avoid suggesting God distances himself from the reality of our lives. Like Job, we are willing to say "the LORD giveth," but unlike him, we are not prepared to say "the LORD taketh away." (Job 1:21).

Similarly, in First Samuel 1:6, Hannah's infertility is described by the biblical narrator with the words "The LORD had closed her womb." After "the LORD remembered her" and she conceived Samuel and dedicated him to the LORD in fulfillment of her vow, she made this prayer of praise and thanksgiving which included the words:

> "The LORD brings death and makes alive; he brings down to the grave and raises up. The LORD sends poverty and wealth; he humbles and he exalts."[15]

It is perhaps the Hebrew concept of "struggling with God"[16] which enables the Bible to be frank about God bringing things to bear that we experience as painful. This would include God using his sovereign power to weave the inclinations of sinful hearts and all the consequences of that sin into his plans so that he can be said to "bring" or "send" war, death and poverty, using them as instruments for his good purposes. It is important to say however that this does not mean that war, poverty and death are good things in themselves. They are against his pleasurable or desired will and will thankfully be ended when the fullness of his kingdom comes. God has no evil in him.

Some argue that the Bible (and the world for that matter) is just too violent for us to believe in the goodness of God. Charles Darwin, for example, not only had moral objections to parts of the Bible, he could not reconcile the vast amount of suffering associated with, and indeed necessitated by, evolutionary theory, to both humans and animals, on the one hand, with the goodness of God on the other. Interestingly though, the Darwin who hated controversy and conflict and was so sensitive to pain and suffering was no pacifist. In 1861, the year the American Civil War broke out, Darwin, an ardent Abolitionist, wrote to his American friend Asa Gray.

> "Some few, and I am one even, wish to God, though at the loss of millions of lives, that the North would proclaim a crusade against slavery. In the long run, a million horrid deaths would be amply repaid in the cause of humanity."[17]

---

15. First Samuel 2:6–7
16. The Hebrew word "Israel" literally means "contends with God"
17. Letter dated 5th June 1861 cited by Spencer, Darwin and God, 87

So it appears that Darwin, so troubled at the theological implications of "nature red in tooth and claw," was more than willing to see in this instance a justification for terrible slaughter according to a higher purpose.

Dawkins and Barker should reflect that if a mere mortal can make that kind of moral evaluation, then why cannot Almighty God who is perfectly just and wise. Moreover, he himself knows what it is like to suffer and cannot be accused of theorizing while keeping himself at a safe distance. God has in Christ himself tasted the most horrid of deaths in order to bring salvation to a world he knew would otherwise be lost to ever increasing evil.

Chapter 8

Ethnic Cleanser?

"We don't hate sin so we don't understand what happened to the Canaanites"
—Clay Jones

Ethnic cleansing refers to the systematic eradication of people of a particular background from a particular area of land. The core motivation for it today seems to be hatred of a people for what is intrinsic to their social-cultural identity. Ethnic cleansing has been distinguished from genocide although the two often go together. The goal of ethnic cleansing is to rid an area of territory of a particular people who are seen as a malign influence or contaminating the "purity" of the nation. *Genocide* refers not just to expulsion but the intent of total annihilation. Genocide is usually motivated by a desire for ethnic cleansing and clearly ethnic cleansing is achieved by genocide. The term "ethnic cleansing" came to prominence during the Balkan conflicts in the 1990s. A more recent example is the driving out of Rohingya Muslims from Myanmar.

To accuse God of being an ethnic cleanser is to imply that he has the character of a racist or religious extremist, and he is guilty of "crimes against humanity." What is the evidence Dawkins and Barker give for this claim? A straightforward reading of the Old Testament is all the evidence we need, they argue. Barker cites the commands God gave the Israelites in the books of Exodus, Deuteronomy and Joshua. He claims that the reason Saul angered God in First Samuel 15 was because he wasn't effective enough at his job of ethnic cleansing. In fact, the Bible says Saul angered God because of his disobedience regarding plunder taken from the Amalekites and his fear of man rather than God in this matter. But I will deal with Barker's allegations in chapter thirteen because they relate more to the accusation that the biblical God is genocidal.

Christians do have to accept that the biblical God did, through Moses, command his people to enter the Promised Land and be his instrument in the process of driving out the Canaanite tribes who resided there. This did mean attacking their fortified cities as recorded in the book of Joshua. It meant destroying all traces of Canaanite religion within the territory given to the Israelites. If we say that the Old Testament God is not the real God, as some theologians do[1], then the Old Testament, which Jesus believed was, in its entirety, the true Word of God, becomes worse than useless. It would be evil because it so seriously distorts the character of God. Jesus' credibility is then destroyed too.

The greatest act of "cleansing" in the Bible was the flood in the time of Noah[2], an act of judgment by God that Jesus said should provide a warning of the dreadful reality of final judgment at the end of the age.[3] There was nothing "ethnic" about it and nor did it involve God commanding any humans to take part in the "cleansing." In terms of the overall death toll, or the percentage of human life destroyed, this was the most devastating action God did in the Old Testament. Everyone, young and old, male and female, rich and poor other than Noah and family were drowned, so this is the "Act of God" that we should logically have most ethical problems with. If the driving out of the Canaanites involved "indiscriminate slaughter" as Professor CS Cowles wrongly claims,[4] then the drowning of all of humanity bar Noah by God must be considered as more "indiscriminate."

But if the all-knowing all-wise creator of the universe thought (much to his grief, the Bible says) that the whole of sinful humanity had spiraled down so much that he had to start over through Noah's descendants, then who are we to argue? Are we more just or merciful than God? With the rainbow covenant God made with Noah he promised that never again would he destroy all mankind like he did with the flood. Was that because he felt he had been too hasty or unjust? No. His covenant promise meant that, in his mercy, God committed himself to doing what it took to bring salvation to a

---

1. See CS Cowles's contribution in *Show No Mercy*, Grand Rapids: Zondervan, 2003 with other contrasting contributions from Eugene Merrill, Daniel Gard and Tremper Longman III
2. see Genesis chapters 6–9
3. Matthew 24:37–39
4. Cowles *Show No Mercy* 15, 17, 27

world where every inclination of man's heart was evil.[5] He knew that this had to culminate in the only way justice and mercy could be reconciled, his self-offering in the person of his son, born as a man, and able to make atonement for mankind's sins as a perfect, once and for all sacrifice. And this is the doctrine some claim as unjust, cruel or sadomasochistic!

This plan involved initially planting a people he would train in holiness in a territory he set aside. In the previous chapter I explained how he didn't just arbitrarily kick out an innocent group of people from their land to provide living space for his chosen ones. He waited till the corruption of the Canaanites was so bad and the land so defiled that the land itself could be said to have "vomited the inhabitants out."[6] We're talking here about the most debased form of worship imaginable. Child sacrifice (not babies, but children old enough to know what was about to happen and be terrified) ritual orgies, abuse, incest, bestiality, perversion and cruel oppression of every kind characterized the Canaanite kingdoms by this time. The Canaanite gods practiced incest—Baal, the fertility god was believed to have had sex with his mother Asherah, his sister Anat, and his daughter Pidray.[7] Canaanite gods had sex with animals. The evil Jezebel from Tyre, who actually became queen of Israel at a particular low point in their history, was a typical Canaanite ruler. She worshipped Baal with all the degrading and disgusting practices this involved. She was so immoral she thought nothing of falsely accusing of an innocent man of blasphemy so he could be stoned and her husband free to seize his property.[8]

The Israelites were always vulnerable to making spiritually compromising alliances with heathen peoples around them and in their midst, marrying their sons and daughters into these peoples and thereby taking on their vile gods and immoral practices. God wanted this to be prevented, even at the cost of bloodshed.

The psalmist recounts the terrible consequences of Israel disobeying the command to destroy Canaanite religion within the borders of the Promised Land, and their taking on of Canaanite practices.

> "They did not destroy the peoples as the LORD had commanded them, but they mingled with the nations and adopted their customs. They worshipped their idols which became a snare to them. They sacrificed their sons to demons. They shed innocent

---

5. Genesis 8:21

6. Leviticus 18:28

7. Jones, *We Don't Hate Sin So We Don't understand What Happened to the Canaanites*.

8. First Kings 21

blood, the blood of their sons and daughters whom they sacrificed to the idols of Canaan and the land was desecrated by their blood. They defiled themselves by what they did; by their deeds they prostituted themselves. Therefore the LORD was angry with his people and abhorred his inheritance. He handed them over to the nations and their foes ruled over them. Their enemies oppressed them and subjected them to their power. Many times he delivered them, but they were bent on rebellion and they wasted away in their sin."[9]

There was nothing inherently racist about God's desire that they rid the land of the Canaanites. Israel included people from various other nations who joined them and became part of the covenant people.[10] There is a constant emphasis in the Old Testament on the compassionate and fair treatment of ethnic aliens within the borders of Israel, who acknowledged Israel's covenant God. What God wanted was not purity of ethnic blood lines but purity of *worship*. He wanted to rid the land of Canaanite religious practices. The invasion under Joshua was intended to be a *spiritual* cleansing of the land rather than ethnic cleansing as such.

But is this "spiritual" cleansing any better than a racially or religiously motivated ethnic cleansing? Well God, being God, has the right to punish or drive out people from certain places if they deserve it. God showed great patience with the Canaanites, even allowing his chosen people to suffer in Egypt hundreds of years in order to give the Canaanites more time to repent of their wicked ways. He then justly drove them out, as part of a salvation plan that would benefit the whole world. The idea was to remove their evil customs within the land set aside for the Israelites, the holy land, rather than protect the Israelite blood line from ethnic contamination. God did not want the Israelites intermarrying with them and being enticed into worshipping idols with all the dreadful consequences which would follow from that. (See chapter two). This is the context of the "show no mercy" command in Deuteronomy 7.

> "When the LORD *your God brings you into the land you are entering to possess and drives out before you many nations—the Hittites,* Girgashites, Amorites, Canaanites, Perizzites, Hivites and Jebusites, seven nations larger and stronger than you— and when the LORD *your God has delivered them over to you and you have defeated them, then you must destroy them totally. Make no treaty with* them, and show them no mercy. Do not intermarry

9. Psalm 106:34–43
10. See chapter 11

with them. Do not give your daughters to their sons or take their daughters for your sons, for they will turn your children away from following me to serve other gods, and the LORD's anger will burn against you and will quickly destroy you. This is what you are to do to them: Break down their altars, smash their sacred stones, cut down their Asherah poles and burn their idols in the fire. For you are a people holy to the Lord your God. The Lord your God has chosen you out of all the peoples on the face of the earth to be his people, his treasured possession."[11]

After the Fall, God had driven Adam and Eve from the Garden of Eden and put cherubim and a flaming sword to guard the entrance. This was so they would not eat from the tree of life and live forever in a state of alienation from God—everlasting hell in other words. The judgment of expulsion had mercy within it. It was the same with the spiritual cleansing of Canaan. The promise to Abraham was that his descendants would be a blessing to all peoples.[12] Terrible though it seems, the spiritual cleansing of the land by God through the agency of the Israelites and the establishment of the Jewish nation was a necessary part of the plan for the salvation of all the peoples of the world, *including the Canaanites*. It was just and it was confirmed as just to the Israelites by the God who had just performed supernatural wonders such as the plagues of Egypt and the parting of the Red Sea.

DOES THE OLD TESTAMENT JUSTIFY OR ENCOURAGE ETHNIC CLEANSING TODAY?

In the context of Barker's accusations, it is very important to say that it is a misuse of the Bible to claim it justifies anything like "ethnic cleansing" today. The Bible repeatedly emphasizes that the reasoning behind the invasion and the displacement of the Canaanite peoples, and the destruction of all their religious, political and cultural infrastructure, the timing of it, the pace of it, the fear it engendered, and the method was all very much under the controlling direction of God himself. It was a unique command given to Israel at a particular time in its history. God had promised this land to Abraham's descendants by oath in Genesis 15 and explained they would be aliens in a country not their own, would be enslaved and ill-treated there for four hundred years allowing for the sin of the Amorites (another name for Canaanites) to reach its full measure, before they could enter it.

11. Deuteronomy 7:1–6
12. Genesis 12:3b

You can see the emphasis God puts on himself being the one in control, with the repeated use of the pronoun 'I' in Exodus 23.

> "*I* will send my terror ahead of you and throw into confusion every nation you encounter. *I* will make all your enemies turn their backs and run. *I* will send the hornet ahead of you to drive the Hivites, Canaanites and Hittites out of your way. But *I* will not drive them out in a single year, because the land would become desolate and the wild animals too numerous for you. Little by little *I* will drive them out before you until you have increased enough to take possession of the land. *I* will establish your borders. . . ..*I* will hand over to you the people who live in the land and you will drive them out before you. Do not make a covenant with them or with their gods. Do not let them live in your land, or they will cause you to sin against me, because the worship of their gods will certainly be a snare to you."[13]

So, this was not case of God sitting back and giving the Israelites, as his favorites, *carte blanche* to do whatever they liked to establish themselves in whatever territory they could grab. At every point God directed them and went before them.

God's commands to Israel *then* cannot be translated into an argument that ethnic cleansing could be theologically justified *now*, because the New Testament reveals that, we are now in a different era of salvation history. The Old Covenant, based on God's people being territorially set apart from the heathen nations (as well as ritually and ceremonially distinct) was never kept faithfully enough by the Israelites but has been fulfilled by Christ the perfect Israelite. The national and territorial symbolic markers regarding God's salvation have been rendered obsolete in Christ. Now the people of God transcend national and territorial boundaries. God in Christ commands us to "go into all the world to make disciples, baptizing them in the name of the Father, Son and Holy Spirit."[14] He does not command us now to set up one religiously pure nation to be kept culturally apart from other nations.

It is biblically unsound (not to mention arrogant) to claim that somehow Old Testament Israel has been re-incarnated as Britain or the USA or any other so-called "Christian" country. We do not promote faithfulness to God by seeking to expel people of a different ethnic or religious make-up. We do the reverse. Forced removal of large groups of people, unless ordered by God against a people who deserve it and carried out in precisely the way

13. Exodus 32:27–33
14. Matthew 28:19

instructed by God (and the Bible reveals that the era of God directing Israel, let alone other nations, to do this, is over) is highly likely to be unjust. In thus acting unfairly, inhospitably or cruelly, we offend God, sin against others and bring Christian faith into disrepute.

That is not to say that Christians within a nation should not contribute to national debate about multi-culturalism and the nature and extent of any immigration controls. There will always be a spectrum of political ideas and beliefs among Christians. Those more on the right wing of the political spectrum do tend to emphasize God's continuing role for nation states, with their distinct national identities, and are suspicious of anything that seems to weaken national sovereignty and cultural identity. Those on the left tend more to internationalism and support the development of transnational institutions, as a check on nationalism and its potency. Some will be keen on freedom of movement and some will prefer tighter border controls. The Brexit saga in the United Kingdom throughout 2019 saw all these tensions played out. Bible-believing Christians in Britain were found on opposing sides of the issue.

While Barker might concede that there might be few today who would brazenly try to use the Old Testament to justify a deliberate campaign to establish ethnic or religious "purity" by force, he nevertheless claims nations influenced by the Old Testament might be more ready to assume it is their "manifest destiny" to establish control and eventually displace others whose presence is deemed not to be conducive to the public good. That is what he says happened in America in the nineteenth century.

Barker descends from the Delaware Indian tribe, the Lenni Lenape. In reading his book, one can surmise that the level of his vitriol against the biblical God has a lot to do with his anger and resentment at the way the British and European Christians who settled in the New World, and their descendants, came to displace native Americans as the dominant cultural group.

The historical scholarship regarding the relationship between the settlers and the indigenous peoples in what is now the United States is vast and complex. What is undoubtedly true is that the Bible was very influential in forming the values, mindset and vision of many of the settlers, beginning with the early Puritans who set sail from Plymouth on the *The Mayflower* in 1620. The very term "New World" encapsulates the sense of hope that God was doing something new in enabling Christians to leave the corrupt, oppressive and decadent nations of Europe and build "a new Jerusalem" in a vast area of rich and fertile land, comparatively thinly populated. Still today, there is a legacy of this in the way many Americans believe they have a calling to uphold ideals of democracy, human rights, honest wealth creation and freedom in the world.

However, as with every movement of people throughout a fallen world, since the origin of Christianity, there was a combination of peace-loving idealism, desire to honor God, make Christ known and build a just society, with the sad reality of disease, hunger, greed, broken covenants and attitudes to 'savages' based on arrogance and fear. So the steady flow of settlers crossing the Atlantic brought with them diseases which killed huge numbers of Indians who had not developed immunity to them. When more arrived and multiplied, disputes regarding land were inevitable. Were the warrior Indian tribes to remain independent, with their vast hunting lands impermeable to whites or should they be integrated into the political institutions and legal structures of the fast growing, technologically advanced, agrarian majority, with all the difficulties this would present? The relevant question is whether the Bible was an influence for good or for bad in the conduct of Christians in all this moral complexity.

READING BOTH TESTAMENTS IN THE LIGHT OF EACH OTHER

I would accept that if the Old Testament is not studied carefully enough, through the eyes of the Gospel revealed in the New Testament, then passages simplistically lifted from it might be used to promote in people's minds the idea of ethnic cleansing. However, those who pay heed to Jesus' words in John 18:36. "My kingdom is not of this world. If it were, my servants would fight to prevent my arrest," and Paul's words in Ephesians 6:12 about the true nature of spiritual warfare, would understand that Jesus's kingdom is not established by flesh and blood "Holy War." The conquest of the land under Joshua was a unique command at a particular point in history, involving the establishment of the promised Israelite kingdom in a land where the inhabitants had become utterly depraved.

Although I believe God still has purposes for the Jewish people (as taught in the New Testament book of Romans—see chapters nine to eleven), some politically extreme religious Jews who have not yet recognized Jesus as the Messiah and do not accept the authority of the New Testament, might be prone to cite the book of Joshua to bolster the view that they have God's authority or encouragement *today* to displace non-Jews from land promised to the descendants of Abraham, Isaac, and Jacob.

They might be supported by some Christians who do not balance their reading of Old and New Testament in a healthy way. Those who spend *all* their time in the Old Testament can take on very right-wing views. For them everything is about the inexorable march of nationalistic prophecy. Their hope is fixed on God raising up the right political leaders to establish righteous laws and punish the wicked now. Jesus' teaching about allowing the tares to grow alongside the wheat until harvest time, peace-making, mercy, tolerance, humility, compassion are forgotten, downplayed, or relegated to the "private spiritual sphere." Neglecting the New Testament means that, ironically, the great themes of mercy, compassion and concern for the poor and oppressed in the Old Testament are missed too. The state of Israel can do no wrong. Military spending should take priority over other things. For "dual covenant" dispensationalists Jewish people don't even need to believe in Jesus, their long-promised Messiah, because they have their own fast track "dispensation" to whatever it is God has promised them. Attitudes to Arabs and Muslims can be contemptuous. Old Testament punishments become in vogue but principles of social justice and wealth redistribution are ignored.

On the other hand, those who neglect the Old Testament, reject it as false, or believe that it is no longer relevant to our understanding of the character and purposes of God, create a Jesus in their own image, because they have severed him from his Jewish identity and cut off the Christian faith from its roots. Jesus is reduced to a socially liberal "hippy" figure, who is divorced from the revelation of God in the Hebrew scriptures, regarding God's plan of salvation. The Old Testament is misrepresented as portraying a nasty, primitive Jewish God. Somehow by the time of the New Testament, God has become a civilized "Christian." He has been on an anger management course. Jesus has given him a complete makeover. Jesus tells everyone to forget the nasty old Scriptures. God is meek and mild, like me, he claims. He never gets angry, and he won't punish anyone's sins. In fact, he is very relaxed about personal sin, especially sexual indiscretions (wink wink). Everyone gets to go to heaven. You don't have to repent or believe in anything. Just try to live an authentic life, being true to who you feel yourself to be.

Those who want the Old Testament without the New fail to see the direction in which the Old was heading, and those who want the New without the Old fail to see the weighty questions regarding sin, justice and redemption to which the New Testament provides the answers and therefore they fail to understand the New properly. The New is built on the foundation of the Old. We now look at those foundations through the perspective of the New, but if we take away the foundation the New crumbles into thin air. You can't claim to really know the Old Testament and fail to see the Jesus it all points to, and you can't know Jesus without also knowing the God of the Old Testament.

True Christianity, in which the Old Testament is viewed in the light of the New, and in which the New is built on the Old, provided, and still provides, under God's sovereign hand, the only true hope for American Indians like everyone else in this world.

For the Lenape Indians, the "trail of tears" led eventually to Oklahoma.

The challenge for them and the other descendants of the American Indians is whether they will choose to forgive their fellow Americans and reflect on the mercies God has shown themselves, despite their own sinful ways. Clyde Ellis, of the *Oklahoma Historical Society* says that Christianity gave many of Oklahoma's Indian people a way to accommodate the changing social and cultural contours of their world, and in doing so to maintain an important sense of ethnic identity and pride.[15]

Nothing in either the Old Testament or the New justified Christians in behaving in a fearful, arrogant, greedy, oath-breaking, cruel way. Where such sins were committed they should be confessed by acts of "representational confession." Any amends or reparations that can be made should be explored.

The only way that annihilation of the Native American way of life could have been analogous to the invasion of Canaan by the Israelites is, if God, after dramatic signs and wonders had commanded New England settlers to drive American Indians from their land, who would otherwise have corrupted with their vile practices the theocratic nation state God had told those settlers to set up for the salvation of the world. Since the New World settlers lived in a different era of salvation history the two situations could not have been analogous.

---

15. https://www.okhistory.org/publications/enc/entry.php?entry=AM011

Chapter 9

Misogynistic?

"Dear God, are boys better than girls? I know you are one but please try to be fair."

—SYLVIA (FROM *CHILDREN'S LETTERS TO GOD*)

In Nick Hornby's funny and perceptive 1998 novel *About A Boy* Will Freeman (played by Hugh Grant in the film version four years later) is a thirty-six-year-old man, who lives off the royalties of a hit Christmas song composed by his late father. Free to immerse himself in 1990s culture without having to work, he spends his time watching *Countdown* on TV and listening to Nirvana. Wanting to meet available women without too much effort, he has the idea of attending a single-parents' support group, pretending that he himself is a single dad, and whose fictional two year-old son conveniently "spends lots of time with his mother." At the first meeting of the support group, at which he is the only man, he listens to the tales of woe told by the single mums and how their lives have been ruined by the male of the species. Despite this, these women treat him sympathetically, believing he has suffered too and is a kindred spirit. Will Freeman comes away from the meeting he has fraudulently attended, guiltily feeling that "all men are bastards" and the reader, at this point, is tempted to agree with him.

After reading Barker's chapter seeking to justify Dawkins's assertion that the God of the Old Testament is misogynistic, a piece of work which presents him as the creation of sexist men, controlling and demeaning women in all sorts of ways, many people might feel the same way. Misogyny is the dislike of, hatred of, or contempt for, women. To describe the biblical God as misogynist is a serious accusation because it claims that this God reflects a vile attitude to half the human race based on their gender.

Barker argues that this "fictional" God, wanting to choose the most demeaning insult to describe the people who so often displeased him, reached for images to do with menstruation or loose women, thus reinforcing the association of women's bodies with un-cleanness and making female unfaithfulness the archetypal form of evil. He says the Covenant was with men only, because circumcision was only given to them. The monetary value given to females in the Old Testament is less than for men, and women are deemed to be the property of men. Ancestry is delineated from father to son. Women only inherit property if there is no male heir and they must marry a male relative to keep it in their father's family. Only men can be priests. Sorceresses are singled out for the death penalty. A woman is unclean for longer after giving birth to a daughter than if she gave birth to a son. They must undergo a cruel test if suspected of infidelity by men, and if she is accused of not being a virgin after her wedding night proof has to be forthcoming in the way of bloodied bed sheets or she will be stoned. A woman's promise can be annulled by her husband or father. If a woman is raped, she can be made to marry her attacker.

As if all this wasn't enough Barker claims that the misogynistic male writers of the Bible wanted to provide a foundational religious justification for their denigration of women and therefore invented a story in which God made Adam first and then his sidekick Eve, who was duly portrayed as the one who caused the downfall of the entire human race. Genesis chapter three was written so women could be blamed for *everything*.

As in each chapter of his book *God: The Most Unpleasant Character in all Fiction*, Barker gives two or three pages of argument and then several pages of selectively presented biblical passages with his own pithy headings indicating how these verses prove this unpleasantness.

But with all these quotes there is no real contextual work accompanying them, only the skewed headings, and perhaps some trite words in brackets afterwards. Sometimes he seems to deliberately misrepresent the biblical God to bolster his case, editing the passages in ways that significantly distort the true picture. Barker cites passages where cruel, unjust or unpleasant things happened to women and then implies that God approved. There are a lot of things that happen in the Bible which are not approved by him, even by people who are otherwise generally commended for their faith. Not everything in the Bible is "biblical!"

STORIES IN THE BIBLE THAT GRIEVE THE HEART OF GOD

An example is the fallout from the terrible events recorded in Judges chapter nineteen. A Levite returning to the hill country of Ephraim with his concubine stopped in a place called Gibeah, where the people were of the Israelite tribe of Benjamin. Some of them surrounded his lodging place and wanted to gang rape him. In a successful attempt to protect himself, he callously sent his concubine out to them and they raped and abused her throughout the night and by the morning she was dead. The Levite cut up her body into twelve parts and sent them into all the areas of the twelve tribes to publicize the atrocity. All Israel gathered to punish this crime and because the Benjamites would not surrender the wicked men of Gibeah, the other Israelites attacked the Benjamites and after much bloodshed on both sides Israel eventually killed all but six hundred of their fighting men.

Despite winning the civil war the Israelites were grieved that one of the tribes was almost wiped out and they wanted the six hundred men to be able to marry and have children to restore the tribe to Israel. However, all the tribes had taken an oath not to let their daughters marry Benjamites. The solution for their problem was to destroy the people of Jabesh Gilead who had not joined the punitive expeditionary force and take the virgins among them as wives for the Benjamites. But there were only four hundred of them leaving them two hundred wives short. So they told the remaining two hundred Benjamites without wives to hide in the vineyards of Shiloh and when the girls came out to dance, they could grab one each and take them away as their wives. In this way the people of Shiloh would not be breaking their oath because their girls would have been taken by force rather than with agreement.

Barker misrepresents the treatment of women in this sorry tale as something God commanded. But these grotesque stories at the end of the book of Judges are bracketed with the commentary "In those days, Israel had no king; everyone did as they saw fit." In other words, they were chaotic and lawless times, where the people were not living the way God wanted at all. The rape of the Levite's concubine is presented as the lowest point in Israel's moral decline in the book of Judges. Far from indicating a misogynistic God, it shows that the story of those who are powerless and marginalized deserve to be told. The victim of the tribe of Benjamin's evil behavior was an unnamed woman who didn't have the legal status of a wife. Yet her suffering is included and given as the casus belli of a bloody civil war.

The exposure of the abuse of women by the Hollywood mogul Harvey Weinstein in 2019 showed how important it is that the voices of victims are heard. Everyone in movie-making circles it seemed to know what he was doing, but no-one with any power took any action to ensure people were listened to and protected by bringing him to account. No-one comes away from viewing the film or reading the book *The Color Purple* saying it is misogynistic because it portrays an African American woman, Celie Harris, suffering rape, incest, and domestic violence. It is lauded as giving her a posthumous voice. So why is the Bible accused of misogyny by simply reporting the evil of it?

And Barker always treats prophetic forewarnings of disasters which would affect women as things that God took pleasure in, rather than was grieved about. So one of the spiritual consequences for David after he had committed adultery with Bathsheba and had her husband killed was that one of his own sons would rise up in rebellion against him. Absalom slept with his father's concubines on the roof of the palace as part of his strategy to show Israel that he was serious about usurping his father's throne, using these poor Jebusite women as pawns in his struggle for power.[1]

Nathan prophesied that God would do this, as a way of saying that David's actions brought judgment on himself which inevitably affected others.[2] When God permits the negative consequences of our actions to happen, theologians sometimes call this God's *permissive* will. He allows the effects of sin to run their course sometimes and because he is sovereign, it was a Jewish way of saying things that God brings about the consequence. But what happens or what he causes to happen (because, apart from anything else, he created the world of cause and effect) is not something he wants or takes pleasure in because it is a result of sin and disobedience. Sin and disobedience are obviously not his *desired* will and so neither are the consequences.

There are a lot of other biblical passages cited in this chapter. To go through each one by one would probably require a whole book in its own right, but I will try to group the remaining citations under various themes.

ASSOCIATING WOMEN AND THEIR SEXUALITY WITH SHAME

First, there are the passages in which Israel or other nations are compared to an adulterous woman or a prostitute. There is no denying this. However, we must also remember that the reason why "the worst kind of woman" is regarded as an appropriate analogy for the idolatrous behavior of cities or the nation of Israel is because the "best kind of woman" also is used as a metaphor for the people in whom God delights.

1. Second Samuel 16:21
2. Ibid.12:11–12

Much of the Old Testament uses the institution of marriage or betrothal as a metaphor to explain the relationship between God and his people. God delights in "virgin" Israel to whom he is betrothed. Hosea 2:19–20 says

> "and I will betroth you to me forever. I will betroth you to me in righteousness and in justice, in steadfast love and in mercy. I will betroth you to me in faithfulness. And you shall know the LORD."

In ancient Israel betrothal was much more than engagement. It was almost the equivalent of marriage, but the betrothed couple were yet to consummate the relationship. So virgin Israel must await the consummation of her relationship with Yahweh, and in the meantime she is to be a virgin. That is to say Israel was to have no other gods. Frequent references to Israel prostituting herself to other gods need to be seen in the light of God's justified indignation at idolatry. (See chapter one on God's jealousy).

As I said in chapter one, the passionate love that God has for his beloved accounts for the right kind of jealousy which he feels when betrayed. What the biblical God thinks about women and sexuality can be seen in the book of Song of Songs, where the erotic love between a man and a woman is symbolic of God's love for his beloved bride Israel.

It is important to note that virginity is the pure and holy state of one who is not yet married. There is no implication here that sex is at all shameful within marriage, as some church fathers implied and Roman Catholicism has often insinuated, with its unbiblical insistence on the "immaculate conception" and perpetual virginity of Mary, and compulsory clerical celibacy.

As well as pictured as a virgin betrothed to God, Israel is often referred to as the daughter of Zion. Israel is cherished as a daughter is cherished. His daughter Israel is the "apple of his eye." God is proud of her. In Isaiah 37, the daughter of Zion is a confident, secure young woman, scornful of the arrogant, godless Assyrians who had come to invade and plunder but then had to retreat with their tails between their legs. Proverbs 31 exalts the "wife of noble character" who is not only a "domestic goddess" but a successful businesswoman and a charitable benefactor in the community. She is the original superwoman.

It is a fact that many cultures use noble women as symbols of what they hold most dear. The New Testament refers to women as "the glory of man"[3] indicating the esteem in which the concept of womanhood is held. Even today, nations tend to be referred to using feminine pronouns. Britannia is a woman. We more readily ascribe the status of "goddess" to a beautiful woman or a woman who is domestically accomplished than we accord the

---

3. 1 Corinthians 11:7

status of a "god" to a man for his looks or capabilities. The quid pro quo of this is that the metaphor of ignoble women might be sometimes used to symbolize the worst aspects of society.

God even uses feminine imagery to describe his relationship with Israel.

> "As a mother comforts her child, so will I comfort you; and you will be comforted over Jerusalem."[4]

What about menstruation being a symbol of uncleanness? Israel was certainly not alone in seeing menstrual blood as bringing ritual impurity, but does this mean God is implicated in sexist male culture? Well no. Bodily discharges of *men* also brought ritual impurity. Yes, women were going to be ritually impure more often than men because of the nature of the woman's body. The life-giving womb was also the source of regular blood flow which symbolized death, and thus could not be allowed to ritually contaminate the ceremonial purity of the sanctuary where the presence of the life-giving God was manifest.

Why did women have a longer period of uncleanness when they gave birth to daughters than they did when they gave birth to sons? Is this about women being denigrated? No. We need to understand that ritual uncleanness does not imply that a woman had more moral guilt than anyone else, just as a man with pus oozing from a sore had no more moral guilt than anyone else. Ritual impurity is a symbolic matter. It does not imply inferiority in someone who happens to be temporarily "unclean." There have been some ingenious theories offered as to why ritual uncleanness lasted twice as long after the birth of a daughter.[5] My view on this is that again, it is a symbolic, ritual matter. Women were ritually impure more of the time than men throughout their lives. Thus, giving birth to someone who in time will become a menstruating woman is accompanied by a greater period of symbolic uncleanness. That women are valued as much as men in God's eyes and that a woman is not considered inherently more sinful than a man, is confirmed by the fact that the sacrificial offering a new mother is to bring after the days of her purification are over is the same whether she had a boy or a girl—a year old lamb for a "burned offering" and a dove or pigeon for a "sin offering."[6]

---

4. Isaiah 66:13

5. These range from claiming that the postnatal blood which seeps out has a higher chemical toxicity after a female is born than a male, to the teaching of one Jewish rabbi that, after the birth of a male, the woman repents more quickly of her vow, induced by the pains of pregnancy and childbirth, not to have sex with her husband ever again!

6. Leviticus 12:6

DOES GOD SEE WOMEN AS INTRINSICALLY INFERIOR IN WORTH?

But what about Leviticus 27, Barker would say, where the LORD gave Moses instruction on what people were to do when they made a special vow to dedicate persons to the LORD by giving "equivalent values." The key here is to understand that the "value" was not set according to the intrinsic worth of someone to God, but the persons economic marketability in a society where manual labor was the norm. Working men, due to their greater physical strength could plough the ground or harvest crops twice as quickly as women. Thus males between the age of twenty and sixty were priced at sixty shekels of silver, and females at thirty. Between the ages of five and twenty it was twenty shekels and ten shekels respectively. This difference represents both the greater physical capabilities of male young men and also the future capabilities of boys. The ratio for children under five was five shekels to three. There being little difference if any in the physical strength of children at that age, the differing amount reflected future earning potential only. A male over sixty was priced at fifteen shekels and a woman at ten shekels. The difference ratio for this age group was the least, reflecting the fact that, increasingly, the physical capabilities of men and women over sixty become more equal.

The fact that these differing economic valuations did not imply intrinsic difference in status or worth to God is shown by the fact that the dedication price for a woman between twenty and sixty is twice as much (thirty shekels) as for a man over sixty (fifteen shekels). In the admittedly patriarchal culture in which the Bible is set (in common with virtually all historical cultures), there is no way older men would have been considered of less innate worth to God than younger women despite the valuation being double for the woman in this case.

WHY MALE PRIESTS ONLY?

Why was the priesthood restricted to men? It was not just restricted to men, but to the descendants of Aaron within the tribe of Levi. But why did God not make his daughters priestesses, like the pagan nations did in their priestly lines? Here, I could do no better than refer to the typically erudite and insightful essay by CS Lewis "Priestesses in the Church."[7] Lewis was arguing against the ordination of women. I differ from Lewis, believing that the Bible (Old and New Testaments) allow the possibility of women in spiritual leadership. However, Lewis's reasoning was based on a high church or

---

7. http://www.episcopalnet.org/TRACTS/priestesses.html accessed 16/04/19

Anglo-Catholic understanding of ministerial orders within the Church of England. Lewis saw "priests" in the Church of England as similar to priests in the Old Testament, where they had a sacerdotal role, offering sacrifices on behalf of the people and in a powerful symbolic way, representing God to the people. In his writing, Lewis interestingly makes no objection to a woman representing men and women to God. His problem is with a woman representing God to men and women in a symbolic way at the "altar." Although he admits that any woman may be as godly, holy, wise, capable, skilled at preaching and pastorally gifted as any man, he says there is a supra-rational (rather than *irrational*) case for restricting priesthood to men, because of the way God has chosen to reveal himself. He is Father. Jesus is the Son. Jesus was incarnated as man. Christ is the "bridegroom" and the church is the "bride." All this masculine imagery serves a real theological purpose which should not be jettisoned, which he thought having what he called "priestesses" would lead to.

In relation to the reason why *Old Testament* priests had to be male, Lewis's essay explains things beautifully. Some feminists may protest, but there is nothing misogynistic about believing that God has revealed himself to us using masculine to feminine imagery and that while men and women are equal in worth, they are not interchangeable as regard certain functions. We no longer live in Old Testament times and we are not under the Old Covenant, and so we are no longer commanded to invest the function of "representing God" to a singular priest because, under the new covenant, through the Holy Spirit poured out at Pentecost, *everyone* who is in Christ now represents God to the world—a concept known as the "priesthood of all believers." Thus, ordination to ministerial roles should be about recognizing spiritual leadership, which Jesus taught us is essentially about service. A woman should therefore not, in my opinion, be denied a role serving as a discipleship leader, vicar, pastor, chaplain, evangelist, missionary, bishop or theological college principal, if she has the right character and gifts, and certainly not because Old Testament priests were male. We might as well say spiritual leaders in the Church of England today have to be Jewish descendants of Aaron with no physical defects.

COMPLEMENTARITY, PATRIARCHY AND SUBVERSIVE TEXTS

But does a husband still have a role in "representing God" to his wife? The New Testament indicates that he does, but only in so far as he loves his wife sacrificially as Christ loves the church. There is such a thing as biblical headship, but we wrongly associate being the 'head' with being the "boss." The husband is the "head" of the wife in the sense that he is the initiator of the covenant relationship (still reflected by the ongoing tradition of the man proposing marriage to the woman). Even in our Western culture today, so influenced by philosophical notions of equality, most wives are happy to take the surname of their husband and for him therefore to be the source of the family name and "head of the household." "Head" here can mean something akin to "source." The husband is to use the responsibility given to him by his physical strength and capacity to make his pioneering mark on the world, to sacrificially cherish his wife and the wife should accordingly give him respect for this. But just as it is inappropriate for a man to wear the uniform of a "priest" today and be seen as representing God thereby, *irrespective of the content of his moral character*, so it is wrong for a husband to be considered as representing God to his wife *irrespective of his conduct towards her*, but simply because he is biologically male.

It was not misogynist for data to be organized on patrilineal lines. Some aspects of the way the Old Testament was written might reflect a patriarchal culture fallen away from what was originally intended by God, and certainly the stories of cruelty and injustice to women portray a society in which the curse of the fall brought about manifest oppression of women by men. But the mere fact that censuses and genealogies focused on the male line simply reflects the view that men represent their nuclear families as head of the household. Also, census taking normally had a military or taxation purpose. Women were probably quite grateful to be spared conscription and responsibility for household tax affairs.

What about circumcision being only for men? It is ironic that today, when the UK has just started to act to try to prevent female circumcision (called Female Genital Mutilation) that Barker claims restricting it to men is misogynist. It is much less traumatic and dangerous to circumcise men. It must also be remembered that in Israel it was not envisaged that anyone should remain unmarried. The covenant sign of circumcision would therefore have been present in the woman's body when joined together with her husband in sexual intercourse. Women were just as much part of the covenant as men.

What about the way in which women were under the authority of their fathers while unmarried and under their husbands when married, as regards property and vows, and what about polygamy? Here it is admitted that Old Testament law reflected the reality of the power imbalance between the sexes caused or exacerbated by the Fall. However, Barker completely fails to acknowledge the rights that women did have under Old Testament law and the places where the biblical narrative honors women and subverts male chauvinism and points forward to times of greater equality.

Examples of this are provided by Genesis 16 and 30, First Samuel 1, Numbers 27, Joshua 15, Job 42. Ruth 4, and Proverbs 31.

In Genesis 16, we have an example of how women in the Old Testament were treated with dignity and value. After Sarai had reacted to the arrogance of her maidservant, Hagar, and had driven her out of the house, the angel of the LORD found the run-away at a well. He said, "Hagar, servant of Sarai. . ." Amy Orr-Ewing says,

> "It would be easy for us to miss the significance of that address. This is the only instance in many thousands of Ancient Near Eastern texts where a deity, or his messenger, calls a woman by name and thereby invests her with exalted dignity."[8]

She continues,

> "Women and men were also equal in prayer. Covenant women prayed directly to God without the priestly mediation of their husbands. For example, when the carnal Jacob defaulted in his responsibility to pray for his barren wife (Genesis 30:1–2), in contrast to his godly forbears, who prayed for their children and wives (cf. 24:7, 12–15; 25:21), Rachel petitioned God directly, and he listened to her and opened her womb (30:22–24). Barren Hannah too went directly to God in prayer, independently of her husband Elkanah, and the high priest, Eli, both of whom were insensitive to her need."[9] (First Samuel 1:1–20).

In Numbers 27, the daughters of Zelophehad petition Moses to be allowed to inherit their dead father's property, given that he died leaving no sons. Moses consulted the LORD who told him they should indeed inherit and it became a lasting ordinance for these circumstances.

In Joshua 15, Caleb promises his daughter Acsah to the man who attacks and captures *Kiriath Sepher* (Barker cites the giving of daughters as a reward as misogyny but it was a way of securing a brave and respected husband for one's daughter). Othniel succeeded in this, but then seemed to be reluctant to ask his formidable father-in-law for a piece of property as a dowry. Acsah takes on this responsibility and goes to her father and not only gets land in the Negev, but asks for not just one, but *two* springs of water, which were highly valuable assets. Caleb does this for her.

---

8. Orr-Ewing, *Why Trust the Bible?* 87
9. Ibid. 88

In the last chapter of Job, when Job has his health and wealth restored and has sons and daughters, he gives his daughters (who unlike the sons, are named and famed for their beauty) an inheritance along with their brothers. So, in these three stories we see women being given ownership of considerable amounts of property, unusual for the ancient near east.

In Ruth 4, the women of Bethlehem tell Naomi, Ruth's mother-in-law, that her daughter-in-law, because of her faithfulness and courage, was better than seven sons. This was quite a statement for those times. Proverbs 31 extols "the wife of noble character" who looks like a businesswoman, philanthropist and domestic goddess all rolled into one. She is certainly no downtrodden drudge; barefoot, pregnant and chained to the kitchen sink.

POLYGAMY

The practice of men having more than one wife, whether those extra wives had equal status or less (in which case they were called *concubines*) was never approved by God. The fact that he is not recorded as directly punishing it seems to be a concession to human weakness. However, all the biblical examples of polygamy contain the clear message that it has come about through a lack of obedience to God or trust in him and brings some kind of trouble. So Abraham only took Hagar, his wife Sarah's servant, as a concubine because both Sarah and he did not trust God to enable Sarah to have a child. The ongoing Middle East conflict between Arab and Jew is the fruit of this, since Jews trace their ancestry from Isaac, the miracle child the Bible says was born as a result of God's promise to Abraham and Sarah, and Arabs descend from Ishmael, the one born of the surrogacy arrangement with Hagar the Egyptian.

Jacob would have been happy with just one wife, Rachel, but was tricked into marrying her sister Leah too and took both his wives' servants as concubines (under their instructions, in the furtherance of their pro-creational rivalry). In both cases jealousy and unhappiness resulted, although God, as ever, redeemed the situation for those who loved him. King David's polygamy resulted in him having many sons who had different mothers and who became rivals for the throne, causing much bloodshed, and King Solomon's polygamy was against God's command not to marry women from other nations who would turn his heart to other gods (which they did).

God did restrict some of the abuses that polygamy might otherwise have given rise to. Barker actually includes God's rule that the firstborn son's inheritance rights should not be overlooked if he was the son of a least favored wife.[10] Why Barker thinks this is evidence of God's misogyny is not clear.

WOMEN AS MERE CHATTELS?

It is true that, in the tenth commandment a man is forbidden to covet his neighbor's *wife*, as well as his ox or ass, his manservant or maidservant or anything else that belongs to him.[11] Barker assumes this means the wife is relegated to being a mere chattel of her husband. However, it is common to use the possessive pronoun to indicate relation, not necessarily possession as property, like a field or an animal. So, in the relational sense, a man belonged to his wife as much as a wife belonged to her husband (see the mutuality of belonging and affirmation of womanly desire in the Song of Songs). Even with servants, the master did not "own" them in the absolute sense that they could do what they liked with them without legal consequence as they could under Roman law in New Testament times. By contrast, a husband was not given legal sanction to beat his wife, as he was his (non-Hebrew) slave, who was regarded as more "his" in the property sense. (Although if he permanently injured his slave, he was to let the slave go free as compensation, a remarkably humane law compared with other ancient societies.)[12] If a husband divorced his wife, he could not just cast her aside without legal ceremony. He had to write her a proper certificate of divorce. This would have enabled her to re-marry without being accused of adultery. Although she could not unilaterally divorce her husband, as he could her, she could have made life unpleasant enough for him in the home to force him to divorce her, thus achieving the same effect.

It was forbidden for the husband to re-marry his ex-wife if, in the meantime, she had married another man, even if that man died.[13] This would have prevented men from passing their wives around temporarily as sex slaves, "Islamic State" style, and also would have caused them to think twice before divorcing. Also a man could never divorce a wife who he had wrongly accused of prenuptial infidelity,[14] or a wife who he had previously seduced when she was a virgin, which was a very significant protection for women for when their husband's ardor had cooled.[15]

10. Deuteronomy 21:15–17
11. Exodus 20:17, Deuteronomy 5:21
12. Exodus 21:26–27
13. Deuteronomy 24:1–4
14. Ibid.22:19
15. Ibid.22:29

What about when it appears that a man has not just seduced a woman, but *raped* her? Well he would be subject to the death penalty if she was married or betrothed. If she was not, the man had to either marry her, if her father was agreeable, or pay a large fine. In our culture this of course seems an appalling prospect, as we might wonder how a woman who has been made to have sex against her will could possibly want to marry the man who had violated her? But we need to understand, that the culture of the time was so different to modern Western ways. In Britain today, even sex within marriage that is deemed to be non-consensual is now classed as rape in law. But in the culture in which the Bible was written, marriage and sex rarely came about by women making autonomous choices. In Bible times women would have preferred that the man who had, in his passion, "taken her," be himself then compelled to look after her and honor her as a wife, rather than leave her desolate.

This was exemplified by the case of Tamar, who was raped by her half-brother Amnon. If the man was a complete monster, then it is unlikely that any woman's father would have allowed a marriage in these circumstances. Tamar thought King David would allow Amnon to marry her, and she pleaded for Amnon to ask his permission, but Amnon was not interested, as after he has satisfied his lust, he then hated her, perhaps because of his sense of guilt at what he had done. Amnon was later killed in revenge by Tamar's full brother Absalom, another example of the bitter legacy of David's polygamy.[16]

A further indication that wives were not regarded as mere chattels was that adultery was not punished as a property offence but as something more serious. Unlike in pagan legal codes, no property offence attracted the death penalty. However, adultery was a capital offence for both the man and the woman.

An indication of how God's law sought to provide for the marital happiness of women as well as men is given in Deuteronomy 24:5 which says

> "if a man has recently married, he must not be sent to war or have any duty laid on him. For one year he is to be free to stay at home and bring happiness to the wife he has married."

Does this sound like the command of a misogynist God?

---

16. Second Samuel 13

CRUEL TESTS?

It could be the passages people find most difficult, relate to the test for unfaithfulness, if the husband suspected adultery, and the need for proof of virginity if the husband suspected his wife was not a virgin on their wedding night.

Let's look at what Barker calls a "cruel test," laid down in Numbers 5:1–29. If a husband suspected his wife of adultery and had jealous feelings, but had no proof, he was commanded to take his wife to a priest, with a grain offering and his wife would make a solemn oath that she had not been unfaithful and drink some holy water with curses written on it regarding infertility. If she was telling the truth these curses would have no effect, but if she was lying then she would become barren.

If the wife had been guilty of adultery, then she escaped the death penalty (a penalty that applied to men equally remember), since there was no witness and the adulterous man could not be identified. She suffered barrenness it was true, but is this misogynistic? The test in some ways seems like a supernatural version of a modern paternity test, where a husband suspects that the child his wife has given birth to is not his. If a husband is feeling suspicious and jealous then it is better for a test to be made, to clear things up. In ancient Israel, it likewise would have been better for an innocent but suspected woman to undergo this test rather than have her husband treat her unpleasantly throughout their marriage because of his unfounded jealousy. If there were no test, the husband could have been tempted just to assume his wife's guilt and use it as justification for treating her badly. But the existence of the test was a protection for the woman, because the husband would have had to find out for sure. If she was innocent, she would be vindicated. If she was guilty, then she would suffer barrenness but would not be subject to the death penalty. Her inability to have children might simply be due to the loss of marital intimacy rather than a medical reason, but the Hebrew is unclear exactly what the curse would have done.

What about the situation where the husband doubted his wife's virginity on the wedding night? This is covered in Deuteronomy 22. We must remember that a wedding usually happened in order to consummate a betrothal, which was a more committed arrangement than a modern engagement. So if the woman had had sexual relations with another man after betrothal but prior to the marriage, this was considered adulterous behavior. The rupture of the hymen after intercourse for the first time would have produced its mark on the bedsheets and so the girl's parents would have had a straightforward way of proving her virginity if this was called into question. Like the test for an unfaithful wife, this provision functioned as a protection for an innocent wife, since the husband was forced into seeking the truth, rather than continuing the marriage in a state of anger and suspicion which would have been most unpleasant for the wife. If the wife was guilty, then it was as if she had committed adultery and the penalty for adultery, when proved, was death for both women *and* men. So this law cannot be said to be misogynistic.

HARSH PUNISHMENTS?

What about the death penalty for sorceresses[17] and priests' daughters who became prostitutes.[18] These punishments of course seem very severe, but they are actually no more severe than punishments decreed for men who committed offences of similar magnitude. In a previous chapter I spoke about the pernicious effect of tolerating witchcraft within Israel. Sorcery was generally associated with women, which is why the command referred to sorceresses specifically, but the death penalty for some other offences is stipulated as being for men, although women technically could have committed the offences too, such as sacrificing children to Molech, consulting mediums, kidnapping someone for ransom, and cursing one's father and mother. If later societies within Christendom were being consistent with the Old Testament when they put to death women who really were witches, then they should have put to death a whole range of other people as well, mainly men.

What about hand amputation for a woman who seizes a man's genitals?[19] If a woman seized a man's genitals, then this was regarded as a humiliation. It might even have extinguished the possibility of that man having descendants—the equivalent of his line being "cut off" from Israel (this was considered worse than death). That is why it was a serious offence. Professor Paul Hogan makes a convincing case that, as regards the punishment, the translation of the Hebrew should refer to the shaving of the groin area. The usual Hebrew word for hand, *yad*, is not used here but the Hebrew word which is, *kaph*, can be used to refer to the *palm* of a hand, or some rounded concave object like a dish, bowl, or spoon, or even the arch of a foot. It would be a strange command to cut off the palm of a hand. *Kaph* can refer to the curve of the woman's groin area and the "cutting off" was not mutilation but shaving of the pubic hair. This makes more sense according to the retributive "eye for an eye" principle, because the text does not specify there was any lasting injury to the man. So this was an example, not of mutilation for mutilation, but humiliation for humiliation. Also, in

---

17. Exodus 22:18
18. Leviticus 21:9
19. Deuteronomy 25:11–12

the Old Testament there is no other case where mutilation is a specified punishment. (The "eye for an eye" principle was not meant to be applied literally, but required some kind of equivalence—the punishment should be equal to the crime—no more or no less. This was an important contrast to the Babylonian code of Hammurabi, which insisted that certain crimes should be punished by the cutting off of the tongue, breast, hand or ear, or the dragging of the convict around a field by cattle.[20])

There were serious punishments for men who harmed a pregnant woman accidentally while fighting. If, as a result, she gave birth prematurely, the offending man had to pay a fine. If however, there was serious injury or miscarriage, then it was "life for life, eye for eye, tooth for tooth, hand for hand, foot for foot, burn for burn, wound for would, bruise for bruise."

So, while the punishments for women might today be considered harsh, because the punishments for men were equally severe, they are not evidence of unfairness towards women or misogyny.

SEX SLAVES?

What about the treatment of women as booty after battle? In relation to captives taken in war, the relevant chapter is Leviticus 21:10–14.

> "When you go to war against your enemies and the Lord your God delivers them into your hands and you take captives, if you notice among the captives a beautiful woman and are attracted to her, you may take her as your wife. Bring her into your home and have her shave her head, trim her nails and put aside the clothes she was wearing when captured. After she has lived in your house and mourned her father and mother for a full month, then you may go to her and be her husband and she shall be your wife. If you are not pleased with her, let her go wherever she wishes. You must not sell her or treat her as a slave, since you have dishonored her."

This law balanced realism in the context of war with humane provisions designed to protect women. Notice how different this is to Barker's misrepresentation of the situation when he quotes Judges 5:30 "Have they not divided the prey; to every man a damsel or two" and informs the readers of his book that these words form part of a hymn of praise to God. This is an outrageous piece of chicanery designed to replace the truth as revealed in

---

20. Copan, *Is God a Moral Monster?* 121

Leviticus twenty-one with the impression that God approved of the rape or casual appropriation of women after battle.

The words quoted by Barker were indeed part of a song of praise (co-wrote by Deborah, a victorious woman ruler of Israel, please note), who had triumphed over a Canaanite army led by a general called Sisera, who had oppressed Israel for twenty years because he had nine hundred iron chariots at his disposal. (Sisera fled the battlefield after his defeat and fell asleep, exhausted, and was killed by a woman called Jael who drove a tent-peg into his skull). However, Deborah and her co-songwriter Barak were not referring to the *Israelite* soldiers taking girls after winning the battle, but to Sisera's worried mother consoling herself with the hope that her delayed son was doing just that as part of the plundering. I will quote the passage in full so you can see the context. They sang. . .

> "Through the window peered Sisera's mother; behind the lattice she cried out, 'Why is his chariot so long in coming? Why is the clatter of his chariots delayed?'
> The wisest of her ladies answer her; indeed, she keeps saying to herself,
> 'Are they not finding and dividing the spoils: a woman or two for each man, colorful garments as plunder for Sisera, colorful garments embroidered, highly embroidered garments for my neck— all this as plunder?'"

STRONG HEROIC WOMEN

As I said above, Barker completely ignores all the ways in which the Old Testament honors women of courage and faith, and how it often deliberately contrasts them favorably over against weak, foolish or faithless men.

Mention has already been made of Deborah who led Israel in the time of the Judges. Her male general Barak would not entertain the idea of going into battle without her. Then there is the story of Samson's conception in Judges 13. An angel of the LORD appears to the wife of a man named Manoah to tell her that, despite being barren, she will give birth to a boy and gives her full instructions as to how she is to bring him up as a Nazirite. She tells all this to her husband, who cannot take it in. His spiritual dimness then turns to panic when the man returns and instructs him to make an offering to the LORD, and then, revealing he truly is an angel, ascends amazingly in the flame of the sacrifice. Thinking they will now die for having "seen God," his wife calms him by saying that God is not going to kill them, having just accepted their burnt offering and given them instructions about how they are to bring up a miracle child.

Other women heroes include the foreigners Rahab who lived in the garrison town of Jericho and acted as a double agent for the invading Israelites,[21] and Ruth, the Moabitess, who showed great faithfulness to her Israelite mother-in-law and is the heroine of a book which bears her name. Ruth married Boaz, who was the son of Rahab, and she became the great grandmother of King David and so both Ruth and Rahab feature in Matthew's genealogy of Jesus at the beginning of his Gospel. As well as undermining the case for biblical misogyny, this also provides evidence that the biblical God is not racist (see chapter eleven).

Then there is Abigail the beautiful wife of the mean-spirited and stupid man Nabal, who saves much bloodshed through her skillful diplomacy with David and when her husband (who she despised) was struck down by God for his foolishness, David proposed to her and she gladly accepted. Barker's version of the story is that God killed the poor woman's husband just so David's harem could have one more woman added to it. The truth is that when David did, years later, have another man killed (Uriah the Hittite) so he could take his beautiful wife Bathsheba for himself, God convicted David (through the prophet Nathan) of how wicked this was in his sight.

Then there is Huldah the prophetess who lived during the time of the young King Josiah, much later in Judah's history. The neglected book of the law was discovered in the Temple and the king's chief ministers went as a delegation to ask Huldah, a married woman, what they should do in response to what they read. Her voice was seen as the authoritative voice of God.[22]

Last, but not least, there is Esther, who saved the entire Jewish population within the Persian Empire from a holocaust and, like Ruth, has a book in the Bible named after her.

EVE

Finally, let's consider the first three chapters of Genesis. Chapter one verse twenty-seven says that women are equally made in image of God and "very good." In chapter two creation of the woman comes about to remedy something which is "not good," namely the fact that the man is alone. God says he will make a "helper" for the man. This of course sounds like she has an inferior role. Her job will be to tidy up after Adam, wash his socks and cook his meals. That is, until we realize that the same Hebrew word translated

21. Joshua 2
22. Second Kings 22

"helper" is used to describe God himself in Genesis. Of course, by this God is not being designated as inferior, but the one who enables the man to flourish.

What though about Genesis chapter three, which Barker claims is foundational in entrenching a theological justification for the hatred of women? Given that in a sinful world, misogyny is indeed a sad fact, it is not surprising that men have been tempted to read Genesis three with a chauvinistic spirit, thinking that it justifies them in seeing women as inferior or more blameworthy than men for the mess that the world is in. But what if the situation in this chapter was interpreted by a woman who perhaps has been influenced by a spirit of misandry? Could it be read in a way that points the finger mainly at *men*?

Listen to this possible commentary by Eve, shortly after the ill-fated episode (written for a church drama by the author).

> "Adam is a typical *useless* man! He's terrible at communicating for a start. When I simply mentioned that the fruit of the tree in the middle of the garden looked nice he shouted at me and told me I mustn't touch it or I'll die. It turned out that God did *not* say we couldn't even touch it, so when I held it in my hands and nothing bad happened, I naturally assumed Adam had got it wrong and it would be alright to eat. That serpent smooth-talk was so convincing, and Adam was giving me no moral support whatsoever. Why didn't he say something and help me out when this charmer was appealing to all my womanly instincts? Bloody men! They like the 'go forth and multiply' bit of the relationship. But when it comes to emotional engagement they might as well be off in their cave somewhere. Well of course I desired wisdom, wouldn't you? Someone around here needs to have some competence. Of course, if *he* had been the one being tempted *I'd* have been the first to help. After all, I truly am God's gift to him, though he can't see it—the one to bring help, strength, encouragement, wisdom, and comfort into the relationship, like God does, but in the flesh, so to speak. But does he reciprocate? Not likely. While *I'm* facing the fight of my life with the concentrated forces of evil, what is *he* doing? Just standing there, clueless! When the serpent wasn't around, he was all talk, but as soon as the pressure was on, he bottled it. I want a strong man, someone who I can respect, but he lets this snake captivate me so I just *had* to walk all over him. And he has the cheek to blame *me*. '*That woman* who you put here with me made me do it,' he said to God. That wasn't his attitude when he first saw me without my fig-leaves on, I can tell you."

THE NEW TESTAMENT

But hang on a moment, you might say. Doesn't the apostle Paul in First Timothy chapter two verses 11–15, give the definitive male sexist interpretation when he says

> "A woman should learn in quietness and full submission. I do not permit a woman to teach or to assume authority over a man; she must be quiet. For Adam was formed first, then Eve. And Adam was not the one deceived; it was the woman who was deceived and became a sinner. But women will be saved through childbearing—if they continue in faith, love and holiness with propriety."

At first this looks like biblical sexism has continued from the pages of the Old Testament into the New and been spiritually revamped in the process. But again, we must look at the context to get an accurate understanding of the meaning. Paul was writing to a young church leader called Timothy (whose faith, incidentally, is credited to the witness of his mother and grandmother). Timothy lives in Ephesus, a place where the Greek goddess Artemis is worshipped (the Romans called her Diana). Thousands of Temple prostitutes "assisted" men in worshipping Artemis. Women were regarded as not only the originators of men in the sense of giving birth to them, but in the primal religious sense too. In the context of sexual seduction they gave men a revelatory connection with the divine. It didn't matter that women weren't educated like men and often married young. They could still be Temple prostitutes. The kind of "knowledge" they had didn't require formal education. They could babble away in ecstatic utterance without engaging their minds at all and through this communicate supernatural power. The promoters of Artemis worship feared childbirth (understandably, in an age when women often died in the process). But they believed Artemis would keep them safe if they worshipped her.

The Greek word *authentein*, translated "to have authority," is not used elsewhere in the New Testament in the context of God-given authority and some scholars think it means something pejorative like "controlling or even violent dominance" rather than something good and necessary for human protection and flourishing. Women were not to behave aggressively and manipulate men.[23]

Furthermore, there were the beginnings of gnostic influences infiltrating the young church community that Timothy led. The gnostics prized the knowledge of secret spiritual wisdom and they argued that the bodies of Adam and Eve, like the rest of the material world, were created by an evil

---

23. https://margmowczko.com/authentein-1-timothy2_12/

demigod. All material things were by nature bad and so the only hope of salvation lay in liberating the soul from the prison of the body through the secret knowledge and ecstatic experience that came with it. They argued that in eating the "forbidden fruit" Eve *liberated* the world by prizing open the way to achieving spiritual understanding.

The fact that Paul wanted women to *learn* (be properly educated in the Christian faith) was revolutionary, carrying forward Jesus' novel policy of allowing women (like Mary) to "sit at his feet" (be students). The Greek pagan philosophers like Aristotle taught that women were, ontologically, genetically deformed males and manifestly inferior. Some Jewish rabbis, following their chauvinistic spirits and man-made traditions instead of knowing the God of their Scriptures as they should have done, taught that it would be better to burn the Torah than teach it to a woman, of all things. Rabbi Eliezer, a later contributor to the Jewish collection of writings known as the Mishnah, a few years after Jesus, said "if any man gives his daughter a knowledge of the Law it is as though he taught her lechery."[24] Into this cauldron of misogyny Jesus and then Paul began the emancipation of women. One of the great theological statements Jesus gave about himself was to Mary's sister Martha, when he said "I am the resurrection and the life. Whoever believes in me will live, even though he dies."[25] Of course Paul wanted women to learn in "quietness and full submission" (not literal "silence"). Shouldn't all those who are learning do this?

However, Paul also wanted to correct the false teaching that women were created first and were the originators of men in the primal sense. Furthermore, woman was not the wise liberator of man when she ate the forbidden fruit but was deceived and became a sinner. Despite the frightening experience of going *through* childbirth in a fallen world, women will be saved, not by following Artemis and getting involved in Temple prostitution, but "continuing in faith, love and holiness, with propriety." So, a knowledge of the context Paul was addressing helps to make sense of what Paul was saying in First Timothy 2, which would otherwise contain much that would be baffling.

The Gospels show Jesus honoring women in all sorts of ways. The longest one to one recorded conversation Jesus has is with the Samaritan woman at Jacob's well, near Sychar. She then evangelizes her whole village. Jesus had women disciples. When Jesus is with some disciples in a house and is told that his mother and brothers are waiting outside to see him and

---

24. Orr-Ewing, *Why Trust the Bible?* 81
25. John 11:25

take him in hand, he points to his disciples and says, "here are my mother and my brothers,"[26] indicating women were among them.

He included women in his travelling circle. Luke 8:1–3 says,

> "After this, Jesus traveled about from one town and village to another, proclaiming the good news of the kingdom of God. The Twelve were with him, and also some women who had been cured of evil spirits and diseases: Mary (called Magdalene) from whom seven demons had come out; Joanna the wife of Chuza, the manager of Herod's household; Susanna; and many others. These women were helping to support them out of their own means."

Amy Orr-Ewing comments,

> "By mentioning these women by name, the tradition offers praise and gratitude to them for their financial contributions to the ministry of Jesus. A sharp contrast may be seen here with authors such as Ben Sirach of Jerusalem (c. 195 BC), who reflect a more prevalent attitude of the time with statement such as: "Bad temper, insolence and shame hold sway where the wife supports the husband." (Sir. 25:22)...

What about First Corinthians 14:34 where Paul says, "women should remain silent in the churches"? Again, the word "silent" should be interpreted as "quiet" or "orderly." Paul cannot have meant literal silence, because just three chapters before in chapter eleven he has been giving instructions on how women were to prophesy in church gatherings! The context of the Corinthian church was, like other congregations across the Greco-Roman world, one where women were not used to formal education and might call out disruptively. They needed to learn to behave in a decent and orderly way. It was like when a judge today bangs his gavel down and barks "silence in court." He is not commanding literal silence, but seeking to establish dignity and respect so that the business of the court can proceed effectively. An important principle of biblical interpretation (the discipline theologians call *hermeneutics*), is that we must first "travel to Corinth," as it were. Instead of jumping too quickly to try to interpret the relevance of scriptures to us in our context, we must first undertake proper *exegesis*, which is the working out of what they were saying to their original hearers in their original context.

We see several prominent women mentioned in the New Testament, with significant influence in the church. It is women who first discover the resurrection at the tomb. In the early church we have Priscilla, who with her husband was a theological teacher to Apollos, a bold and eloquent

---

26. Matthew 12:46–50

preacher.[27] It seems Lydia hosted a church in her home.[28] Phoebe was a deacon, entrusted with Paul's letter to the Romans and greatly commended by him.[29] Junia was called "outstanding among the apostles."[30]

THE RISE AND FALL OF WOMEN'S RIGHTS

In reviewing Alvin Schmidt's book "How Christianity Changed the World," Bill Muehlenberg says

> "In spite of the claims of some today that Christianity oppresses women, the historical record shows just the opposite. Women were oppressed in almost every culture prior to the coming of Christianity. By elevating sexual morality, and by conferring upon women a much higher status, the Christian religion revolutionized the place and prestige of women. For example, the great importance given to marriage meant that women were spared much of the abuse and mistreatment that they were accustomed to. By rejecting polygyny, prostitution, homosexuality and bestiality—all common during the time—the early Christians not only sheltered women but protected children and family. During this period Christian women actually outnumbered Christian men. Admittedly there were some anomalies later in the church's history, when chauvinistic and anti-feminine views were allowed to re-enter parts of the church. But such aberrations must not detract from the truly revolutionary elevation of the status of women achieved by Christianity."[31]

In the last five hundred years, the nations of the world most influenced by the Bible and the Reformation Theology which promoted knowledge of it have been the nations that have led the world in treating women with dignity. The elevation of the status of women was given a boost by Protestant reformers like Luther who delighted in the married state and rejected the Aristotelian misogyny which was still influencing the Roman church. Henceforth, women did not have to be cloistered in a nunnery in order to be regarded as godly—they could be socially esteemed wives and homemakers, and witness to Christian truth alongside their husbands.

27. Acts 18:26
28. Acts 16:40
29. Romans 16:1–2
30. Ibid. 16:7
31. https://billmuehlenberg.com/2005/09/07/a-review-of-how-christianity-changed-the-world-by-alvin-schmidt/

However, in the West today the sexual chaos promoted by the forces of rebellion against biblical truth is harming women especially and reversing social progress. So called "no fault" divorce, now being brought into the UK, makes a mockery of the covenant vows. Marriage becomes just another contract, easily voidable by either side at will, thus undermining one of the essentials for biblical marriage which is covenanted permanence. (The other is sexual differentiation, which has also been rendered unnecessary by "same-sex marriage."). Apart from the very meaning of marriage disappearing, men have little incentive to marry anyway when it is culturally acceptable to have sex with women as they please without any tiresome residue of the idea of commitment. (Increasingly the evidence is that men are disinclined to have "normal" sex with real women anyway when pornography, often violent, is more and more socially acceptable and so readily available online).

If contraception fails, many women have, since the 1960s viewed abortion as the natural fallback option. The early feminists who fought for women's political emancipation would be horrified at the gullibility of "progressive" women today who have swallowed hook line and sinker the lie that easy abortion benefits women. Historically, the group most in favor of abortion was upper class men, wanting to "sow their wild oats" with less socially advantaged girls without the inconvenience and embarrassment of siring children. Yet abortion on demand has become a shibboleth social liberals and modern feminists cling to with a blind passion.

The culture of sexual incontinence and abortion is one that far from liberating women, makes rape and abuse much more common, as is being demonstrated on university campuses all over Britain. With the breakdown of the practice of marriage, it is common for women to be abandoned by the fathers of their children, sometimes even before they give birth. The way the welfare state works in the UK often gives perceived advantages to women who have children with absent men, such as priority in social housing. Children grow up without fathers, and often seek out membership of gangs to feel they belong somewhere. Some women do a heroic job of bringing up children without fathers, but it is a terribly difficult task, particularly for less socially privileged women. It is no wonder some women in the West are attracted to Islam, which while subjecting women to strict social boundaries (similar to ancient near east cultural mores) at least gives them protection from the sexual anarchy which they know allows men greater opportunities to exploit them at will, and lessens the chance they will experience the chaos of family breakdown. It is our godless, sinful world which encourages misogyny, not the Bible, which saves us from it.

Chapter 10

Homophobic?

phobia (NOUN)—*an extreme fear or dislike of a particular thing . . . especially one that is not reasonable*

—The Cambridge Dictionary

Dan Barker in *God: The Most Unpleasant Character in all Fiction* relies heavily on the story of the destruction of Sodom and Gomorrah in Genesis 19 to justify Dawkins's assertion that the biblical God is homophobic. In fact, he spends virtually the whole chapter on it, save a passing reference to two Levitical passages which he glibly interprets as saying "gays are bad" and "gays should be killed."

In Genesis 18, three mysterious guests visit Abraham, who bows low and offers them hospitality, eventually recognizing that one of them is the LORD. The LORD says that Sarah, his wife, who is past childbearing age, will miraculously have a child within a year. She laughs in disbelief, but when challenged she is afraid and denies laughing. The LORD explains to Abraham that they have come down to see if the people of Sodom and Gomorrah are as wicked as he had heard. While the two angels head towards Sodom, the LORD remains to tell Abraham what he intends to do. I summarized their conversation about justice in chapter three of this book. Chapter nineteen says that when the angels reach Sodom in the evening it is Lot, Abraham's nephew, who gives them hospitality.

When it was late all the men from every part of the city, old and young came and surrounded the house and demanded Lot hand over these two strangers for an exercise in ritual humiliation—homosexual rape. Lot is horrified. Handing over guests who had come under his protection to such a fate would have been considered the worst thing he could do in the circumstances, going against all codes of ethical conduct everywhere, such as to bring terrible judgment on him and his family. In sheer desperation he goes out and offers the mob his two virgin daughters as an alternative. They regard this as a provocation and tell him they will treat him even worse than the visitors for having the nerve to judge them for what they want to do.

The angels pull Lot back inside the house, strike those nearest the house with blindness and tell him to get himself, his wife, his daughters and the men they were pledged to marry out of the city at once, because they are going to destroy the place. The men betrothed to his daughters don't take him seriously when he passes on the angels' warning, and as he hesitates, the angels grab his hands and that of his wife and daughters and lead them safely out of the city. They tell them to flee to the mountains and not look back. Lot's wife though, does look back, lingering over the city where her heart is. God then rains burning sulfur down on the cities of the plain, and she was not far enough away and was turned into "a pillar of salt."

Lot and his two daughters then go and live in a cave on the mountain. Thinking that they would now not be able to find husbands to give them children and preserve their family line, the older daughter, persuades the younger to agree to a plan whereby they get their father drunk on two successive nights so they can in turn have sex with him and get pregnant. The plan works and they each have a son, the father of the Moabites and Ammonites respectively.

The sordid and terrible tale seems to exert great fascination on Barker, even though he spends much time pouring scorn on the story's veracity. His friendship with Dawkins should incline him to show more respect for the scientific evidence that the destruction of Sodom and Gomorrah really happened.

In 1908, a massive blast near Siberia's Stony Tunguska River flattened some two thousand square kilometers of uninhabited forestry. Curiously, no crater was discovered and scientists explain the strange phenomena by postulating a meteor explosion some five to ten kilometers above the land. A multi-disciplinary team of scientists, analyzing the archaeological evidence, believe a similar occurrence caused the demise of a Middle Bronze Age civilization in a once fertile plain near the banks of the Dead Sea around the time of the biblical account.

The fertile soil would have been stripped of nutrients by the high heat, and waves of the Dead Sea's briny anhydride salts would have—tsunami-like—washed over the surrounding area. At the same time, the explosion's fallout caused blisteringly hot, strong winds, which deposited a rain of mineral grains, which have been found on pottery at a place called Tall el-Hammam. Radiocarbon dating of organic archaeological evidence has shown that mud-brick walls of buildings suddenly disappeared around 3,700 years ago, leaving only stone foundations.

The scientists analyzed samples from twelve seasons of Tall el-Hammam excavations to conclude that the most logical explanation for the settlement's demise was a meteor explosion. They wrote

> "Based upon the archaeological evidence, it took at least six hundred years to recover sufficiently from the soil destruction and contamination before civilization could again become established in the eastern Middle Ghor,"

According to a 2013 *Biblical Archaeology Review* article by Tall El Hamman Excavation Project co-director Dr. Steven Collins, the site is a strong candidate for the biblical city of Sodom. In the article, among other biblical citations, Collins quotes from Genesis 19:24–25:

> "Then the Lord rained down burning sulfur on Sodom and Gomorrah—from the Lord out of the heavens. Thus he overthrew those cities and the entire plain, including all those living in the cities—and also the vegetation in the land."

On the ground at the site, Collins witnessed such destruction firsthand. In a vivid description he writes, "The violent conflagration that ended occupation at Tall el-Hammam produced melted pottery, scorched foundation stones and several feet of ash and destruction debris churned into a dark grey matrix."

In a jointly authored paper between Phillip J Silvia and Collins, they conclude

> "The destruction not only of Tall el-Hammam (Sodom), but also its neighbors (Gomorrah and the other cities of the plain) was most likely caused by a meteoritic airburst event. . .The memory of the destruction of ha-kikkar, with its large population and extensive agricultural lands, was preserved in the Book of Genesis and ultimately incorporated into a traditional tale that, drawing on the layer of ash that covered the destruction of one of its major cities, remembered a place consumed by a fiery

catastrophe from 'out of the heavens' (Genesis 19:24). The Bible gives the city's name: Sodom."[1]

Barker's theory is that, because the destruction of Sodom is bracketed by two accounts dealing with fertility, the motive of the writers was part of a broad "macho agenda" in which the need for men to have offspring one way or another led them to represent homosexuality in a bad light and ripe for God's judgment. He says that the biblical writers wanted the men of Sodom, as "crazed homosexuals," to be seen to be judged for "the refusal to provide offspring for the patriarch" by not accepting his offer of his daughters. He says that the writers also then assumed the daughters' priority in their new cave refuge would be to provide descendants for their father. Thus the fiery judgment account was designed as a foundational story for developing a homophobic culture, in order to ensure Israelites avoided non-procreational sex.

It is amazing what lengths people will go to distort biblical narratives if they themselves have an agenda, which of course Barker does. Let's try to apply some sane exegetical principles to understanding Genesis 19.

First, it is anachronistic to say that the text infers that all men of Sodom, young and old, were "homosexuals," crazed or otherwise. Apart from being statistically ridiculous the idea of categorizing a group of people who sometimes practice, or who are drawn to practice genital acts with others of the same gender, as "homosexuals" or "gays" is a modern invention. The Bible does not concern itself directly with the concept of "sexual orientation." Some of the males probably were titillated at the prospect of "carnal knowledge" of these exotic looking men. Others perhaps were just interested in reveling in the symbolic dominance over these foreigners or just there to view the pornographic spectacle from a distance. The numbers present would have been considerable, and there is a particularly demonic dynamic that can operate through large crowds of men, like in the gladiatorial arenas of Rome and football violence today.

Barker's suggestion that Lot offered his daughters to them for his own procreational purposes is as daft as anything else in his book. Lot is presented as man in desperate straits with no way out open to him from his own resources. To have handed his visitors over would have been to act as an accomplice to the most wicked act he could imagine—subjecting defenseless guests to the humiliation of anal rape before a vast, jeering crowd. It is in this context that we should view his apparent offer of his two virgin daughters to them as a substitute object for their lust. People understandably see this as cowardly and immoral and an example of the gross disregard

---

1. https://www.timesofisrael.com/evidence-of-sodom-meteor-blast-cause-of-biblical-destruction-say-scientists/

men had for women and girls. Lot was willing to sacrifice his own daughters as mere pawns to protect his "honor" and that of his male guests!

It is certainly true that no modern-day action film hero would even contemplate such a course of action. But we are not dealing with a character in a fictional fairy-tale but the grim reality of a man in an impossible situation. I'm inclined to think, along with some biblical commentators, that Lot's "offer" of his daughters was intended to shock the people of Sodom into realizing what a terrible course of action they were proposing. If all the men of the town were there, this would have included the men who were betrothed to his daughters. It's as if Lot were saying "what you are threatening is so evil, it would be better for you to violate my own daughters, betrothed to your own countrymen here, than for me to allow you to proceed with your obscenely wicked plan." Their enraged reaction that he, an alien among them, is presuming to judge them for what they want to do, seems to confirm this interpretation. His desperate attempt to shame them backfired.

Having said this, the Bible does not present Lot as being a man who is a great example of faith, even though such examples were not immune from sinful or cowardly behavior. Abraham, generally praised for his faith, twice passed his wife off as his sister to save his own skin (despite God's guarantee that he would live to have descendants) risking her honor in the process. It is true that Lot is referred to as "righteous" by the apostle Peter in Second Peter 2:7–8, but this seems to be simply because he was distressed and tormented in his soul by the filthy goings-on he witnessed in Sodom and was therefore rescued. Lot in Genesis 13 and 14 is portrayed as making the decision to settle among the cities of the plain of the Jordan. The plain was well watered and fertile, but the people in the cities were described as wicked and "sinning greatly against the Lord." Lot then had to be rescued by Abraham when the king of Sodom was defeated in battle and the victors carried off Lot and his possessions into captivity. By the time of the visit of the angels, he seems to be a tired, broken man, unable to summon up the energy to make a decisive break with the place he had settled in, despite its wickedness and the dramatic warning he had from the angels of its impending doom.

When he does eventually make it with his daughters to a cave in the mountains, his daughters did not concoct their incestuous plan for the reason of honoring him, as their father, by providing him with descendants. If this was the biblical writer's assumed priority for all concerned, as Barker claims, why did the plan have to involve constructive rape? No, they did it because they wanted children for themselves and were willing to take away their father's ability to consent to get what they wanted. Had he not been so drunk and known what was going on he would not have agreed to impregnate his daughters.

Genesis 18 and 19 seem to contrast three different kinds of people. First, there are those who, like Abraham, trusted God for their deepest hope—that of having descendants—and who believe in God's justice and righteousness. Second, there are those like Lot's daughters who had some knowledge of God through the witness of their great uncle Abraham, but like Sarah earlier on who persuaded Abraham to enter into a surrogacy arrangement to produce a child, thought they should pursue their own way of doing things. Finally, there are the people of Sodom, who are portrayed as being as godless and wicked as they could possibly be. Attempted male on male gang rape of travelers seeking hospitality was the detestable culmination of arrogance, violent lust and lack of compassion for the vulnerable, according to the prophet Ezekiel in his commentary on the story.[2]

Does the story give insight on the question of the morality of homosexual acts today? It is certainly not obvious that the behavior of the men of Sodom had anything in common with consensual genital acts between people in a "loving, stable, same-sex relationship" in the twenty-first century.

However, Barker is probably right in assuming that the biblical story does have some relevance to those looking to the Bible for guidance about the general legitimacy of homosexual activity. Robert Gagnon in *The Bible and Homosexual Practice* (page 78) says that "while the story of Sodom, because of the added factors of inhospitality and rape, is not an ideal passage for studying the Bible's views on same-sex intercourse, it remains a relevant text." This is because, in the light of prohibitions on same sex intercourse (both consensual and non-consensual) in Leviticus chapters eighteen and twenty, to "sodomize" someone was to degrade them in a particularly shameful way because it involved destroying their masculinity.

LEVITICUS

Leviticus 18:22 says "Do not lie with a man as one lies with a woman; that is detestable." This would certainly include penetrative anal sex between males, and probably indicates disapproval of all genitally intimate acts between male Israelites.

Barker is right that this verse cannot be dismissed by liberal Christian revisionists as saying that what is referred to is only "ritually" detestable, in the same way that eating pork or shellfish is, and therefore not something that should restrict us today. In chapter two I explained how Christians should seek to abide by the principles in laws which reflect God's unchanging moral character and what he does and doesn't approve of.

2. Ezekiel 16

Leviticus chapter eighteen lists a range of sexual prohibitions, including incestuous sexual relationships, taking a wife's sister as a rival wife, approaching a woman for sex during her monthly period, having sex with animals and also a prohibition on offering a child to be sacrificed to Molech, which perhaps had a sexual aspect to it, given its inclusion in a list where every other prohibition clearly relates to sex. That these are all highly "moral" commands directly reflecting God's unchanging character rather than "ritual" ones abrogated by Christ's redeeming work is shown by the words at the end of the chapter. Verse 24 says

> "do not defile yourselves in any of these ways, because this is how the nations that I am going to drive out before you became defiled. Even the land was defiled, so I punished it for its sin, and the land vomited out its inhabitants."

So these commands in chapter eighteen reflected moral principles and standards that God wanted to see *all* people adhere to, not just Israelites, and he punished those who consistently broke them. Thus they are relevant today in guiding us about what God sees as good and what he doesn't. Incest, bestiality, sex during a woman's flow of blood, sacrificing children and male homosexual intercourse are all deemed *morally* detestable in God's sight and things Christians will want to avoid if we are seeking to live holy lives in response to what Christ has done for us.

Of these, the ban on sex during a woman's menstrual flow seems exclusively about safeguarding ritual purity and may appear not to contain any moral principle relevant to us today. This is probably because our culture is different both from those where husbands are considered to generally have a "right" to sex with their wives, and the biblical ideal where husbands and wives freely give themselves to each other sexually in recognition that their bodies actually belong to each other (See First Corinthians 7:4–5a). The suspension of sexual intercourse as a marital duty during the wife's period therefore provides her with a protective rest from sex and it was (and is) immoral for this not to be respected and observed by their husbands. Orthodox Jews and Muslims recognize this still today as a moral issue alongside any concerns about ritual purity. But in post-Christian, promiscuous Western culture, those who advise people on "safe sex" echo the standard line that consensual sex is fine for women and girls with any man at any time, providing a condom is used. However, in a loving, stable, socially recognized relationship (biblical marriage) a man should have the patience to wait for a woman's period to be over before approaching her for sex.

So is Barker right that God is "homophobic"? Leviticus 18 does put "lying with a man as with a woman" in a list of morally prohibited things, a list which also includes sex with animals, incest, and child sacrifice. This is clearly not only unacceptable to those who believe homosexual intercourse is equally valid to heterosexual intercourse, but is also deeply offensive to them, and many today would therefore conclude the biblical God is "homophobic."

They would feel their case is strengthened by Leviticus 20:13 which is part of a chapter outlining the punishments for contravention of the prohibited acts in chapter eighteen. The death penalty is stipulated for "lying with a man as with a woman" (both for the penetrator and the one allowing himself to be penetrated). However, it should be noted that the death penalty is also stipulated for adultery (for the man and woman), among other things. Any country in the world that decided to criminalize sodomy solely on the basis that Old Testament law does, should, to be consistent, also criminalize adultery.

QUESTIONING THE TERMINOLOGY

Before going further, however, let's examine what is understood by "homophobic." It used to mean having an irrational fear or hatred of anyone who is suspected of homoerotic feelings or identifies themselves or is identified by others as "gay." One classic scenario would be an overly macho character, perhaps with suppressed homoerotic inclinations himself, bullying or mocking those he perceives as effeminate or who identify with gay subculture.

Another scenario could be a hypocritical religious leader denouncing gay people for their proclivities whilst being tolerant of adultery and fornication. For some, the term "homophobia" carries painful memories of bullying or violence towards them or the past stigma attached to those suffering from HIV-AIDS. Some think of 1950s Britain where the police, judicial system and much of society regarded "queers" with contempt and where there was a lot of general prejudice towards those who were "different" as exemplified by hotel signs saying "no blacks, no Irish, no dogs."[3]

In the 2019 film *Downton Abbey*, set during the 1930s, morally self-righteous police are portrayed as raiding a joint where gay men are simply dancing and enjoying each other's company and carting them all off to the

---

3. See Wilson, *More Perfect Union*. The implication that the opponents of the concept of "same sex marriage" in the UK were motivated by prejudiced sentiments akin to racism fuels much of Wilson's rhetoric. I'm sure some of them were, but I have endeavoured to persuade Bishop Alan Wilson (who is my area Bishop) that opposition to the Church of England embracing same sex marriage and the LGBT+ agenda can be based on sincere theological principle and a desire to radically live out the Gospel rather than a merely reactionary spirit. https://www.youtube.com/watch?v=QY8Oai6_Cek

cells. Some think of certain African countries today where AIDS is spread mostly through heterosexual promiscuity but where the authorities treat homosexual offences with a harshness which implies they are the biggest threat to public health and wellbeing. Others think of areas of the world controlled by Islamist extremists where those identified as being homosexual are thrown off high buildings.

However, the term "homophobic" has evolved and now it is often used to describe anyone who has a conscientious objection to the concept of "same sex marriage"[4] or believes that homosexual behavior is one manifestation of human sinfulness among all the others, including heterosexual immorality. Such people may be compassionate, kind and earnestly seeking to love their gay neighbor as themselves, but if they express any disquiet with what is considered the new orthodoxy on LGBT+ matters, however mild, then they are denounced as "homophobic." The Christian Legal Centre provides support for those who are losing their jobs or otherwise persecuted for expressing biblically orthodox Christian views. Orwellian thought control is terrifying many into acquiescence with the full LGBT+ agenda.[5]

---

4. Now called "equal marriage" by those who control the language used regarding sexuality and gender in politics and the media. How could any right-thinking person ever oppose something so sacred as "equality"?

5. For some time now in the UK we have seen people lose their jobs or university places for expressing a traditional view of marriage. Now we are seeing the same thing happen over the transgender issue. Recently a tax expert for the Centre for Global Development, Maya Forstater, did not have her contract renewed because of her resistance to transgender ideology expressed on Twitter. The judge in the Employment Tribunal hearing, Mr Justice Tayler, held that her views "did not have the protected characteristic of philosophical belief" under the Equalities Act of 2010. Her stance that she should not be forced to recognize a person's chosen gender if it was at odds with their biological sex was, he said, "not worthy of respect in a democratic society." https://www.theguardian.com/society/2019/dec/18/judge-rules-against-charity-worker-who-lost-job-over-transgender-tweets Clearly, in our "egalitarian society" so called "progressive" beliefs are more equal than others.

In the UK, many senior people in the Church of England, and other denominations, are either pushing the LGBT+ agenda themselves, going along with it, or just lying low for fear of being crushed by the oncoming cultural juggernaut. Although concerns about transgender ideology are still felt across society, this thinking has penetrated the church quickly and with ease, with the Church of England General Synod recently encouraging parish clergy to use the service of renewal of baptismal vows to mark a person's "transition" from one gender to another rather than to remind them of their identity in Christ. See Ian Paul's helpful analysis of the House of Bishop's guidance https://www.psephizo.com/sexuality-2/a-plea-to-the-bishops-on-trans-guidance-please-listen-and-respond/

In *The Madness of Crowds*, Douglas Murray, who himself identifies as a gay man, outlines the corrosive effect on society of identity politics and the rush to persecute those with traditional views on sexuality and gender.

THE NEW TESTAMENT

It is frequently averred that because Jesus didn't say anything directly about homosexuality, this means that it was not something he thought was morally problematic. A moment's thought reveals what a feeble case this "argument from silence" makes. The argument assumes that in Jesus time, there was the kind of debate there is today in the church, about the rights and wrongs of homosexual practice and that therefore if Jesus had wanted to endorse the status quo, he would have made a point of doing it. However, in Jesus time Jewish people were united in understanding that the Torah forbade it as serious sin, like other forms of *porneia*, the Greek word used to denote all forms of sexual immorality. Therefore the fact that Jesus is not recorded as talking specifically about homosexuality when speaking of *porneia* is evidence that he concurred with the unanimous Jewish view that homosexual practice was included in what was understood to be sexual immorality. When Jesus differed from what was assumed generally to be the case in ethical matters he was not afraid to say so, e.g. marriage and divorce, and the validity of taking personal revenge for wrongs.

There are New Testament passages which clearly confirm the sinfulness of homoerotic, genital acts. First Corinthians 6:9 says that both the active and passive male partners in willing and persistent anal sex belong to a category of people who will not "inherit the kingdom of God." Also, First Timothy 1:10, like the Corinthians passage, uses the word *arsenokoitai* (a Greek compound word referring to the Hebrew "he who lies with a man as with a woman") to describe a category of people who are rebels and lawbreakers.

Romans 1:27 describes men who

> "abandoned natural relationships with women and were inflamed with lust for one another. Men committed indecent acts with other men and received in themselves the due penalty for their perversion."

Romans 1:26 also sees lesbianism as a feature of a fallen world.

> "Even their women exchanged natural relationships for unnatural ones."

Revisionists dispute that the meaning of "natural" in this passage relates to God's purposes in creation. Some say the word is referring only to those who are "heterosexual" by nature, who give up their personal "orientation" to pursue what is not "natural" *for them*. Another way of getting round these verses is to say that what is natural is *culturally determined*.

They argue that in the Apostle Paul's time it was considered "unnatural" for people to practice gay sex as it was for men to have long hair like women, but in our culture today it is socially acceptable both for men to have long hair and to have sex with each other and therefore the latter is as "natural" as heterosexual sex. However, what is meant by the terms "natural" or "unnatural" varies according to the context. In some contexts, it can indeed refer to people's subjective feelings and in others something primarily cultural. Something could seem "natural" to a particular human being with particular tendencies or to a society according to its customs and traditions. And it can also mean something that is intrinsic to the way God created humanity.

The context of the word "natural" in Romans chapter one, which is idolatry leading to futile thinking and the giving over of men in the sinfulness of their hearts "to impurity for the degrading of their bodies" shows that "natural" makes a lot more sense if it means "the way God designed us to be," rather than "someone's subjective feelings" or "current social mores or customs." Furthermore, the Bible does not concern itself with the issue of "orientation" (which, ironically, is the reason some revisionists claim its passages on sexuality are irrelevant to us today when the idea of "orientation" is regarded as a modern, educated insight). Also, homosexual practice was widespread and often socially acceptable in the Greco-Roman world of Paul's day so it cannot be said that it was against the cultural mores of the time.

Some say that this passage is only referring to the behavior of people who, in an excess of sexual desire overspill normal heterosexual behavior and add homosexual behavior to satisfy their wanton lust, and/or people who transgress the customary male role of always being the "active partner" in sex.[6] However 1:27 does not read like this. There is nothing there that suggests the problem is *excess*. The problem is *abandonment* of one thing and its substitution by another. The *acts* themselves are indecent, rather than the oversexed desire to indulge in them. Also 1:27 speaks of *exchange* rather than intemperate *addition*. Also, the argument that the problem was that people were going against what were considered "natural" gender roles is just another version of the argument that the word "natural" means "what was understood as natural in that culture." As explained above, these verses are talking about God's creative design and purpose.

However, it is important to point out that Romans 1:24–32 is set in the context of Paul's teaching that everyone is under God's righteous judgment. Distortion of sexuality is something that follows on from idolatry in society generally, rather than a deliberate choice made by certain, especially wicked,

---

6. Vines, *God and the Gay Christian*, 103–11 cf. Gagnon, *The Bible and Homosexual Practice* 176–8, 361–95

people. The culmination of wickedness is greed, depravity, envy, murder, strife, deceit, malice, gossip, slander, God-hatred, insolence, arrogance and boastfulness, disobedience to parents, senselessness, faithlessness, heartlessness and ruthlessness. These are sins that everyone must repent of and guard against.

The answer therefore to the question "Is God homophobic?" will depend on your definition of homophobia. We are all made in God's image and we are all sinners who need the grace and mercy of God. We are all called to repentance and holiness of life. Sex is not to be a rival god and sexual intercourse is not to be regarded as essential for a fully human life. If it were, Jesus could not have been fully human.

SAME SEX FRIENDSHIP AND INTIMACY

Throughout the Bible close same sex friendships are celebrated and affirmed. Examples of friends sharing deep love, intimacy, trust and loyalty are David and Jonathan, Ruth and Naomi, Jesus and John. But none of this necessarily implies any homoeroticism. It would be blasphemous to suggest that Jesus, as the sinless Son of God, was guilty of any homoerotic genital acts with men, just as it would be to suggest he had sexual relations with a woman, as an unmarried man.

We should understand that the cultural context of both Old and New Testaments was one where non-genital same sex physical and emotional intimacy was a feature of people's lives, much more so than in our hyper-individualist Western culture where men only relate in an emotionally and physically close way to each other in certain rare circumstances. For example, men reclined on each other when eating together in Jesus' time. The Leonardo Da Vinci painting, *The Last Supper*, depicting Jesus sitting in the center of a long table, flanked by the apostles, is stylized art. In fact, they would have been reclining on each other around a low table in a circle. In some middle eastern lands today, where sodomy is a serious criminal offence, you see men holding hands in the street with other men as a sign of friendship and intimacy and this is completely socially acceptable (in contrast to public displays of affection between opposite-sex people which are not acceptable).

One of the problems in our society today is loneliness. Many of us lead socially isolated lives. We crave intimacy and people equate this with sex. But it is a false equation. It is possible to have physical, emotional and spiritual intimacy without sex and to have sex without any intimacy whatsoever. A person who identifies as gay or same-sex-attracted should not think the

Bible's message means they are to experience no intimacy. Our society is moving in the direction of assuming that two men or two women who share a home must be indulging in gay sex but of course this is an unwarranted and harmful assumption , as it might discourage people from living together who are simply wanting company and friendship. People who admit to being same sex attracted but are committed to remaining chaste should be able to live in a shared household, without finding temptation unbearable, if they are getting support and encouragement from fellow believers.

In a stable gay relationship today, there would probably be many aspects of that relationship, physical, emotional and spiritual, that could be completely affirmed by faithful Christians, especially genuinely sacrificial care. Many a gay man dying of AIDS has been tenderly cherished and nursed by his partner. But these expressions of love are things that can be affirmed in any intimate, loving relationship, such as between very close friends and family. Homoerotic genital practices themselves between people of the same sex do however fall outside the biblical revelation of what real love is, just as perverted sex or sadomasochistic behavior or sex without total commitment is not an expression of real love among heterosexuals.

Does that mean God has an irrational fear or sneering contempt for people who have homoerotic thoughts and feelings? Nowhere does the Bible teach this. It is true that lust offends God but the New Testament makes clear that this is lust of *any* sort.[7]

> "For this is the will of God, your sanctification: that you abstain from sexual immorality; that each one of you know how to control his own body in holiness and honor, not in the passion of lust like the Gentiles who do not know God."

Lust can be defined as the *cultivated* desire for and pursuit of sexual gratification outside the boundaries God has given for our human flourishing. But being *tempted* in a particular way is not of itself sinful. Jesus was tempted in every way we are but was without sin.[8] It is how we *respond* to temptation that matters.

IDENTITY VERSUS MORALITY

The difficulty today for those who want to submit to the Bible's authority in the area of sexual relationships is that Western society has embraced a paradigm which is not biblically centered. Nowhere does the Bible divide people

---

7. First Thessalonians 4:3–5 (English Standard Version)
8. Hebrews 4:15

into tribes according to "sexual orientation," and today there is actually no great enthusiasm among leading gay influencers like Peter Tatchell and Matthew Parris to find a "gay gene" to prove homosexuality is hard-wired. They do not like the argument, often heard in the church to justify homosexual behavior, that "it is OK because they cannot help being who they are," believing that it is more accurate to understand sexuality as a spectrum, along which most people do have a choice about what kinds of sexual relationships they pursue. It is just they think the homosexual option should be as morally acceptable as the heterosexual one, whatever the blend of personal desires and feelings.

However, there has been nevertheless a tendency to want to define people's identity by their thoughts and feelings in relation just to sexuality, let alone gender identity as well. The proliferation of sexuality categories represented by initials testifies to this – as I write we are up to a veritable alphabet soup of LGBQQAOPPBDSMDS.[9] This ignores the reality that all of us have thoughts and feelings in relation to which we must operate an ethical filter if we are to be moral creatures. Deep down we all know that our thoughts and feelings should not shape our foremost sense of identity in a way that overrides what is ultimately right and wrong, which is why people characterized by behaviors that are near universally considered wrong such as bestiality, pedophilia and necrophilia, do not have their initials added to the list.

The current Western social more in the "#metoo" era is that, in the area of sexuality, we should "give expression to who we are" unless that expression takes place without valid consent (such as sex with minors, animals and the rape, assault and harassment scenarios) or where there is a power imbalance deemed unacceptable, making any apparent consent invalid (the "casting couch" scenario).

This "free love" approach ignores the more indirect forms of harm done to people when sexual activity takes place outside the boundaries laid down by God to protect people from being hurt. The institution of biblical marriage, which in a fallen world is never going to be as good as it could be, nevertheless does, overall, help to minimize the power imbalances which inevitably arise between two people in a sexual relationship and which in sinful societies allow people to damage one another.

People who have exchanged marriage vows in public, invested a considerable degree of emotional, financial and practical commitment to each other and who have bought in to the institutional respectability which

---

9. Lesbian, gay, bisexual, queer, questioning, asexual, omnisexual, polysexual, pansexual, bondage, discipline, sadist, masochist, dominant, submissive.
The number of gender categories has now reached three figures and so these are too many to list.

marriage still affords, therefore give each other a certain amount of power which helps to equalize the relationship and moderate what might otherwise be deepening power imbalances. A man in his forties or fifties, for example, who has invested in a marriage is, on average, likely to feel somewhat more deterred from leaving his wife to go off with a younger model, or subjecting her to abusive treatment, than if he has just been living with a woman outside of marriage. A married man or woman is generally more frightened of any infidelity becoming known about than a person who just has a "partner." The relative stability of married relationships as compared to co-habiting relationships testifies to this, even though it is true that people (mainly powerful men) can use marriage as a "front" to conceal their hypocrisy in sexual matters.

A testosterone-fueled teenage boy has sex with his insecure girlfriend and after the relationship breaks down he breezily moves on to other girls but she falls into self-harm. An attractive, socially confident woman sleeps with a dependable, but less gregarious, man but will not agree to marry him, in order to keep her many options open. This destroys his confidence and he becomes depressed. A man and woman, both divorcees, embark on a relationship involving sexual intercourse. She, childless, wants the commitment of marriage and the chance of children, but he has got used to his independence, already has his own children, and spins her along, causing her pain and frustration. A female celebrity has lots of younger boyfriends, and as a desirable woman, more experienced and wealthier than her younger partners, she holds most of the cards. But when she gets older, her insecurities grow, and her latest "lover" has the upper hand, leading her to desperate anxiety that he will go after other women. When this is suspected, violence follows and even suicide.

Making a choice to refrain from something we are drawn to does not mean we are denying our identity and living an inauthentic life, failing to be "truly ourselves." Some people are especially prone, whether through hereditary or other factors, to particular temptations, like ill temper, destructive, narcissistic or addictive behavior. According to the Gospel this should induce compassion but also a call to repentance and transformation through the power of the Holy Spirit. It is the same with sex. If we are going to define people by those they are tempted to lust after then a married man with even just an average sex drive who honors his marriage vows could be described as a "non-practicing adulterer." We already see signs that in the future many people will see their sexuality as fluid, and they will be unwilling to be pigeon-holed. This will mean that either they will act in whatever way they please at the time, as that will be the current expression of "who they are" *or* they will choose to follow a moral compass which gives objective guidance about what is right and wrong for everyone.

IS GOD TRANSPHOBIC?

Because Dawkins did not, in *The God Delusion*, specifically accuse the Old Testament God of being transphobic, Barker does not refer to this issue or cite any biblical texts about it. However, I know of a verse in the Bible which some Christians have been troubled by. Among a collection of various laws given to the people of Israel recorded in Deuteronomy 22, verse 5 says

> "A woman must not wear men's clothing, nor a man wear women's clothing, for the LORD your God detests anyone who does this."

Most English translations use the word "abominable" to describe those who are cross-dressing. One translation, the *Good News* version, used the word "hates" instead of "detests." What are Christians today to make of this verse? Is it relevant to the issues around people who identify as transgender or transvestite?

The first thing to say is that this verse is among commands that were given for society in Israel and they say nothing explicit about life outside Old Covenant Israel, then or now, unlike the injunctions in Leviticus 18. Some of the commands seem to be akin to the clearly ritual separations of one thing from another, e.g. verse 6 which prohibits the planting of two kinds of seed in their vineyards, and verse 11 which forbids the Israelites wearing clothes of wool and linen woven together. For the reasons given in chapter two Christians do not feel bound by them. Other verses in this chapter carry moral principles which Christians would feel have relevance to situations today, such as the Israelites making parapets around their rooves to protect the health and safety of occupiers and visitors. This moral principle does have to be translated into something more culturally appropriate for people who have sloping rooves which aren't designed for people to go up and sit or walk around on. But in Mediterranean houses with flat rooves and staircases to provide access to them, this part of God's word can still be more directly applied as part of our overall Christian duty to love people and protect them from harm.

The verse immediately before, verse 4, is about coming to the rescue of your brother if his donkey or ox has fallen on the road. This is a plainly moral command, grounded on the principle that Israelites were to see their fellow Israelites as brothers who they should not ignore when they needed their help. Where Cain asked God sulkily "am I my brother's keeper?" the law of Moses says "yes, you are." So, a Christian today should sense a duty to help another member of the community who is in a crisis situation.

So in 22:5 is the "abomination" a ritual one, in the same way that eating unclean animals was "an abomination" or does God find something timelessly morally objectionable in cross dressing which therefore extends the command's relevance to today and gives a negative view of transvestitism or transgenderism? I'm not completely sure. It could be that the command is a mix of both types of law and that for Israelites, it both contravened the idea of "separating one thing from another" but also involved the Israelites immorally rejecting their sexual or gender identity which God had given them.

What about the word "hates" or "detests," or as some translations have, "find disgusting?" It is conceded these are strong words, and in the kind of direct speaking which is a feature of the Hebrew culture, they are directed to the people rather than the behavior. This indicates to me that this command had moral dimensions. But whether it does or not, how can a God of love be said to "hate" or "detest" or "find disgusting" a certain category of people?

It must be said that this is not the only place where this particular Hebrew way of saying things, literally translated into English, gives rise to problems of understanding. In Hebrew, to "hate" someone did not mean to literally "hate" them as we would use the word generally in English. It meant something like "to regard any obligation to them as secondary to something higher and thereby in some way rejecting them or what they want."

Jesus used this Hebrew way of speaking when he said to be his disciples we must "hate" ourselves, our nearest kin and our spouses.[10] What he meant was certainly not that we should dishonor or harm our families, or fail to look after them, because elsewhere he commanded we should do all those things and he condemned the idea we should use religious excuses to get round our duty of care to them.[11] No, he meant we must put him first and not use family or the desire for personal fulfilment as an excuse for holding back from wholehearted devotion to him.[12]

In Malachi 4 God says ". . . I have loved Jacob, but Esau I have hated." Esau despised his birthright and sold his inheritance rights for a bowl of red lentil stew,[13] and God chose to fulfil his greatest covenant promise to Abraham through Jacob, the younger twin of Esau, instead. God did not intend Esau harm, nor was he even indifferent to his fate. But he *chose* Jacob

---

10. Luke 14:26
11. Mark 7:8–12
12. Luke 9:59
13. Genesis 25:29–34

and *rejected* Esau for his covenant blessing. The Israelites were commanded by God *not* to despise the descendants of Esau, the Edomites, even though the Edomites forbade the Israelites to peacefully pass through their territory when they came out of Egypt, and continually tried to cause trouble for them. It was their gloating over the destruction of Judaea and Jerusalem which finally led to their downfall.[14] King Herod, who tried to kill Jesus by murdering all the baby boys in the vicinity of Bethlehem was called an Idumaean (the Greek name for a descendant of Edom).

As Christians, we are, as Hebrews 12:16 says, not to be godless like Esau, exchanging our birthrights for a single meal. To reject the body I have been given, choosing my own gender identity, and claiming that "God made a mistake by putting me in the wrong body" seems to me to be similar to what Esau did. Esau claimed he would die of starvation if he didn't exchange his birthright for a bit of soup. Grasping at the alphabet soup of alternative gender identities may give temporary relief from suicidal thoughts and threats, but it will not sustain the soul or help society in the long term. Those who embrace transgenderism find it is not the answer to all their problems and causes a lot *more* problems to themselves and others. I know a woman with young children whose husband, soon after the birth of the third one, started to identify himself as a woman and take cross sex hormones. The woman's family and church community gave all the kindness, understanding and support they could to this troubled man, but the pain and confusion for his wife and children was devastating and the consequences of his rejection of his masculinity, husband-hood and fatherhood will continue to detrimentally affect his wife, children, grandchildren and great-grandchildren in the years to come.

THE NEW TOTALITARIAN ORTHODOXY

Because in many ways we worship the god of Eros and the idea of sexual fulfilment, consensual human sexual intercourse of some kind between people of legal age is seen as something that is as necessary for life as eating and breathing. Sexual drives other than the bestial and the ones that are obviously predatory towards the vulnerable are seen as relating to our core identity as people. So it seems axiomatic that those who have different sexual leanings should face no inequality of treatment.[15] Thus fairness

---

14. Ezekiel 35:15

15. Bestiality and paedophilia are still seen as taboo, but in the current philosophical climate, this can only logically be maintained because animals and minors are deemed unable to give valid consent. Consent is *everything* today, which is why

demands that "gay" people should have access to the things that "straight" people have access to, including marriage and children, conceived if necessary by artificial means. These children can be sacrificial offerings to political correctness.[16]

Using a person's preferred gender pronoun when it doesn't correspond with their biological sex is not considered a kind, protective or gracious accommodation to their mental state, but an obligation to be enforced by law.[17] If someone believes, deep down, that they are really an amputee inhabiting the body of an abled-bodied person, then they should be treated kindly but diagnosed as delusional. Their request to have limbs removed by the health service would be refused and they would be referred to a psychiatrist. Likewise, a skeletal anorexic girl who believes she is grossly overweight is rightly seen as having a mental illness.

However, if someone believes they are a woman in a man's body or a man trapped in a woman's body then the transgender lobby is eager to penalize anyone daring to question this and the state is willing to pay a lot of money for cross sex hormone treatment and a surgeon to castrate their genitalia or cut off their breasts. But for a counselor to agree to help someone who experiences gender dysphoria and who *wants* their sense of gender to correspond with their biological sex, or for a therapist to agree to help a man (even a man with a wife and children) who *voluntarily* wishes to diminish his unwanted homosexual *feelings* are both regarded as shamefully immoral and should result in them being professionally struck off or even subject to criminal proceedings. This is because they are seen as colluding in the person's denial of something intrinsic to their very being.

---

sadomasochistic behaviour is regarded as acceptable if carried on between consenting adults. In the bestselling novel *Fifty Shades of Grey*, a woman signs a contract designed to allow her rich and privileged male partner to fulfil his sadistic fantasies upon her. His aim is to ensure that at every stage of proceedings she is seen to have given technical and legal agreement to the satisfaction of his desires. More and more defendants accused of murdering sexual partners for their own sexual gratification are claiming, with some success, that they were indulging in consensual "rough sex," for example, involving asphyxiation. Lawyers call this the "Fifty Shades Defence."

16. See Lopez and Klein *Jephthah's Children*

17. In view of the sad reality that many transgender people have experienced nastiness and bullying, both before and after transitioning, and the likely fragility of their mental state, I agree that if "misgendering" an individual person is done with the intent to humiliate, expose, bully or harass them then it should attract appropriate sanction in school, college or the workplace. Any behaviour intended to and reasonably likely to *incite violence* against transgender individuals or transgender people generally should rightly be a criminal matter. A Christ-centered church following biblical principles should extend kindness and a gracious welcome to people who identify as transgender, as they should to everyone.

For many this all appears progressive, compassionate, inclusive and just. To disagree with this new ideology is seen as rejecting someone's core identity and unacceptable in any public forum because it might threaten someone's feeling of having a "safe space" to be "who they are." It is a heresy, a "hate-crime" and should be punished severely. Notice how extremely illiberal this is. In effect, gay people must stay gay. Transgender people must stay transgender. Like the world of Islam,[18] there is to be no back door for those who want to change their beliefs and practices.

The Church of England General Synod has been influenced by current campaigners like Jayne Ozanne who claims that something called "conversion therapy" has caused her mental health problems. It is true that there have been things done by certain psychiatrists and psychotherapists which have been ineffective, been based on a lack of understanding, and/or been damaging, even cruel, and things done by Christians in ministry that have lacked true spiritual insight and loving care. However, when the Synod in 2017 called on the government to ban "conversion therapy" *without defining what it was*, it was a victory for the new ideology, because it signaled alignment with the *Stonewall* view of sexuality and gender rather than the Bible's. LGBT+ activists are hostile to any Christian teaching or healing ministry, no matter how responsible, caring and loving, which is based on traditional, biblical Christianity, and carried out in the power of the Holy Spirit.

The fact is that when people are brought to a knowledge of sound biblical truth, and are ministered to in a godly, spirit-filled, Jesus-centered, loving, gentle, sensitive, truthful, non-condemnatory environment, they will experience healing in all aspects of their lives. This is a process we all need to go through because we have all been damaged by sin, and this may include areas of our lives to do with sex, sexuality and gender identity because of particular experiences. As a result of this inner healing, some of us may experience a change in our sense of "orientation" or "gender identity."

For example, I know people who used to identify as "gay" or "same sex attracted" but who now experience heterosexual feelings and are even happily married with children born in the normal way. Some may still experience homosexual feelings to a greater or lesser degree. It may be claimed that these people are essentially bisexual, but if the definition of a bisexual

---

18. I have met persecuted Christian believers from a Muslim background in Pakistan, Egypt, Sudan and even the UK. They are a target because they are deemed to be apostates from Islam. In a similar way, people who have left a homosexual lifestyle out of loyalty to Christ or who have experienced a change in their psycho-sexual outlook towards heterosexuality or have re-transitioned back to accepting their biological sex are hated by LGBT+ ideologues, and their voices are silenced by censorship and intimidation.

person is someone who has at some time experienced crushes on people of both sexes then most people should be classified as such.

I also know of a case where a male to female transgender person began to attend a church and was treated as a woman and even baptized using the female name they were known by. (The baptism was not, however, being used as a way of marking their transgender identity, but simply their new identity in Christ). After a period of time experiencing the life of the church community, the truth of the Gospel and the general love, support and prayers of people in the church, this person, getting up at home one morning, looked in the mirror and experienced a sudden change back to having an identity as a male person, and thereafter freely decided to come to church as a man. The LGBT+ "support group" he had been affiliated to assumed he had been subjected to some kind of sinister "conversion therapy." It was furious and accused the church of brainwashing someone they thought of as their own.

The stories of those who have moved away from homosexual practices are censored.[19] Those who admit to having "same-sex- attraction" but who commit themselves to chastity because they believe this is the right thing to do as Christian disciples, are mocked, even by some other people in the church, as being sad, repressed creatures, who will be forever unhappy because "they are not being true to who they are." Even evidence from research carried out by people such as Dr Robert Spitzer of Columbia University, who was influential in the American Psychiatric Association deleting homosexuality from its list of mental disorders in 1973, that voluntary reparative therapy can help many find "good heterosexual functioning" has long been dismissed as bogus.[20] But as a self-declared "atheist Jew" he can hardly be accused of "Christian fundamentalist bias."

In a similar way, research into the phenomenon of people regretting having "gender reassignment surgery" and seeking to "de-transition" and reverse the surgery is blocked by universities, afraid of the abuse the transgender lobby is likely to hurl at them on social media and its effect on their reputation in the so-called "liberal" circles which control the academic world.[21]

The sense of gender identity is becoming increasingly self-determined in young people rather than reflecting the physical nature of their bodies. Once the evidence of physical differentiation into two genders (confirmed

---

19. https://www.lifesitenews.com/news/cinema-bans-movie-about-ex-gays-being-silenced

20. https://www.ncbi.nlm.nih.gov/pubmed/14567650

21. https://www.theguardian.com/education/2017/sep/25/bath-spa-university-transgender-gender-reassignment-reversal-research

by Genesis 1:27) is rejected, proliferation of gender identities could be limitless. As I write *Facebook* now offers seventy-one options for one's preferred gender term and the BBC now recognizes one hundred gender identities. This goes alongside a spectacularly dramatic increase in the numbers of children and young people seeking help for gender dysphoria. Puberty blockers are being doled out to children without any understanding of the long-term harm to them, which can include sterility for life.

Politicians from historically sane parties are now advocating that full legal privileges should be accorded to anyone simply on the basis of their declared gender. Thus women's and girls' showers, changing rooms, sleeping quarters, refuges from domestic violence, hospital wards, prisons should be open to biological men who declare themselves transgender women, even if they have a history of sexual offences or violence against women and retain their male genitalia and appearance.

In February 2020, a candidate for the position of leader of the UK Labor Party, Lisa Nandy was asked at a hustings whether a person called "Zoe Lynes" (previously known as Christopher Worton), a transgender male to female convicted of raping a girl, should be sent to a female or male prison. She replied: "I believe fundamentally in people's right to self-ID. I think trans women are women, I think trans men are men, so I think they should be accommodated in a prison of their choosing."[22] Health trusts have issued guidance to hospital nurses to respond to women complaining that the bed next to them is occupied by a male-bodied person who identifies as transgender, as if they were guilty of racism. They were told to say "your complaint is similar to you complaining about being next to a black person."[23]

We should not really be surprised at all this. Philosophical transgenderism and sexual revisionism are related. We are seeing a return of a form of gnosticism, which was widespread in the ancient world and held that our bodies are the work of a lesser demigod and that what really matters is the "spark of pure divinity" within us. What we know we are "on the inside" is what is true (or "true for us"), whatever the physical nature of our body may indicate.

People therefore assume it is philosophically justifiable to say they are "born in the wrong body" and the fact that the male sexual organ is plainly designed to penetrate the female one is deemed irrelevant to the question of the ethics of sexual practice. Anyone who fails to affirm a person's self-analysis of their own psycho-sexual identity is accused of inflicting harm.

22. https://metro.co.uk/2020/02/18/labour-split-dawn-butler-says-trans-women-never-put-female-jails-12260746/

23. https://www.thetimes.co.uk/edition/scotland/staff-guidance-into-trans-patients-on-womens-wards-is-under-review-cfq2c7nrf

However, to a person who is spiritually self-deceived or delusional, truth and reality, however they see it, will always appear to be threatening to their own sense of mental well-being. Therefore, they are likely to attribute their mental health problems to those who deny reality is merely subjective, and hold to objective truth, rather than their own internal disorder and confusion.

IN BUT NOT OF THIS WORLD

So it has to be admitted that the biblical paradigm is becoming in some areas as counter-cultural as it was in pre-Christian times. The Bible says that we are a unity of body, soul and spirit.[24] Our bodies are God-given and good and what we do with them matters[25] and we are created in God's image, male and female. The rare, traumatic cases of some people being born with deformed genitalia or even chromosomal abnormality does not negate this truth. Genesis 2:24, affirmed by Jesus in Matthew 19:4–5, speaks of a man leaving the relational orbit of his parents and being united to his wife, and the two becoming "one flesh"—a spiritual, psychological and physical union facilitated by the Creator's design of our complementary sex organs.

The Bible teaches that both covenanted permanence *and* sexual differentiation are essential components of marriage and marriage is a God-given estate which has a mystical dimension, being a model of Christ's relationship with the church.[26] The Bible teaches that sexual intercourse belongs inside marriage and that marriage is the publicly recognized sexual union of man and woman for life. Sex outside of marriage is regarded as a serious sin. Sex is designed by God as an expression of total and sacrificial commitment to one's opposite sex spouse, rather than merely a vehicle for individual pleasure seeking. The biblical injunctions against adultery and fornication are as strict as those against homosexual intercourse.

If the Bible is judged as homophobic by the world, because it is radically counter to contemporary Western liberal cultural mores, then it is also "phobic" about all sex outside of marriage, something which Western society now considers normal. So-called "casual sex" (although there is really no such thing) is shamelessly encouraged in all the forms of media. The idea that it could be right to keep oneself a virgin till one's wedding night meets mocking disbelief, but that is the biblical standard and anything below that standard is declared sinful.

24. First Thessalonians 5:23
25. First Corinthians 6:12–20
26. Ephesians 5:32

It must be admitted, however, that the context in which we live today is one where the great majority of those who call themselves Christian do not believe in or practice this standard, and few Christian leaders now teach it with sincere conviction. Therefore, any objection to homosexual practice is understandably seen as grievous bigotry against a minority group rather than part of a radical desire for sexual purity across the board, out of love for Christ who calls every disciple of his to lay down their lives in costly obedience.

> "Then he called the crowd to him along with his disciples and said: "Whoever wants to be my disciple must deny themselves and take up their cross and follow me."[27]

The Bible is sympathetic to those who do not feel good about the body they have.[28] Loving, welcoming and respecting people does not, however, mean we should deny God's truth. The biblical message includes compassion for those who feel drawn to using their sexual organs in ways for which they were not designed.[29] However, the call to repentance, new life, transformation and inner healing applies to all. Forgiveness for sexual sins and rejecting the bodies God has given us is plentifully available in Christ but the biblical God will judge all the sexually immoral who refuse to repent.[30]

Although marriage is the assumed state for people of age in the Old Testament, the New Testament teaches that, in the light of the Gospel of Jesus, there are important advantages to *not* being married and in (horror of horrors) living a celibate life. Married life, which when at its best (and it is often not), provides a foreshadowing of the blissful union of Christ and the church, something which all believers will be part of, is not actually held out as the greatest form of love. Jesus says the highest expression of love is when someone lays down his life for his friends, which of course is what he did.[31]

Because of our socially fragmented lives and the worldliness of so many conventional churches, there is a great need for people to be helped to live lives that are marked by loving social intimacy and chastity (which means practicing either celibacy with the social and economic freedoms this brings, or faithful, biblical marriage—a covenanted sexual relationship between a man and a woman, to the sexual exclusion of all others). It may be that the answer will be new communities of people living under some sort

---

27. Mark 8:34
28. Romans 7:24
29. Ibid.7:21–23
30. Hebrews 13:4
31. John 15:13

of rule of life together, like the old monastic communities. This will mean community members being prepared to live in a radically counter-cultural way, being accountable to one another in a way that truly promotes sexual purity as the way of love for God and for each other.

The biblical meaning of the word "marriage," after years of being weakened through the prevalence of divorce, pre-marital and extra-marital sex among heterosexuals, is finally being destroyed by the state itself in many countries. Culturally, for some time it has been all about the wedding day rather than the life together afterwards. The "Big Day," is designed to fulfil a fantasy and to impress others. However, with regard to the couple's life ahead, the wedding now signifies merely a vague and often short-lived arrangement based on feelings, voidable without serious relationship-destroying behavior[32] and requiring no sexual differentiation. Therefore committed disciples of Christ may need to find a new word to describe the kind of covenanted sexual relationship that the word used to signify.

Furthermore, the direction of travel in our culture is towards a growing divorce between biological sex and gender identity. It could even be that the very concept of gender based on innate bodily sexual characteristics, rather than self-chosen identity, is abolished. Might the state at some time in the future decree that all children are brought up as "gender neutral" until such a time that they are deemed to be able to give consent to be identified as one of many gender options available? May the good, living God of the Bible save us from such a "brave new world."

---

32. The introduction of "no-fault" divorce in the UK will remove the requirement to assert that the relationship has irretrievably broken down due to adultery, intolerable behavior, desertion or long-term separation. Current proposals in the UK will mean no reason at all need be given for divorce. See https://christianconcern.com/comment/mps-back-no-fault-divorce/

Chapter 11

Racist?

"Then Peter began to speak: 'I now realize how true it is that God does not show favoritism but accepts from every nation the one who fears him and does what is right.'"

—ACTS 10:34–35

It is ironic that Dawkins and Barker accuse the biblical God of being racist. Racism as a concept developed in the atheistic and pseudo-scientific wake of the evolutionary theories of the nineteenth century. When people at football matches shout monkey chants at black players who have the ball, they are harking back to the racist idea that those with an African heritage are closer in the evolutionary chain to the apes than are White Europeans. There is nothing in the Bible to support this. The Bible knows only one race—the human race. Yes, the Bible traces various groups of people from particular individuals, but biblically speaking, we are all descended from Adam.[1]

The evidence Barker cites in support of this allegation concerns God's choice of Israel as a people to be in a covenant relationship with him; his dealings with other people groups; the removal of certain groups of people or nations from the Promised Land when Israel entered; the commands to avoid inter-marriage with the pagan nations around Israel; the prohibition of certain people groups "entering the assembly of the LORD even down

---

1. Acts 17:26

to the tenth generation"; the regulations regarding slaves; and the curse on Canaan and his descendants, because of what his father Ham had done to his father Noah.

I dealt with the allegation of racist "ethnic cleansing" in chapter eight and I will deal with the issues around "genocide" in chapter thirteen and slavery in chapter twenty-seven.

In chapter eight we saw that the driving out of the Canaanite civilization, built as it was on degrading idolatry and evil, corrupt practices like child sacrifice, shrine prostitution, ritual orgies, incest, and bestiality was a *spiritual* cleansing rather than an ethnic one. It was purity of *worship* God wanted rather than purity of blood line based on ideas of racial supremacy.

Barker argues in chapter eleven of his book that when the Bible says God told the Israelites that "the LORD your God has chosen you out of all the peoples on earth to be his people, his treasured possession,"[2] this shows that they put in the mouth of their fictional god words to justify their racist sense of superiority. "Can there be a stronger example of prejudice, for their god to elevate them above all the other peoples of the earth?" he says. But he ignores the very next verse where God says that it was *not* because of their superiority in number (which carried the connotation of military and cultural dominance) that God chose to set his affection upon them,

> "for they were the fewest of the peoples. But it was because the LORD loved you and kept the oath he swore to your forefathers that he brought you out with a mighty hand and redeemed you from the land of slavery, from the power of Pharaoh, king of Egypt. Know therefore that the LORD your God is God; he is the faithful God, keeping his covenant of love to a thousand generations of those who love him and keep his commands. But those who hate him he will repay to their face with destruction; he will not be slow to repay to their face those who hate him. Therefore, take care to follow the commands, decrees and laws I give you today."[3]

The Bible says that neither were the Israelites chosen because of their moral rectitude.

> "After the Lord your God has driven them out before you, do not say to yourself, 'The Lord has brought me here to take possession of this land because of my righteousness.' No, it is on account of the wickedness of these nations that the Lord is going to drive them out before you. It is not because of your

2. Deuteronomy 7:6
3. Deuteronomy 7:7–11

righteousness or your integrity that you are going in to take possession of their land; but on account of the wickedness of these nations, the Lord your God will drive them out before you, to accomplish what he swore to your fathers, to Abraham, Isaac and Jacob. Understand, then, that it is not because of your righteousness that the Lord your God is giving you this good land to possess, for you are a stiff-necked people."[4]

Barker also ignores the reason why God chose Israel. It was for the blessing of *all the nations*.[5]

THE CURSE ON CANAAN

But isn't Barker right in arguing that the biblical God has it in for particular people groups? What about the Canaanites? Canaan was a grandson of Noah. Why were he and his descendants cursed by Noah and then subjected to God's wrath as a result? The answer can be found in Genesis chapter nine. This is another "X-rated" portion of Scripture, with a connection to the story of the destruction of Sodom and Gomorrah which we looked at in the previous chapter.

Noah, we are told, as a man of the soil, planted a vineyard, and drank its wine. He became drunk and lay naked and exposed inside his tent. Ham, the father of Canaan "saw his father's nakedness" and told his two brothers Shem and Japheth outside. But they took a garment, laid it across their shoulders, and respectfully walking in backwards, with their faces turned the other way so they could not see their father's nakedness, they covered their father with the garment. When Noah recovered from his drunken state and found out what his youngest son "had done to him," he said, "cursed be Canaan! The lowest of slaves he will be to his brothers."

At first reading, this story seems incomprehensible. Why should Ham "seeing his father's nakedness" be such a terrible thing and cause such severe consequences? What was it that he "did" to his father? And why should Noah curse *Canaan*, Ham's son, rather than Ham himself? It makes no sense unless we understand that the biblical Hebrew often uses euphemism, especially when it comes to sexual matters where it was considered indelicate or even shameful to spell things out in explicit terms. So, in Leviticus 20:17 the phrase "seeing her nakedness" refers to a brother's incest with his sister. The NIV translates this as "has sexual relations" to aid our understanding but for some reason, in *this* case (perhaps due to the horrendous nature of

---

4. Ibid 9:4–6
5. Genesis 12:3; 28:14, Psalm 72:17

the act) it retains a more word for word, euphemistic translation. This is the key and then everything makes sense. Ham is not just innocently passing by and getting an unexpected and fleeting glimpse of his father lying on his bed in the nude. He goes inside the tent (which is implied when it says he then tells his brothers outside "what he has done") and commits an unspeakable act—incestuous, homosexual rape of his own father! What possessed him to do such a thing—and then boast to his brothers afterwards about it?

Robert Gagnon draws on a Mesopotamian omen text and the Egyptian myth of Horus and Seth to deduce that homosexual rape was used as an attempt to emasculate, disgrace and dominate over one's rival.[6] By raping his father and informing his brothers of the act, Ham hoped to usurp the authority of his father and elder brothers (he was the youngest), establishing his right to succeed his father as patriarch and making his lineage predominant over his brothers descendants. When Noah awoke from his stupor and realized what Ham had done to him, he reversed what Ham had hoped to achieve by cursing Ham's firstborn son Canaan. Shem and Japheth had carefully avoided even merely literally "seeing their father's nakedness" and so, whereas Ham was guilty of the vilest possible behavior, their actions were by contrast scrupulously pure. So Noah pronounces a blessing upon them and their descendants.

Thus the nations, or people groups descended from Canaan did share an abominable spiritual inheritance. They were known for their vile sexual practices and they were the people who inhabited Sodom and Gomorrah as well as the territory later given to the Israelites by God. The curse that came about through Ham's sin only operated through Canaan, Ham's firstborn. Some nineteenth century people with a vested interest in the slave trade tried to argue that all of Ham's descendants, through his other sons, who spread out across Africa, were also under the curse and this justified their enslavement by European and North American nations. Arabs (descendants of Shem, as are Jews, hence the name *Semites*) have also enslaved Africans from the sons of Cush, Canaan's brother, in the Upper Nile region (now South Sudan), and still do to this day. But apart from the fact that in God's eyes, those used to fulfill a curse on others are still held liable for their greed, arrogance, and cruelty, it was the *Canaanites* only who were cursed with slavery and then driven from the Promised Land because of entrenched spiritual iniquity. Unlike racist theory, it had nothing to do with them being thought to be further back in the evolutionary chain or studies into the size of their brains. Nor did it have to do with mere prejudice. Canaanite religion *was* particularly evil.

6. Gagnon *The Bible and Homosexual Practice*, 63–71

OUTRAGEOUSLY BIGOTED "HONOR-KILLING"?

What about God's treatment of the Midianites? I will consider the command to attack a particular group of them in chapter thirteen. But to justify the charge of racism, Barker concentrates on the judgment on Israelite men who had allowed themselves to be seduced by Moabite and Midianite women into sexual immorality and worship of the Baal of Peor. In particular, he focusses on the killing of the Israelite Zimri and Cozbi, the daughter of a Midianite chief by Phineas, Aaron's grandson.

The story Barker cites can be found in Numbers chapter twenty-five. However, to understand this chapter we must know some background. Israel had spent forty years of wandering in the desert places and was now moving north, on the east side of the Dead Sea in order to then cross over the river Jordan from east to west and enter the Promised Land. God had told Moses not to attack the territory of the Moabites because that was not part of the land promised to them. They asked the Amorites, the overlords of Moab, for permission to travel peacefully along The King's Highway across the plain of Moab but were refused, and they suffered unprovoked attacks from Sihon, king of the Amorites and Og King of Bashan. God enabled Israel to defeat them both, and this meant they could camp peacefully north of Moab, just east of the Dead Sea and the Jordan, listening to the teaching of Moses (recorded in Deuteronomy) and being made ready to cross the Jordan when God gave the command.[7] When the incident in Numbers 25 occurred, Israel was camped at Shittim, just five miles from the Jordan.

Although the Israelites had shown no hostile intention towards Moab, Balak, the king of Moab was full of dread about so many Israelites being nearby. He realized that Israel, having defeated the Amorites, was too strong to be attacked by normal military means. So he and his allies, the Midianites, came up with a plan to use sorcery against them. They hired Balaam, a prophet who lived in a town on the banks of the Euphrates to come and curse them from various mountain top positions overlooking the plain where they were. Balaam warned Balak that he would only be able to prophesy what God gave him to say, and instead of cursing the Israelites he ended up blessing them in four oracles and cursing Moab! This is all told in Numbers 22–24.

Balaam was a complex character though. He clearly heard from God and attributed to God his powers and yet his heart was corrupt and he was open to being paid for divination and giving advice to Moab and Midian regarding how best to weaken the Israelites. So in Numbers 31 we learn

---

7. Numbers 21 and Deuteronomy 1

from Moses that Balaam had advised them that they should seek to turn the Israelites away from the LORD, who was the source of their blessing and strength. He suggested that they should send a considerable number of women to sexually entice the Israelite men and seduce them, not only into sexual immorality but into joining their sacrificial feasts with meat and wine and then worshipping the Baal of Peor, the fertility god. Balaam correctly predicted that this would bring down God's wrath upon them.

What happened while the Israelites were at Shittim remained a source of shame and regret to the Israelites for many years to come.[8] Those who were inclined to rebel against Moses' God-given leadership and who wanted to pursue alliances with pagan nations and take on their gods, used the opportunity that this mass honey trap provided to undermine the very purpose of Israel's existence, to be a nation holy to the Lord. This accounts for the severity of the command God gave to Moses to execute the ringleaders of this rebellion and to expose them in broad daylight before the LORD. This is an example of the principle of propitiation on which biblical atonement is based. This action was necessary in order for God's fierce but justified wrath to be turned away from the Israelites. Moses may have gone further than this command when he ordered Israel's judges to put to death all those who had joined in the worship of Baal. However, we are given no indication in Scripture that Moses was reprimanded by God about this. The situation was extremely serious. Already twenty-four thousand Israelites had died of the plague God sent in judgment upon them.

Moses and the whole assembly of Israel were weeping at the entrance to the tent of meeting, in sorrow and distress at their sin and the righteous punishment of God. Then, right before their eyes, the son of a leader of a Simeonite family (Zimri) brought the daughter of a Midianite leader (Cozbi) into a tent for sex in a public act of amoral disregard for God and the mourning community. It is hard for us to imagine the heinousness of this act. Try to picture a leader of a neo-Nazi movement, responsible for stirring up hatred and persecution of Jews in Eastern Europe, clothed in Nazi regalia, sacrificing a pig in the foyer of the Yad Vashem holocaust memorial center in Israel, and you might begin to come close. Already, Midian and Moab had invested time, money and resources into escorting a large group of women north to Shittim, using sex as a weapon of war to destroy the Israelites, who, although they didn't always realize it, depended on their relationship with God for their survival. Having suffered the judgement of God for their foolishness in succumbing to the evil plan of their enemies, the Israelite community is weeping in remorse. Zimri brazenly demonstrates

---

8. Deuteronomy 4:3–4; Joshua 22:17; Psalm 106:28; Hosea 9:10

utter contempt for God and for the faithful Israelites by publicly staging an insulting act of blatant rebellion.

Phinehas, son of Eleazer and grandson of Aaron, takes responsibility to enact God's judgment on them by driving his spear into them both as they were engaging in sexual intercourse. In this he bravely confronted this man's family and tribe and all who were leading the people towards idolatrous Baal worship. God applauded his action because by this act Phineas averted his righteous anger that would have destroyed all of Israel for their gross unfaithfulness. He established a covenant of lasting priesthood for Phinehas because "he was zealous for the honor of his God and made atonement for the Israelites." Psalm 106:28–31 says what Phinehas did "was credited to him as righteousness for endless generations to come."

This story is certainly sobering for thoughtful and sensitive Christian believers today, but for aggressive atheists like Barker, it presents an opportunity to slander God's character in almost every way. So, Barker presents the scenario as the racist murder of a nice young couple, whose tender love for each other and desire to start a family together had braved an intolerant religious divide. He claims that the Midianites, being related to the Israelites as fellow ancestors of Abraham, would have naturally fraternized with them and that Zimri and Cozbi's relationship was just one romantic inter-faith story among others, cruelly stamped out by an extremist priest whose insecure, jealous god who didn't want the Israelites to experience any religious freedom of choice. It was an abominable "hate crime," a savage "honor killing" sanctioned and rewarded by a bloodthirsty racist bigot of a fictional god!

In an episode of *Spooks*, a BBC drama about the British security and intelligence services MI5, the team comes up against an Israeli terrorist group called "the sons of Phinehas." One MI5 operative explains to a colleague that their inspiration was an Israelite who murdered a man and his foreign lover for "polluting the blood-line of Israel." Like Barker's biblical understanding, this is a travesty. It had nothing to do with racism or bloodlines, but everything to do with national survival. Later, after the Israelites had enacted God's judgment on the Midianite men and women who through their evil plan had tried to destroy them, they absorbed the virgin Midianite girls into their community rather than killing them. Barker would no doubt dispute that this was an act of mercy, but he cannot deny this proves they were not worried about "purity of bloodline."

THE "ALIENS WHO LIVED AMONG THEM"

Old Testament expert David Firth, in his book "Including the Stranger" examines the inclusion of foreigners into the people of Israel in the books of the "Former Prophets," i.e. Joshua, Judges, First and Second Samuel, and First and Second Kings.

In the book of Joshua, we have the Canaanite prostitute Rahab helping the Israelite spies sent to discover information about Jericho, because she knew that God had given the Israelites the land. She becomes incorporated into the people of Israel and becomes an ancestor of King David and of Christ.[9] Canaanite women, even prostitutes, are not seen as contaminators of Israel's bloodline, but can be accepted if they bow the knee to Yahweh. Firth calls attention to the writer of Joshua's contrast between Rahab, an "outsider" who became an "insider," and Achan, the Israelite who stole some of the "devoted things" taken when Jericho was attacked. Achan was the archetypal "insider" (from the tribe of Judah) who became an "outsider," and is treated as an unbelieving Canaanite.[10]

Also Caleb, one of the two worthy spies alongside Joshua himself, was a Kenizzite, a descendant of Esau and who lived in Canaan. At some point he had become part of Israel.[11] When the covenant is renewed at Mount Ebal[12] special mention was made of the aliens who were with the Israelites citizens. They were included in the call to worship and serve Yahweh only. When the Covenant is again renewed at Shechem[13] Joshua stresses that Abraham came from a background of worshipping other gods but was called to follow the one true God. The important defining characteristic of an Israelite was not ethnicity but a willingness to:

> "Throw away the foreign gods that are among you and yield your hearts to the LORD, the God of Israel."[14]

In the book of Judges Caleb's nephew Othniel becomes the first "judge" of Israel[15], the Spirit coming on him and enabling him to rescue Israel from the king of Aram, into whose hands God has given the Israelites who had already forgotten the LORD in order to serve the Baals and the Asherahs. The

---

9. Matthew 1:5
10. Firth, *Including the Stranger*, 24–27
11. Ibid. 36–7
12. Joshua 8:30–35
13. Joshua 24
14. Ibid. 24:23
15. Judges 3:7–11

LORD uses foreigners like Shamgar[16] and Jael the Kenite[17] to bring relief to Israel from their enemies, as well as of course using foreign armies to bring his discipline to bear on Israel for its idolatry. Israel increasingly behaves like the ungodly Canaanites who they failed to completely dislodge and the result is disunity, violence and a spiraling down into vile behavior mirroring the actions of the citizens of Sodom and Gomorrah in Genesis 19 before their destruction.[18] All this shows that their ethnicity did not protect the Israelites from judgment and did not preclude non-Israelites from salvation or from being agents of God's blessing, as well as judgment.

Although there are some parts of Judges where the characters of Israelites are assessed by their interaction with foreigners, such as Samson and the Philistines, this is a stronger theme in the two books of Samuel. Most of First and Second Samuel deal with the story of king David who succeeded King Saul who lost favor with God because of his disobedience. David is of course an iconic figure, the great warrior-king, and shining example of faith in the God of Israel in many ways. But at key moments in his life, his behavior towards certain foreigners determines whether he is blessed or cursed by God. Let's consider three of these moments.

First, in 1 Samuel 30, while Saul is on the throne and David is living as a fugitive from Israel among the Philistines, he and his six hundred men are seeking to rescue their loved ones and possessions taken by the Amalekites from their home in Ziklag while they were away. David was under great pressure from his anguished followers who were talking of stoning him, but the narrator of the book tells us that "he found strength in the LORD his God,"[19] and "enquired of the LORD"[20] regarding his strategy.

Leaving two hundred of his men who were too exhausted to continue the pursuit, at a ravine, David and the four hundred continued to hunt down the Amalekites. They happen to find a foreign man in a field who was near death and David and his men gave him some of their water and precious food—pressed figs and two cakes of raisins. The man revives and tells David

16. Judges 3:21 Shamgar is a non-Hebrew name. And he is called "the Son of Anath," Anath was the name of a Canaanite goddess

17. Ibid. 4:17–24

18. See the rape of the Levite's concubine in Judges 19 and subsequent civil war. The irony in this story is that the Levite, although it is dusk, decides against lodging among the alien Jebusites in Jerusalem, assuming he'd be better off among the Benjamites in Gibeah. Little did he know what awaited him and his concubine there. It is unlikely the Jebusites would have treated them as wickedly as the Benjamites did, so this is another story where foreigners (and residual Canaanite ones at that) are portrayed more positively (or less badly) than Israelites.

19. First Samuel 30:6

20. Ibid. 30:7–8

his story. He was an Egyptian slave whose Amalekite master had abandoned because he had become ill. He had not eaten or drunk for three days and three nights. He had been part of the raiding party on Ziklag, and after receiving David's assurance that he would not be handed over to his master, he revealed where the Amalekites were, and David was able to take them unawares while they were drinking and reveling in all the plunder they had taken. All the wives, children and possessions taken by the Amalekites were recovered, and David's leadership over his men was firmly established.

So we see here how David had acted in accordance with the spirit of God's laws set out in Leviticus 19:34 and Deuteronomy 23:15:

> "The foreigner residing among you must be treated as your native-born. Love them as yourself, for you were foreigners in Egypt. I am the Lord your God."
> "If a slave has taken refuge with you, do not hand them over to their master."

His kindness to the abandoned Egyptian slave is linked to his seeking the LORD and finding strength in him, and the restoration of all he had lost.

Secondly, there is the occasion when David, now king over all Israel, and having just resoundingly defeated the Arameans, sent his commander Joab to fight their allies, the Ammonites, while he remained in Jerusalem. What then happened was to cast a shadow over David's dynasty forever after. The story is told in Second Samuel 11. David was walking on the roof of his palace when he saw a beautiful woman bathing. He sent someone to find out who she was. The man said,

> "She is Bathsheba, the daughter of Eliam and the wife of Uriah the Hittite."[21]

Knowing her husband, Uriah was fighting at the front with Joab, David sent for Bathsheba and slept with her. She later sent word to him that she was pregnant. David now has a problem. His dirty secret will get out unless he can quickly get Uriah to come back home and sleep with his wife, so that he will assume the child to be born is his. He sends an order to Joab to send Uriah to him at the palace, and when he arrives David pretends to be interested in how the war is going. He then tells Uriah to have some home leave with his wife. Uriah, however, does not go home but sleeps at the entrance to the palace with David's servants.

When David finds out, he asks Uriah why he hasn't gone home and Uriah replies,

---

21. Second Samuel 11:3

"The ark and Israel and Judah are staying in tents, and my commander Joab and my lord's men are camped in the open country. How could I go to my house to eat and drink and make love to my wife? As surely as you live, I will not do such a thing!"[22]

David tries to weaken Uriah's resolve by getting him to stay another day, wining and dining him and even getting him drunk, but Uriah still won't go home. So David resorts to a terrible back-up plan. Knowing Uriah is a man of integrity and won't read the sealed letter he will give him for Joab, he writes a message ordering Joab to see to it that Uriah is set up to die by putting him in the front line of a battle and then withdrawing his fellow soldiers from around him. Uriah unknowingly carries the letter that seals his fate. Uriah does indeed get killed, and when David hears of this he takes Bathsheba to be his wife, after she has undergone a suitably decent period of mourning for her dead husband.

The name Uriah means something like "Yahweh is light."[23] This means that although he was a Hittite, he had come to be a worshipper of the LORD. So this story places the characters of these two men in stark contrast. Uriah, an ethnic Canaanite, is portrayed as positively as he can be. From Second Samuel 23:39 we know that he was one of David's "thirty mighty men of valor." He is shown in this story to be also loyal, deeply respectful of the ark of the covenant and his duty to serve the LORD and his anointed king, and full of integrity and self-control even when drunk! David, on the other hand, the anointed King of Israel, ethnically of the foremost tribe of Judah, is guilty of lust, abuse of power, deceit, conspiring to pervert the course of justice, and the murder of this faithful subject who he has already so grievously wronged.

God sends the prophet Nathan to David, to whom David totally and pathetically incriminates himself. Nathan tells him that he has despised "the word of the LORD"[24] (interestingly Nathan regards this as synonymous with "despising the LORD"[25]), and that what he has done has "made the enemies of the LORD show utter contempt."[26] In modern parlance, he had brought God and Israel into disrepute among the peoples of the world, when the calling of God was for them to be "a light for the nations." His son born to Bathsheba would die and Nathan prophesied to him that "the sword shall never depart from your house."[27]

22. Ibid. 11:11
23. Firth, *Including the Stranger*, 121
24. Second Samuel 12:9
25. Ibid. 12:10 See chapter 29 on the authority of Scripture.
26. Ibid. 12:14
27. Ibid. 12:10

Although a chastened David fully acknowledged his sin and repented with great contrition (according to Psalm 51), the consequences of what he had done were grievous. As a result of this sin and also the sin of taking many wives and concubines (contrary to Deuteronomy 17:17) there was internecine rape, bloodshed and rebellion in his household and much damage to Israel's stability and reputation as a nation under God. David's son Absalom who killed his half-brother Amnon for raping his sister Tamar, recorded in the very next chapter, leads a rebellion against David and is abetted by David's former adviser Ahithophel. He is revealed in Second Samuel 23:34 to be the father of one of David's mighty men called Eliam. Bathsheba's father was called Eliam so it could be that Ahithophel was Bathsheba's grandfather. Perhaps Ahithophel's support for Absalom's revolt, which was part of the curse God brought on David as pronounced by Nathan, was motivated by anger at David's treatment of his granddaughter and grandson-in-law.

Despite all this, God's shows amazing grace to David through foreigners such as Ittai the Gittite and Hushai the Arkite, who continue to show David loyalty during the rebellion. David says Ittai and his men should return home to Gath. Ittai is having none of it. He swears by the LORD he will stick by David. Then David's friend Hushai agrees to do the highly dangerous job of being a double agent in Absalom's camp trying to frustrate the wise advice of Ahithophel as to how Absalom could defeat his father. Through Hushai, God answers David's prayer for this to happen. Absalom rejects Ahithophel's sound advice in favor of Hushai's, which was designed not to help Absalom but to buy David much needed time to strengthen his forces. Knowing this spells disaster for the rebellion he has supported, Ahithophel goes home, puts his affairs in order, and then hangs himself.

Thirdly and finally, there is the account of how David came to purchase the site on Mount Moriah on which his son Solomon was later to build the Temple. Again, this is a story of God's grace, operating through an ethnic foreigner. David has sinned (again) by disobeying the LORD regarding a military census. A plague comes upon the land but as the plague approached Jerusalem, the prophet Gad tells David to build an altar for a sacrificial offering on the threshing floor of Araunah the Jebusite. Araunah wants to give the site, the oxen and the yokes and threshing sledges for the wood of the burnt offering to David at no cost, and pronounces a blessing on David in the name of the LORD. David insisted on paying for it, famously saying, "I will not sacrifice to the LORD my God burnt offerings that cost me nothing."

In First and Second Kings, alongside the usual motif of foreign armies being used to discipline Israel over its idolatry, there is a remarkable emphasis on God working through the two main prophets, Elijah and Elisha, to bring salvation and healing to those *outside* Israel. Even before the ministry of these prophets, Solomon, when dedicating the Temple in Jerusalem, had included a prayer for foreigners which recalls the reason for Israel's existence—that the peoples may know the name of the LORD and reverence him.

> "As for the foreigner who does not belong to your people Israel but has come from a distant land because of your name— for they will hear of your great name and your mighty hand and your outstretched arm—when they come and pray toward this temple, then hear from heaven, your dwelling place. Do whatever the foreigner asks of you, so that all the peoples of the earth may know your name and fear you, as do your own people Israel, and may know that this house I have built bears your Name."[28]

However, despite the prayer Solomon offered, his later actions as king in taking wives from the surrounding nations terribly undermined Israel's vocation, because these wives brought in their gods and turned Solomon's heart away from the LORD. First Kings chapter eleven makes it clear that it was not the mere fact of marrying a foreigner that was problematic (Solomon's marriage to an Egyptian princess is not criticised) but the fact that these were not foreigners who had turned to worship the LORD but who had retained their devotion to their abominable gods along with the detestable practices that worship of them involved.

> "King Solomon, however, loved many foreign women besides Pharaoh's daughter—Moabites, Ammonites, Edomites, Sidonians and Hittites. They were from nations about which the Lord had told the Israelites, 'You must not intermarry with them, because they will surely turn your hearts after their gods'. . . As Solomon grew old, his wives turned his heart after other gods, and his heart was not fully devoted to the Lord his God, as the heart of David his father had been. He followed Ashtoreth the goddess of the Sidonians, and Molech the detestable god of the Ammonites. . . On a hill east of Jerusalem, Solomon built a high place for Chemosh the detestable god of Moab, and for Molech the detestable god of the Ammonites. He did the same for all his foreign wives, who burned incense and offered sacrifices to their gods. The Lord became angry with Solomon because his heart had turned away from the Lord, the God of Israel, who had appeared to him twice. . . So the Lord said to Solomon, 'Since this is your attitude and you have not kept my covenant and my decrees, which I commanded you, I will most

---

28. First Kings 8:41–43

certainly tear the kingdom away from you and give it to one of your subordinates.'"[29]

After Solomon the kingdom was indeed divided between the northern kingdom of Israel with its capital Samaria, and the southern kingdom of Judah centered on Jerusalem.

In terms of faithfulness to Yahweh, Judah's kings were mixed. Israel's on the other hand, were universally idolatrous. In this context, the biblical record shows that God chose to show his healing power to foreigners who were open to recognizing and worshipping him as the one, true God.

During the reign of king Ahab of Israel, who married the Sidonian princess Jezebel, a Baal worshipper, there was a famine and Elijah was sent to a widow from the region Jezebel came from. The widow was about to cook one last meal for herself and her son before they died of starvation. After testing her faith in the LORD by getting her to use what she had to make him a cake of bread, Elijah prophesied that her jar of flour would not be used up or her jug of oil run try till the day the drought ended. This came true and showed that the LORD was sovereign over the provision of food, not Baal, the so-called god of fertility.[30] The later victory on Mount Carmel for Elijah over Jezebel's prophets of Baal was not about jingoistic Israeli nationalism but about who really was the true God of everywhere.[31]

In the story of Elijah's successor Elisha, and the Syrian commander Naaman, we see a parallel to the story of the taking of Jericho, where Rahab, a foreigner, was saved through faith in Yahweh, and Achan, a true blooded Israelite, was condemned. Naaman was a successful general, leading the armies of Aram to many triumphs (and incidentally, the writer of Second Kings attributes his success to the LORD giving victory to Aram through him). However, Naaman had a seriously unpleasant skin disease. A young Israelite slave girl, captured on a raid and who served his wife, said that there was a prophet in Samaria who could cure him. Naaman ended up being sent by the king of Aram in stately fashion to Samaria but then had to submit to Elisha's relayed instructions and humble himself by bathing seven times in the less than salubrious Jordan river. He was completely healed. He then said to Elisha,

> "Now I know that there is no God in all the world except in Israel...please let me, your servant, be given as much earth as a

---

29. Ibid. 11:1–11
30. First Kings 17:7–16
31. First Kings 18

pair of mules can carry, for your servant will never again make burnt offerings and sacrifices to any other god but the Lord." [32]

Naaman urged Elisha to accept the lavish gifts he had brought to pay the prophet, but Elisha steadfastly refused to accept his largesse. After being blessed, Naaman took his leave. But, without his permission, Elisha's servant, Gehazi, raced after him and made up a story about Elisha needing some payment after all—75 pounds of silver and two sets of clothing. Naaman was more than happy to give him 150 pounds of silver and the two sets of clothing. Gehazi intended to keep it all secretly, but Elisha saw in his spirit what he had done, and declared that Naaman's skin disease would cling to Gehazi and his descendants forever. Like Achan, he, an Israelite, was excluded from the life of the people of God, while Naaman received God's blessing, even though he was leading the army of Israel's enemy! This is another example of obedient faith in God being the crucially important thing in determining who is "in" and who is "out," not ethnicity

Fast forward to the New Testament. When the Gospel writer Luke tells us that Jesus returned to Nazareth, the town where he grew up and was invited to speak in the synagogue, he was very well received at first. However, he then unexpectedly challenged the people's small-minded ethnic chauvinism by showing from the Scriptures that being an Israelite did not automatically mean receiving God's favor. He gave the two examples cited above where God chose to bless people of faith from other nations rather than faithless Israel.

> "'Truly I tell you,' he continued, 'no prophet is accepted in his hometown. I assure you that there were many widows in Israel in Elijah's time, when the sky was shut for three and a half years and there was a severe famine throughout the land. Yet Elijah was not sent to any of them, but to a widow in Zarephath in the region of Sidon. And there were many in Israel with leprosy in the time of Elisha the prophet, yet not one of them was cleansed—only Naaman the Syrian.' All the people in the synagogue were furious when they heard this. They got up, drove him out of the town, and took him to the brow of the hill on which the town was built, in order to throw him off the cliff. But he walked right through the crowd and went on his way."[33]

32. Second Kings 5:15–17
33. Luke 4:24–30

If Jesus himself quoted the Old Testament to expose and refute the sort of latent jingoistic prejudice found all over the world, it is a false charge to call the God of the Hebrew Scriptures racist.

INTER-FAITH MARRIAGES

Barker also cites Nehemiah's strictures against inter-marriage of Jews with wives from pagan nations as additional evidence of the biblical God's racism and xenophobia. Again, the reply is that Nehemiah was not concerned with bloodline but was zealous for the post-exilic Jews back in the land to be faithful to God. Marriage to foreign wives usually meant worshipping their gods and he rightly saw this as covenant-breaking behavior. Children were being born of these marriages who had pagan idols in the home and couldn't even read the Hebrew scriptures.

There is a spiritual principle here which was confirmed in the New Testament and applies today. If a Christian marries a non-Christian, then they are showing that either their relationship with Christ is not of first importance, or that they are being foolish in thinking that being "unequally yoked" spiritually is not a serious obstacle to a happy marriage. They might gamble on being able to draw their spouse into sharing their faith, but this is not wise. A committed Christian would want to marry someone who is spiritually compatible with them, who would help them from the start to live a holy, Christ-centered life.[34] However, the New Testament era in which we are now, is different from the Old Testament era in which nationalistic separation from heathen peoples was necessary and needed to be enforced by civil sanction. A committed Christian parent today might be personally grieved if their son or daughter married outside of the Faith, but there is no warrant for inter-faith marriages attracting any civil penalties or violence, nastiness or prejudice.

Furthermore, the Christian faith, with its roots in the Old Testament, is the greatest force for overcoming national, ethnic and cultural barriers. There are, for example, many international, bi-lingual, dual heritage and cross-cultural Christian marriages. Anyone being true to the Faith would much rather marry a committed believer from a different worldly background than someone of the same nationality, ethnic group or social class who was not.

---

34. Second Corinthians 6:14

ACCENTS THAT DON'T FIT?

Barker throws in the strange claim that God wanted forty-two thousand people killed "because of their accent." This relates to the period of the Judges, when Jephthah was leading Israel and the relevant passage can be found in Judges 12. The men of Ephraim were angry that Jephthah, the misfit from Gilead, had fought and defeated the Ammonites without their help and so they threatened to burn his house down. They accused the Gileadites of being renegades from Ephraim and Manasseh. But Jephthah defeated them in battle and captured the fords of the Jordan leading to Ephraim. Whenever a survivor of Ephraim tried to cross the men of Gilead asked him whether he was an Ephraimite. If he denied it they challenged him to pronounce "shibboleth." If he could not pronounce the "sh" and said "sibboleth" they knew he was an enemy Ephraimite and they killed him. According to the New International Version of the Bible and all other translations, a total of forty-two thousand[35] Ephraimites were killed in the battle and afterwards by the Jordan fords. There is no evidence that God approved of Israelites killing in cold blood other Israelites with the wrong speech dialect. On the contrary, the refrain throughout the book of Judges is that "in those days Israel had no king. Everyone did what was right in their own eyes." This story shows that when the one true God is not faithfully worshipped and there is no powerful ruler to restrain evil, there is an absence of godly authority. People have nothing but the lawless instincts they are brought up with and easily fall into tribal violence and clan warfare.

NO FOREIGNERS ALLOWED?

Finally, what about God's command in Deuteronomy 23 that Ammonites or Moabites were not to enter the assembly of the LORD, even down to the tenth generation? It is difficult to know the precise scope of this prohibition, but it was not a racist statute but a didactic inter-generational ban imposed because of their serious sin in the way they treated Israel after the exodus from Egypt. As descendants of Lot, Abraham's nephew, they could have been expected to have helped their cousins, at least with bread and water, on their weary journeying. But instead they hired Balaam to curse them.

---

35. Like other numbers in current translations of the Old Testament, this number seems far too large and I would argue is almost certainly a mistranslation, rather than the original Hebrew being hyperbole. The Hebrew word translated 'thousand' *'elep* is also used to refer to a clan or a family unit or could denote an officer or trained fighting man. No fully satisfactory resolution has commanded common assent. I would suggest 42 trained fighters or officers would be much more realistic as to the number killed.

The ban could have simply applied to those who refused to be circumcised and who remained religiously apart, rather than those who became worshippers of Yahweh. Or it could have just prevented people with a Moabite and Ammonite background participating in the tabernacle worship or civil leadership in Israel.

One thing is clear. Ruth, a Moabitess, who became a worshipper of the LORD, was welcomed into Israel with her mother-in-law Naomi not long afterwards and she became the great grandmother of king David! Ruth's husband, Boaz, was himself the son of the foreigner Rahab, who was a Canaanite from Jericho who feared the LORD and joined the Israelites. So, in the royal line of Judah, the lineage of Christ, there were two foreign women, further proving the biblical God is not racist.[36]

---

36. Matthew 1:5–6

Chapter 12

Infanticidal?

"The King of Egypt said to the Hebrew midwives, whose names were Shiprah and Puah, 'When you help the Hebrew women in childbirth, and observed them on the delivery stool, if it is a boy, kill him, but if it is a girl, let her live.' The midwives, however, feared God and did not do what the king of Egypt had told them to do; they let the boys live."

—Exodus 1:15–17

War is truly a most horrible thing. After defeating Napoleon at Waterloo, the Duke of Wellington, surveying on horseback the desolate battlefield strewn with the mangled bodies of the dead and dying, is reputed to have said "next to a battle lost, the greatest sadness is a battle won." And he was talking about a single day's engagement, not the hardships caused to soldiers and civilians alike during protracted military campaigns. There is the dehumanizing lawlessness, starvation, disease, exposure, rape, brutalization of young and old, mental breakdown, families torn apart, hopes dashed, land ravaged for years to come, resources diverted from life-giving investment, and long-reaching legacies of hatred and bitterness.

For those of us fortunate not to have been caught up in a war, these experiences seem to belong to another world. It's not a world we want to think about. But war has been a feature of human existence ever since we lost our primal innocence. It is impossible to understand history without learning how armed conflict has shaped and still shapes the world we all live in. As a testimony to God's involvement with the real world, the Bible does not shy away from God's engagement with such a ubiquitous aspect of fallen civilization. If there was nothing about war in the Bible, it could not authentically relate to the human experience. The biblical God would be disconnected with life on earth. As with everything that happens in our world, God is sovereign over war and though he does not rejoice in it he uses it, without pleasure, for his purposes which are always good.

As part of his relationship with Israel in the Old Testament, he sometimes commanded the Israelites to make war against certain peoples or nations. As LORD of his people, he was also commander-in-chief of their military capability. If the world was to be saved, there could have been no other way. Before the Flood in the time of Noah, there is no record of God being involved in human warfare, yet the most terrible of divine judgments the world has known hitherto destroyed the earth. After the Flood, God committed himself to doing what was necessary to redeem mankind. This meant he *had* to become involved in every aspect of the human condition, including war.

Theologians debate what is meant by *God's will*. We can distinguish God's *desired* or *pleasurable* will from his *sorrowful* will.[1] The former is reflected in his commands to his people which set out a way of life bringing peace and prosperity. It is his pleasurable will that humanity was created healthy, strong, free and able to enjoy life. It is his pleasurable will that we avoid murder, rape, stealing, lying and vindictiveness. It is his sorrowful will that he expelled us from Eden and denied us the fruit of the tree of life. In sorrow he sends, allows, or uses war with all its consequences. His sorrowful will includes his painful action *or inaction* necessary for the reformation of sinful humanity. This can be understood both as him stepping back and allowing the consequences of our sin to work their way out (his *inaction*) and, more often in the Hebrew way of putting things, his direct carrying out of judgment (his *action*). So, when the Bible says the LORD "hardened Pharaoh's heart" when he would not let the Israelites go, this was a typically Hebrew way of saying that he withdrew his grace from Pharaoh leaving him

---

1. The common distinction made by theologians is between God's decretive will (what he decrees) on the one hand, and his permissive will on the other. However, I think this formulation is less helpful than recognizing the difference between his pleasurable will and his sorrowful will. There are some things that God decrees that he is happy to decree, and there are some things he decrees in sorrow. Likewise, there are some things which he permits which are a delight to him and some which are abhorrent. There has been a tendency to automatically attribute anything which is severe or unpleasant to his "permissive" will in a way that ignores how the Bible sees things.

to the stubborn inclination of his sinful nature. The latter explanation is a way of putting things which we today are generally more comfortable with.

A prominent form of judgment in the Old Testament was carried out by nations in war, with all the terrible slaughter this involved and suffering for men, women, children and animals. In the Bible, like everything else, killing, even atrocious killing, is always subject to God's sovereign will. The God of the Bible is never impotent in the face of evil. Sometimes the Bible tells us that an action resulting in suffering is expressly commanded, other times it does not, yet the Hebrew prophet Amos says rhetorically in 3:6 "if disaster comes to a city, has not the LORD caused it?"

Thus, there are many parts of Scripture where God, through the prophets, warns people of the terrible consequences of their communal sin. Often the biblical writers describe the catastrophes that war will bring as being explicitly "sent" by the LORD. Whether they do or they don't however, biblical theology teaches that when bad things happen it is part of God's unfathomable and sorrowful will. To those who find this hard to accept, I would say that, even if we did not have the Bible with all its problematic passages, believing somehow in an all-loving, all-powerful God would still mean we had to face the problem of evil and suffering in the world. If we believe in God, the only way we can escape facing the hard, theological truth of human suffering is by either jettisoning our belief in God's complete goodness or our belief in his all-powerful greatness. If we want to "protect" God from any responsibility for violence and destruction "on his watch" we have to deny his sovereign power, making him less than God, and a God we could not fully trust to overcome evil.

Therefore, when the prophets warn Israel or another nation that they will face war where "their infants will be dashed to pieces before their eyes," God is sorrowfully announcing that this is the terrible consequence of the way corrupt and decadent nations have to face his just judgment. Isaiah prophesied to the Babylonians that, just as they had destroyed cities of Judah and killed infants within them the same thing would happen to them when they were overpowered by the Medes.[2]

Mass slaughter after battle was a feature of ancient warfare. When fortified cities were besieged, there was often great suffering on both sides. The inhabitants of the city might suffer extreme hunger and parents sometimes literally did "eat the flesh of their children." Jeremiah prophesied this would happen inside Jerusalem when the Babylonians surrounded it unless the people repented of their perverted idolatry, human sacrifice and arrogant

---

2. Isaiah 13:11–18

rebelliousness.[3] The besieging army would also suffer privation, disease and loss of life. If they did take a city, women and girls were usually treated with lustful savagery. Because a quick death for women was often considered a mercy compared to the alternatives, many committed suicide. There was a vicious cycle to the whole thing. The fear of what would happen after defeat led the besieged city to desperately hold out and fight to the end, which of course led to a more protracted affair and greater loss of life for the attackers, and when they did eventually prevail, their appetite for revenge was all the greater.

It is in this light that we have to see the commands given to the Israelite soldiers regarding what they were to do when they attacked the cities of their enemies.[4] Outside of the land God gave to Israel, they were instructed to make the city an offer of peace. If the city accepted the offer the inhabitants would be subject to forced labor but no killing or raping. If they decided to fight, then the Israelites were to besiege the city and when they eventually broke through and prevailed they had license to kill only the men. It might not have been feasible to keep the men alive and preserve their own security. The women, children and livestock were to be spared and taken back to Israel. There was no divine sanction for raping women or killing children. If a man desired a woman sexually he had to take her as a wife and follow the rules laid down in Deuteronomy.[5] If a woman and her children were taken as slaves they had to be treated in accordance with God's humane rules about bonded labor. This was all remarkably merciful and restrained by the standards of warfare at the time and for many centuries afterwards, including most war situations up to this day, despite Christendom's attempts to establish agreed restraints on brutal conduct through the Geneva Convention and institutions like the International Criminal Court.

SHOW NO MERCY

Within the land that God had promised them, the instructions to the Israelites were different and, at a surface reading to modern ears, shockingly unpalatable. When a fortified Canaanite city within Israel was captured, the LORD instructed them to "show no mercy" and "to not leave behind anything that breathes."[6] However, the biblical evidence suggests that the attacks on the Canaanites remaining in the resisting cities was ordered by

3. Jeremiah 19:3–9
4. Deuteronomy 20:10–15
5. Ibid 21:10–14
6. Ibid. 7:2; 20:16–18

God mainly for the purpose of driving the Canaanites as a whole from the land in order to spiritually cleanse it from all the evil idolatry and teach the Israelites there could be no compromise with pagan worship. The single-minded severity of this would have caused the Canaanites to "melt away in fear"[7] God's s purpose was that the majority of Canaanites, especially women and children, would flee before the Israelites arrived. In Exodus 23:27 God says that he will make Israel's enemies turn and run. The phrase "drive out" is used frequently regarding God's strategy and this does not mean the literal annihilation of every Canaanite.

The average population of each walled city at the time was probably around 1000–3000, with many cities having no more than around 700 people. The 31 cities conquered by Joshua probably had a combined population of around 70,000.[8] Many or all of these would have been garrison towns, mainly inhabited by male soldiers but with some female suppliers of ancillary "services." (An example is Jericho where Rahab ran an inn that could have been a brothel[9]). Even if we assume every inhabitant was killed (which they almost certainly weren't), this would only have been a minority of the total population. The phrases "utterly destroy," "show no mercy" and "leave behind nothing that breathes," whether used as part of an instruction by God or the biblical writer's report of what happened, seems to either carry the meaning of total victory in battle or the removal of the Canaanite town dwellers settled way of life in the land they were living in. Paul Copan and Matthew Flannagan have convincingly shown in their book *Did God Really Command Genocide?* that these phrases were commonly used military hyperbole meaning total victory. They don't mean the rounding up of literally everyone, including women and infants, far and near for extermination. When Joshua chapters ten and eleven recount the Israelites "leaving no survivors" in the towns they attacked within the land of Canaan, this does not mean men, let alone women and children fleeing these towns, never to return, were pursued. We will look at the charge of genocide in the next chapter.

The only occasion on which the Bible tells us God directly commanded the slaughter of children and infants was some time after the invasion of Canaan when he instructed King Saul to carry out his judgment on the Amalekites. This is in First Samuel 15.

> Samuel said to Saul, "I am the one the Lord sent to anoint you king over his people Israel; so listen now to the message from

---

7. Joshua 2:9
8. https://www.bethinking.org/bible/old-testament-mass-killings
9. Joshua 2:1

the Lord. This is what the Lord Almighty says: 'I will punish the Amalekites for what they did to Israel when they waylaid them as they came up from Egypt. Now go, attack the Amalekites and totally destroy all that belongs to them. Do not spare them; put to death men and women, children and infants, cattle and sheep, camels and donkeys.'"

It was the Amalekites who, in an unprovoked attack on the Israelites coming out of Egypt, mercilessly cut down those who were weak and straggling as part of a campaign to destroy Israel totally. They continued to launch extremely cruel terror raids on Israel, once they had settled in the Promised Land, burning crops, stealing livestock, taking people as slaves and killing wantonly.

The Amalekites were to be put under the *herem*, the "ban" which was a solemn sentence requiring the Israelites to "devote to the LORD everything in a fortified city or encampment, including livestock and treasures. This often meant killing people who resisted the LORD and it did in this case. The main purpose of the ban was to be an announcement to the world that Yahweh, the God of Israel and one true God was inflicting his just wrath on a group that deserved it and that the Israelites were not attacking with any motive to enrich themselves with slaves, livestock and possessions, but simply carrying out the LORD's will as an act of obedience. This would have caused the nations to "fear the Lord" and see Israel as his instrument of justice. The "ban" was not necessarily a command to exterminate every genetic descendant of a people group at any one time—it was normally limited to a particular subgroup.

King Saul came under God's judgment for disobeying the "ban" and allowing the Amalekite king to live (presumably for ransom) and collecting the livestock for plunder. Barker says he was condemned by God for not being ruthless enough in committing genocide, but in First Samuel 15 Saul admits he was afraid of standing up to his army who wanted to enrich themselves. Given that there are plenty of Amalekites who feature later on in the time of David, and that Saul was only censured for sparing the king and taking the livestock, this might suggest that Saul was not directly commanded by God to pursue every Amalekite wherever they were living.

However, even if the number of Amalekite and Canaanite children who were killed was small comparative to the casualties of modern "just" wars, we still of course shudder to think of an Israelite soldier impaling an infant with a spear or dashing its head against a stone. Could not God have commanded the Israelite soldiers to spare any little ones found?

The first thing which we should say is that it is the influence of Christian ethics on the way we see things today that leads us to question the morality of God's commands in ancient total war. It is the Bible, with its teaching about the inherent worth of an individual made in God's image, the command to love and the hope of redemption that furnishes us with the morality to critique itself! But even nations shaped by centuries of ethical reflection on Christian just war theory have decided till this day that although war inevitably brings great suffering to children, it is sometimes justified.

Thousands of children were killed by just the two atomic bomb attacks on Hiroshima and Nagasaki in August 1945. Although carried out by the US air-force, Britain gave its necessary consent to the devastation as required under a treaty. President Harry Truman was persuaded that the dropping of the atom bomb would quickly end the war with Japan. A slow land invasion against a fanatical Japanese army defending every inch with their lives, would have taken a huge toll of casualties and he believed millions more lives would have been lost. Furthermore the ending of the war, caused by the two atomic bombs, formed part of the answer to the prayers of millions around the globe, including those being worked and starved to death in Japanese prison camps or held as sex slaves for the Imperial Army.[10]

It is possible that Truman and those who advised him got their moral calculations wrong. Human beings are limited in knowledge and wisdom and we have to make the best decisions we can without knowing the precise extent of the consequences of taking some course of action or not taking it. God however has perfect knowledge and can weigh perfectly the morality of certain commands he gave to the Israelites within the great scale of his loving purposes for humankind.

Uniquely, the Amalekites seem to have been in the same moral category as the people destroyed by God in the Flood. There was a spiritual dynamic within each generation which was utterly hostile to Israel and sought to destroy God's chosen people at every opportunity, from the moment they

---

10. About 200,000 girls and women in Asia are believed to have been forced into sexual slavery by the Japanese during the Second World War. It was an official system, created, ironically, to assuage international outrage at the mass rapes of Chinese women and girls in 1937 by the imperial Japanese army during the Second Sino-Japanese War. Emperor Hirohito of Japan set up a series of "comfort stations" to regulate sex. Young women who thought they were being recruited as nurses or laundry workers found themselves interned in military brothels in occupied territories. Girls as young as fourteen were raped by hundreds of soldiers every week. Only a few survived to tell the tale. Japan still has not accepted fully what it did because it is believed to be too damaging to its national honor. https://www.thetimes.co.uk/article/180c4a60-5e19-11ea-8f5d-5d06dfa1e7b9 based on Christina Lamb, *Extracted from Our Bodies, Their Battlefield: What War Does to Women*, London: Collins, 2020

came out of Egypt through to the time when Jews were scattered across the Persian Empire. This was when Haman, descended from the Amalekite king Agag, sought an Empire-wide genocide. This seems to have been the reason why of all the people groups who lived after the Flood, the Amalekites were singled out for total annihilation. Even the Canaanites, with all their evil, debased practices were allowed by God to survive beyond the borders of Israel. In thinking about the morality of God's commands in Scripture, we must factor in God's omniscience. An all loving, all powerful, all-knowing God would never command or even allow the death of an infant unless there was a good reason, even though that reason be an unfathomable mystery to us.

If we are being honest, we will admit that it is easier today for us to accept collateral child casualties when it is not close up and personal. Picturing a soldier picking up a child and killing it is much harder to cope with than knowing children will die horrible deaths from long range bombing or indirectly through the shortage of food and medicines caused by war. In terms of the suffering of any children who were found among the Amalekites, a quick death would however have been a more merciful experience than dying of exposure, thirst, starvation, or attacks by wild creatures alongside the rotting corpses of their parents. A compassionate person today would want a child orphaned in such circumstances immediately adopted into a loving family so they could enjoy a bright future. But even when we have all the modern resources at our disposal to adopt unwanted or uncared-for children, we still abort them in their millions or leave them languishing in loveless institutional homes. At certain times, it simply wasn't possible for Israelite solders to "adopt" children. Even if economically, psychologically and socially feasible, the girls would have been vulnerable to terrible abuse and the boys could have grown up believing it was their duty to avenge the deaths of their parents. When little ones die our confidence in the justice and compassion of God means we can entrust their eternal future to him. Death is sometimes a mercy, even for the young.

Furthermore, to think that your average battle-hardened bronze-age soldier would suffer life-long mental trauma by having to put to death an infant is to read modern sensibilities back into ancient history. Life was often brutal, hard and often short. Children belonging to enemy groups were not viewed with the sentimentality or transformational hope that we might view them. If they were not slaughtered immediately, they would have been left to die a slow death with the soldiers preoccupied with gathering plunder. Instructing the Israelites to "devote everyone and everything within to the LORD" (i.e. completely destroy everyone and everything, not taking women or objects as plunder) was a way of solemnly teaching them that this was God's holy judgment, not a rape and pillage free-for-all. It would have meant killing any non-combatants who were there quickly and decisively as an act of obedience to God, without getting distracted by looking for booty, and thereby prolonging the terrible suffering.

DELIGHTING IN THE SLAUGHTER OF INFANTS?

However, Barker's case that the biblical God is infanticidal goes further than saying God countenanced the killing of children as a necessary accompaniment to slaughter in war. He says that God *delighted* in it and wanted the Israelites to *enjoy* it!

The evidence he cites for this is Psalm 137. He quotes the last two verses of this psalm.

> "O daughter Babylon, you devastator! Happy shall they be who pay you back what you have done to us! Happy shall they be who take your little ones and dashes them against the rock!"

Barker then says

> "Can there be a more terrible sentence ever spoken in fiction or history? The God of the Old Testament is telling his people to enjoy torturing and murdering babies. This hymn was meant to be intoned during worship. 'Sing Hallelujah! Dash babies against the rock!' God wasn't simply acknowledging that we might need to cause collateral damage during wartime—he said we should be glad to do it. . . .. Smashing babies was meant to be a joyous event."

Is he right? If so, this would be a truly appalling indictment of the Bible. But Barker misunderstands this part of the psalm. All Scripture is God-breathed, but to understand any part properly today we must pay attention to the literary genre in which it is found and the whole context. Psalm 137 is a lament by those from Judea who were taken into exile in Babylon after the destruction of Jerusalem in 586BC. This is the psalm in full [*New international Version*]

> ¹By the rivers of Babylon we sat and wept
>   when we remembered Zion.
> ² There on the poplars
>   we hung our harps,
> ³ for there our captors asked us for songs,
>   our tormentors demanded songs of joy;
>   they said, "Sing us one of the songs of Zion!"

> ⁴ How can we sing the songs of the Lord
> while in a foreign land?
> ⁵ If I forget you, Jerusalem,
> may my right hand forget its skill.
> ⁶ May my tongue cling to the roof of my mouth
> if I do not remember you,
> if I do not consider Jerusalem
> my highest joy.
> ⁷ Remember, Lord, what the Edomites did
> on the day Jerusalem fell.
> "Tear it down," they cried,
> "tear it down to its foundations!"
> ⁸ Daughter Babylon, doomed to destruction,
> happy is the one who repays you
> according to what you have done to us.
> ⁹ Happy is the one who seizes *your* infants
> and dashes them against the rocks.

I have italicized the word "your" in verse nine because I think this is where the stress would have come in the line.

It must be conceded that for any thoughtful Christian the use of Psalm 137 in church services is highly problematic. I will come back to the question of whether the last verse or two should ever be used in an act of Christian worship shortly. But for now, let us consider Barker's interpretation, which is way off-beam.

The psalms are a collection of praise songs and laments. They are included in the canon of Scripture in recognition that faith in God and worship of him is not merely a cerebral thing but involves our emotions. We have a heart as well as a head. When it comes to the difficult and painful issues of life, the healthy processing of emotions is an important factor in spiritual growth. God wants us to relate to him not just when we are happy but when we are sad, fearful, alone, perplexed, angry and desperate. These emotions in themselves may be morally neutral—it is what we do with them that determines whether we behave in a right or wrong way.

Imagine you are an Israelite captive in Babylon. How would you be feeling? All you have loved and known has been destroyed. As you are languishing in exile, homesick and body aching after a forced march of hundreds of miles, you call to mind the taunts of your captors who, at the point of a sword no doubt, demanded from you "happy songs from Zion" for their entertainment. They thought it was a joke that you do this while the memory of friends killed, wives and sisters raped and "infants dashed against rocks" was still fresh in your mind.

How do you pray in such a situation? "O Lord make us truly thankful. God bless mummy and daddy, wherever they are, and look after the Babylonians. It must be hard being them." No, the point of the psalms is that we can be *real* with God in prayer and worship. We can pour out our natural emotions. The psalmist is not cursing the Babylonians to their faces in a crude and vulgar way. He is bringing all his impotent grief and rage to God. If he is invoking a blessing on those who in due course will be part of a stronger empire than Babylon and who will then be God's instrument in doing to them what they did to the Hebrews, he is doing so not from cold-hearted glee but with the most basic cry of humanity—a visceral cry for justice.

So, we see that this Psalm is not an instruction by God that the Israelites kill infants, still less feel happy about it. Its inclusion in Scripture indicates divine permission for the Israelites to pour out their true feelings before a God who can cope with that and who they know has seen their suffering and will establish justice. What we don't always appreciate when we ask for justice to be served is that justice is a terrible thing. As John Wenham says, "the Hebrew way of asking for justice was not expressed in abstract terms, in the way our prayers often are. Hebrew modes of thought tend to be concrete. They express a principle by an example. The psalmists often pray that God will vindicate his cause in a manner appropriate to his holy nature, but they know that this is likely to mean in practice the judgment of war, which will bring suffering to men, women and children. And so they couch their prayers in these terms."[11]

Wenham then proceeds to give a more modern example of circumstances in which a man of faith might utter words like this in the presence of God. He asks us to imagine "a devout old Jew, who had lived with the insults, humiliations and terrors of the Nazis and now found himself at Auschwitz standing naked in one of the endless queues which led to the gas chambers. He might well have been beyond feelings of personal hatred against his captors, but his whole soul would nevertheless cry out:

> "O you Nazis, you tormentors, you destroyers, God will terribly avenge you for this. Lord, how can men believe in your name if such evil triumphs? And if little children grow up in a world like this? You cannot let them blot us out utterly. Speed the bombers, blast their homes and families. Beat them to their knees, stop this devilry. Lord, blessed are those whom you call to this dread work of judgment."[12]

---

11. John Wenham *The Enigma of Evil*, 176
12. Ibid p177

But Psalm 137 is part of the *Hebrew Old Testament*. A Jewish person might echo it today, but can a *Christian* ever express similar sentiments and be faithful to Christ? Some churches have removed the last two or three verses from their service books. After the Second Vatican Council, the last three verses of the psalm were removed from Catholic liturgical books. The Prayer Book of the Anglican Church of Canada has also removed these verses and many musical settings of the psalm omit the last verse.

John Bell, from the Iona Community, takes an interesting, nuanced position. He comments alongside his own setting of this psalm: "The final verse is omitted in this metricization, because its seemingly outrageous curse is better dealt with in preaching or group conversation. It should not be forgotten, especially by those who have never known exile, dispossession or the rape of people and land."[13]

I think Bell has got it about right. The shocking verses in psalms do have a place. Comfortable Christians need to realize that there is a world outside their window. Those Christians who suffer violence and rape in many parts of the world also need to know there are people in the Bible who can relate to their experience. Expressing our anger to God is not incompatible with forgiveness. In fact, being honest with God about our true feelings is an important part of the forgiveness process. For minor things, we can and should "forgive and forget" quickly as Christians. But for major things like murder, sexual violence and serious economic loss and oppression, true forgiveness is a process. We cannot be sure we have fully forgiven until we have allowed ourselves to feel the full extent of the injury we have suffered, which may take a long time. Psalms like 137 can help people to acknowledge and express their suppressed pain while on a journey to forgiveness.

To those who have not suffered like the psalmist, however, the last verse in Psalm 137 is likely to seem jarringly vindictive, especially if we don't fully appreciate that for someone who lived in an age before the resurrection, their hope for justice was focused on what would happen in *this* life. If the psalmist saw a wicked, oppressive person, or his children and grandchildren for that matter, prospering, he found this deeply troubling because it seemed to call into question whether God was just. The psalmist longs to see justice *in this age*.

We have the advantage of knowing Jesus and his resurrection and the New Testament of course, building on the character of God as shown in the Old Testament, strongly teaches the importance of forgiveness. We forgive because we ourselves have been forgiven in Christ and in the light of the

---

13. Bell, John L. (1993) *Psalms of Patience, Protest and Praise*. Wild Goose Publications. ISBN 0-947988-56-4.

resurrection age to come, we know God's vengeance does not have to fall in this age for justice ultimately to prevail. Unwise use of certain passages in the psalms for intoned worship could easily lead to people misunderstanding them and thinking they validate a vindictiveness that runs counter to Gospel values. If even as wise a Christian figure as C.S. Lewis thought this,[14] then better they are taught about in sermons and discussed in small groups but kept in liturgical reserve as a resource for any desperate situations where, God forbid, there might be appropriate emotional circumstances.

---

14. CS Lewis, *Reflections on the Psalms*

Chapter 13

Genocidal?

"Does not the potter have the right to do what he will with the clay?"
—Romans 9:21

If people on the streets of countries in the West were asked for the greatest example of genocide, then most would answer it was the extermination of six million Jewish people by the Nazis. Some might mention the more recent Rwandan genocide of 1994 when one million Tutsis were killed in three months. The truth of what happened in both these genocides has largely been accepted by the nations involved. But in 1917, the Ottoman Turks committed a genocide against Armenian and Assyrian Christians, killing one and half million. To this day Turkey has refused to acknowledge what it did.

Definitions of genocide vary. Some explain it broadly as the killing of a large number from a particular people group. Others would say there also has to be the intention of completely exterminating *everyone* from that group. For the Nazis, it wasn't enough to drive Jews out of Germany. They dreamed of a world where *all* ethnically determined Jews had perished. On the other hand, some mass killings, or policies resulting in millions of deaths, may not be classed as genocide if there is not similar intent, even if the total number of casualties is higher. Historians estimate that Stalin's Soviet regime caused between ten and forty million deaths among the Russian peasantry when he enforced farm collectivization, induced punitive famines, and crushed political opposition by sending huge numbers of people to death camps. Stalin said "one death is a tragedy but millions of deaths is just a statistic."

In the Holocaust and the Rwandan genocide, the cultural situation and general means of killing were different, but what they had in common was a heavy propaganda campaign aimed at providing moral justification. The Nazis taught that Jews were a race of poisonous, corrupting *untermenschen* (sub-humans). A conspiracy of Jewish capitalists, who controlled the world's finance, had betrayed Germany's cause in The Great War, they alleged. The economic double whammy of unemployment and hyper-inflation, where a loaf of bread had cost a wheelbarrow full of banknotes, was all down to the Jews. Every evil in society was laid at their door from the killing of the Christ right up to modern times. Likewise, in the run up to the Rwandan massacres, a relentless barrage of radio broadcasts had accused the Tutsis of being the historical arch oppressors of the Hutus and described them as "cockroaches." This dehumanized them in the eyes of their Hutu neighbors who slaughtered them at close hand. To call God genocidal therefore implicates him in horrors of similar magnitude.

THE FLOOD

Barker charges the biblical God with committing the worst ever genocide in terms of numbers killed. He says that the Flood was fiction, but if it *were* true the numbers killed would have been twenty million people. He does not explain how he can be so precise about the death count of an event he claims to be fictional. However, whatever the absolute number of people who perished, the biblical story makes it clear that it *was* the entire population of the world bar Noah, his wife, his three sons and their wives—just eight people.

So, is there a sense in which the adjective "genocidal" fits the facts of Genesis chapter six? Do the facts necessarily impugn God's character? In the American legal system, the killing of a human being by another human being is called "homicide." There are various forms of culpable homicide, such as murder or reckless killing, but there is also a category called "justifiable homicide." Examples of this include soldiers killing on the battlefield, police or security services killing in the reasonable execution of their duty, the administration of judicial execution and self-defense.

Now hypothetically speaking, if the killing of one individual can be classed as justifiable homicide, then it might be theoretically possible in some circumstances to class the killing of a people group, as "justifiable genocide." However, there is no internationally recognized system of jurisprudence which has or could conceivably recognize this. This is because dignifying such a concept would rightly be seen as opening the door for human beings to act in ways that are way beyond our capacities for moral discernment and, apart from anything else, could result in the kind of catastrophic conflict that would endanger the whole human race.

However, the fact that no human-driven genocide could ever be justifiable does not mean that *God* does not have the right to end the lives of any number of people he created and sustains. God is infinite in love, power and wisdom. If he decides that a person or a group of people or a nation or race, or every human being on the planet should, for the overall good of his creation, perish because of incorrigible wickedness and not continue to be mercifully preserved, how can we as sinful, dependent creatures, claim a right to morally judge him?

Some say that the Flood narrative, like the creation account, is mythological. That means that while it might have had some basis in the primeval memory of a great deluge, it is primarily a non-historical story which expresses theological truth. However this does not actually remove the problem of the goodness of God, since Jesus used the Flood story as a warning of judgment to come and so if it teaches by metaphor the severity of God, how great is the reality of that severity of God to which the metaphor relates.

Also, if the Flood is regarded as non-historical, a Christian must then answer the question "at what point does the Genesis narrative start referring to real people and real events?" The genealogy of Abraham, regarded as a real, living ancestor and father of the three great monotheistic world faiths[1], is traced back to Noah (as his is to Adam). Were the patriarchs mythological? The Exodus from Egypt? The settlement in the promised land? The ministry of Jesus? The resurrection? Some theologians and church people see very little factual basis in anything in the Old Testament and even the New. We know, they say, very little about the historical Jesus, and they claim that the resurrection was not a historical event, but a spiritually stimulating idea in the minds of those who came to believe in the mythological Jesus.

When an individual or a government or a committee of scientists makes decisions affecting life and death in what seems an arbitrary way, we say that that person or corporate body is "playing God." This common saying reflects an underlying instinct that some decisions about life and death rightly belong to God, not us. To think that we know better than God how to run the universe is the height of arrogance. To feel morally superior to God is the epitome of pride and vanity. It is this, the Bible says, that is the root cause of all the evil

---

1. Judaism, Christianity and Islam

in the world[2], including all the evils God is accused of being complicit with by people like Richard Dawkins and Dan Barker. This is not to say that we have no knowledge of right or wrong. We are made in God's image. There are places in the Bible (e.g. many of the Psalms) where an appeal is made to God that he remembers to act in accordance with his essential character. But these appeals are made in the context of a relationship of love and trust and with a sense of humility and awareness of God's moral superiority.

The Bible says in Genesis chapter six that "the LORD saw how great man's wickedness on the earth had become, and that every inclination of the thoughts of his heart was only evil all the time." Twice it is said that he was "grieved" that he had made man and that "his heart was filled with pain." Barker sees an opportunity for a sarcastic dig here about God's supposed omniscience. However, the Bible, in speaking to human beings, accommodates its words and ideas in ways which we can relate to. It uses anthropomorphic language to convey emotions God feels which may appear to us to sit paradoxically alongside his other divine characteristics.

The beginning of chapter six speaks about matters which theologians struggle to understand—"the sons of God' intermarrying with the "daughters of men" and producing a race called the Nephilim. Some say the "sons of God" were fallen angels infecting the human race with powerful but morally degraded characteristics. Others say the "sons of God" were strong but corrupt rulers who took large harems and perpetuated their warlike seed. Some say they were members of the godly line of Seth, who were close to God but who intermarried with ungodly women corrupting that godly line and leaving the world without a faithful dynasty of witness to the living God.

Whatever is the correct answer, this strange passage is a reminder that the ways of God are often mysterious and beyond our understanding. He is infinitely greater than us.[3] There are truths in the heavenly, spiritual realm that we have no access to, but which affect our lives on this earth. In this life we "see through a glass darkly"[4] and have to trust God's goodness as well as his divine power.

CANAANITES, MIDIANITES AND AMALEKITES

What about the other examples of genocide, or what looks like genocide, commanded by God in the Old Testament?

2. Genesis 3:6
3. Isaiah 55:8–9, Job 41:11
4. First Corinthians 13:12

I argued in chapter eight that the command to drive out the Canaanites was a spiritual cleansing of the land rather than an attempt at wiping out an ethnic group. The Bible is clear that God's strategy was to drive out the Canaanites and destroy their presence *in the land he gave to Israel* rather than their genetic extermination. Had all the Canaanites fled instead of fighting they would all have survived as refugees outside the borders of Israel. Copan and Flannagan show in chapter ten of *Did God Really Command Genocide?* that under international law today, in order for someone to be found guilty of genocide, there has to be an intention to annihilate a whole people group, or a significant part of the people group, rather than simply an intention to force people off a particular land.

I have dealt with some aspects of the command to attack the Midianites in chapter eleven. The Midianites had followed the advice of a sorcerer called Balaam who recommended that hundreds of their women should sexually entice the Israelites into immoral relations and Baal-worship. Their intention was to destroy the covenant relationship the people had with God and therefore the social and moral fabric of Israel. After the battle in which five kings of Midian were killed and also Balaam, the command to kill the surviving boys and the non-virgin women who had collaborated in the evil plan against the Israelites was given by Moses and is not recorded as a direct command from God. But Moses' command was just, in the context, and also merciful because the virgin women were incorporated into the people of Israel. This alone shows there was no intention to destroy every genetic Midianite, but also it is clear that the Israelites were only commanded to attack those Midianites who had tried to destroy them. There were lots of other Midianite groups as can be shown by the fact that Midianites continued to send terror raids into Israel during the time of the Judges. So the Israelite action was proportionate. For Moses' command to kill the male infants, see chapter twelve.

"BLOT OUT THE MEMORY OF AMALEK."

In Exodus 17:8–16 we read that the Amalekites (descended from a grandson of Esau, Jacob's twin brother) launched an unprovoked attack on the Israelites when they were at Rephidim, having just come out of Egypt. Joshua fought and defeated them, with Moses and Hur at the top of a hill interceding before God with upraised hands. Afterward the LORD told Moses to write down on a scroll his intention to "completely blot out the memory of Amalek from under heaven." Moses interpreted this as war from generation to generation until no descendants were left. In Deuteronomy 25:17–19

GENOCIDAL? 173

Moses reminds the people that the Amalekites attacked their caravan train and mercilessly killed all the weary and worn out who were lagging behind. They must not forget to carry out the LORD's judgment on them. But they did forget. In the time of the Judges, the Amalekites assisted King Eglon of Moab in attacking Israelite territory and also combined with the Midianites to burn crops, steal flocks and terrorize Israelite farming families until Gideon drove them back.

Glenn Miller provides helpful insights into both the initial unprovoked onslaught by the Amalekites on the Israelites refugees from Egypt and their continue campaign of terror against the Israelites seeking to make a peaceful living from the land when they had finished their wilderness wanderings.

> "Imagine an elderly Israelite couple, who after suffering under harsh slavery for 60 years in Egypt finally escape miraculously with their grandchild. They gather the first material possessions they have ever owned—given to them by the Egyptians on the night they left—and are following the main body of Israelites. They are overjoyed by their first experience of freedom and hope for a more 'normal' life for their granddaughter. But they are old, and the decades of physical abuse have left them weak. And so they fall behind the main group of Israelites, and they must rest more frequently and longer. And, as the gap widens, they see a dust cloud behind them, chasing them. They fear that maybe the Egyptians are trying again to enslave them, so they jump up in fatigue and anxiety and begin racing toward the Israelites. But they are no match for the marauding Amalekites, who quickly capture them. They watch in horror as their granddaughter is stripped and evaluated for what price she might fetch at the eastern slave market, with crude suggestions as to what 'use' she might be to the plantation slave bosses. They see her bound and tied to the back of the horses, where she will have to walk behind their caravan until exhausted and then thrown into a slave-cart. They are next: the Amalekites strip them of their clothes, take their few belongings, and then cut them down with the sword. Their last images are of their granddaughter screaming for help as she is driven at spearpoint..."
>
> "The impoverished and undernourished young Israelite family have been able to hide their small crop so far in the growing season. Each previous year, the marauding Amalekites have burned their small crop and killed the few livestock they used for clothes and cheese, and the family has eaten what little the wild land could provide. They sleep under a rock cropping, in fear of detection, and take turns at night watching for predatory

animals, slave-trading bands, and the Amalekites and their allies. Harvest is almost here, and they have actually gathered a few items already (and consumed them hungrily). They suffer from various forms of malnutrition and exposure, and the youngest—Abigail the three-year old little girl—cannot get up due to some unknown sickness. But hope has arisen for the first time in years, and the parents are eager to feed their little ones the food they desperately need. As they are gathering the first pick, with ears always alert, they hear the familiar sound of hooves...And though they run, they are overtaken by the Amalekite raiding party. They watch as their crop is burned to ashes (the raiders only laugh at the sight—they don't take any of the food at all), along with the feeble hope that grew there too. But they have bigger problems now, because they did not reach the hiding place in time. The raiders size up the family and recognize that such youth will fetch a pretty shekel in the slave markets of Damascus. The young wife and two of the healthier children are stripped and tied together with other captured Israelites, to be marched off to be sold to different owners in different parts of the world. One smaller child is simply cut down—screaming in terror–with the sword in the eyes of both parents. Abigail begins to cry in fear from her cot under the rock, alerting the Amalekites for the first time of her presence. The father tries vainly to defend his family as they plead for mercy, but he is rewarded only with the anti-Israelite taunts of hate and the slash of a sword. The last thing he hears are Amalekite words of the leader, to leave the sick Abigail as food for the wolves, rats, and ants—since she wouldn't have any value in the slave trade."[5]

God commanded King Saul in First Samuel 15 to "devote the Amalekites to the LORD" by totally destroying them and everything that belonged to them. "Do not spare them; put to death men and women, children and infants, cattle and sheep, camels and donkeys. This was the *herem*, the "ban," the solemn execution of God's judgment (as above, see the previous chapter for the issues around the killing of children and infants). There was to be no booty taken. The king and the nobles were not to be spared to be held for ransom. Saul disobeyed this command. Barker asserts it was because he was not sufficiently cruel in carrying out his genocidal orders that God rejected Saul as king. This is not the case. Saul admitted to the prophet Samuel when challenged that he had taken King Agag prisoner and the best of the sheep and cattle because he was afraid of his men, who wanted to enrich themselves with booty rather than solemnly carry out the LORD's judgment in

---

5. See Glenn Miller http://christianthinktank.com/rbutcher1.html

faithful obedience to his instructions. Saul did not carry out the *herem* as diligently as he should have done, not because of a peaceable nature, but because he was distracted with plunder and people pleasing.

The failure of the Israelites to eradicate the Amalekites is shown by the fact that they were still around by David's time. They attacked the town of Ziklag, given to David by the King of Gath, burned it to the ground and took the wives and children of David and his men captive. David's men blamed him and talked of stoning him. But God strengthened David and enabled him to defeat them, recovering the wives and children and killing all but four hundred of the enemy who escaped on camels.[6] The remaining ones we are told were killed later by the Simeonites during the reign of Hezekiah.[7] But even then, this did not mean literally every descendant was killed. The architect of the plan to kill all Jews in the Persian empire, recorded in the book of Esther, was Haman, described as an "Agagite"[8] (a descendant of the Amalekite king Agag). His plan backfired, meaning a bloodbath over two days when the Jews were granted the right to defend themselves by making a pre-emptive strike on their enemies. So, we see that the failure of Israel to carry out God's just command completely brought trouble upon them later and resulted in much more bloodshed.[9]

DID THE "TEXTS OF TERROR" INSPIRE THE CRUSADES?

It is sometimes claimed that the Old Testament commands for the Israelites to attack certain other nations provided the religious justification for attacks by genocidal mediaeval Christian warriors on peaceful Muslims living in the Middle East. Paul Copan and Matthew Flannagan do a good job in refuting this historical travesty of the truth,[10] which was initially spread by writers wanting to be cynical about the Christian heritage of the West, and has been taken up by Muslims in the last century as a propaganda tool against Western civilization and a rallying call for Jihad, particularly after the founding of the state of Israel in 1948.

The Crusades should be seen as beginning with a response by Western Europe against the violent expansionism of the Seljuk Turks who had taken over Christian Asia Minor and who were committing terrible atrocities

6. First Samuel 30:1–20
7. First Chronicles 4:43
8. Esther 3:1
9. Ibid. 8–9
10. Copan and Flannagan *Did God Really Command Genocide?* 288–98

against Christian communities and Christian pilgrims to the Holy Land. Constantinople, the center of Eastern Christianity, was in real danger. The Emperor appealed to Western Christendom for help and on the basis of what he said the Turks were doing, Pope Urban II gave a passionate speech pleading that their cry not go unheeded.

> "They destroy the altars, after having defiled them with their uncleanness. They circumcise the Christians, and the blood of the circumcision they either pour on the altars or into the vases of the baptismal font. When they wish to torture people by a base death, the perforate their navels, and dragging forth the extremity of their intestines, bind it to a stake; then with flogging they lead the victim around until the viscera having gushed forth the victim falls prostrate to the ground... What shall I say about the abominable rape of women? To speak of it is worse than to be silent. On whom therefore is the labor of avenging these wrongs and recovering this territory incumbent, if not upon you?"[11]

The initial cause of the Crusades was a just one in that it was conceived as a defensive war, responding to Islamic aggression which threatened the existence of Christians throughout the Middle East and would in time reach far into Europe. The motive was not forcible conversion of Muslims or the plundering of wealth. On the contrary, wealthy people sunk huge amounts of personal capital with no guarantee of repayment, and ordinary people made great sacrifices to undertake the venture when travel was so difficult and expensive. The only biblical texts cited to encourage people to go that we have evidence for are Jesus' words about taking up one's cross, following him, and leaving comfort and security behind in order to lay down one's life for others.

Sadly, although such noble ideas did persist in some, the corrupting effects of war meant the campaigns were not always pursued in a just way. The customary mediaeval intolerance to religious dissent, anti-Jewish prejudice, and on occasion, sheer, out of control bloodlust, led to some appalling atrocities such as rape and slaughter of civilians from Jewish, Muslim and sometimes even Eastern Christian communities. There was also greed, rivalry and infighting during the centuries that the Crusades spanned. None of this was justified by anything in the Scriptures, New Testament or Old.

---

11. Ibid. 290

Chapter 14

Filicidal?

A true Christian disciple knows that God loves his children more than he does

If infanticide is the killing of infants, filicide is the killing by someone of their children, of any age. God's command to Abraham to sacrifice Isaac in Genesis twenty-two forms the main "evidence for the prosecution" for this charge, although Barker also adds Jephthah's sacrifice of his daughter, and grisly prophecies relating to what Israelite parents will do to their children when they come under God's judgment by being besieged by their enemies. The latter I considered in chapter twelve. I'll deal with Jephthah and his daughter first and then come back to the Genesis 22 story to finish.

THE MAN WHO SACRIFICED HIS DAUGHTER

Jephthah was a "judge" of Israel during the period covered by the book of Judges. It was a time of anarchy in the life of Israel. There was no king and everyone did as they saw fit in their own eyes. The years were characterized by a continual cycle of Israel's unfaithfulness to the Covenant, expressed in the breaking of all the commandments, followed by judgment as God allowed their enemies to oppress them. Then they would cry out to the LORD and in his mercy he would raise up military leaders who defeated Israel's enemies and who then ruled for varying lengths of time. The people would then get complacent and turn to idols and the cycle would be repeated.

Jephthah was an outsider from Gilead, having been cast out and rejected by his father's brothers because he was the son of a prostitute. He lived east of the Jordan and led a band of adventurers. However, when the Ammonites started attacking them, the Gileadites swallowed their pride and asked Jephthah to come back and be their commander. He did and Judges 11:29 says "the Spirit of the LORD came upon Jephthah" and he advanced against the Ammonites. And before going into battle, he made a vow to the LORD. Most English translations are similar to this one:

> "If you give the Ammonites into my hands, whatever comes out of the door to meet me when I return in triumph from the Ammonites will be the LORD's, and I will sacrifice it as a burnt offering."

Jephthah did defeat the Ammonites and when he returned home his daughter, his only child, emerged first from his home, dancing to the sound of tambourines. He tore his clothes in misery, explaining that he had made a vow to the LORD that he could not break. His daughter told him he must go ahead with his vow, but please could she have two months to roam the hills and weep with her friends because she would never marry. After this time, she returned and her father "did to her what he had vowed. And she was a virgin."

There are two views as to what actually happened to Jephthah's daughter. The first view which has the support of the way the Hebrew has been translated in all the English versions, is that on her return to her father she was indeed killed as a sacrifice and her body burned as an offering to the LORD. This is what Barker naturally assumes, and he says the favor granted to Jephthah in battle and the absence of divine intervention to stop the human sacrifice (in contrast to the case of Isaac) meant that the biblical God was quite happy to accept this arrangement.

It must be admitted that if Jephthah's daughter was killed as a sacrifice then this is perhaps the saddest story in Scripture. What happened to the Levite's concubine in Judges nineteen was gruesomely cruel and utterly evil, but here we see a father killing his own beloved daughter in fulfilment of what seems to be an unnecessary vow, the scope and consequence of which he did not foresee. Let's assume that she did die at his hands. Is God implicated in this cruel, pointless tragedy?

Let us remember that the times were lawless, and Israel was continually descending to the standards of the heathen nations which did practice child sacrifice. Jephthah, although used by God to help the Israelites, was, because of what had happened to him, a damaged individual, and he probably grew up with a sense of never being good enough or acceptable unless he performed impressive feats. It could be that Jephthah thought that such a vow was necessary to persuade God to secure victory for him. What was he thinking?

Kenneth Bailey argues that, just as in Jesus' time, houses consisted of a ground floor for the animals (into which the animals went at night) and a floor above it for living quarters, Jephthah's house would have been designed in the same way. The animals were let out in the early morning and so emerged first. He therefore surmises Jephthah would have assumed one of the animals would have come out of the house first when he made his early arrival home, before any members of his family did.[1]

If this theory is correct, Jephthah clearly felt that despite his assumption of animal sacrifice only in making the vow, he was still bound by the exact form of his words, which were taken very seriously when uttered in oath.

But why didn't God stop Jephthah in his tracks and tell him in no uncertain terms that he regarded human sacrifice as abominable? Well, the period in Israel's history was very different to the time of Abraham and Isaac. At that time the LORD appeared to Abraham and spoke to him because he was close to God in faith. By Jephthah's time, although the Israelites had had the Mosaic law which completely ruled out child sacrifice, they had fallen away from a close relationship with Yahweh and were out of touch with what he wanted. The book of First Samuel tells us that this period of Israelite history was characterized by an absence of hearing the word of the LORD. Also, there are plenty of places in Scripture where people, including flawed heroes, do things which are clearly wrong and there is no explicit statement of divine disapproval. The readers of Scripture are left to come to their own conclusions about what God thought.

There is however another view that Jephthah's daughter was not killed but offered to the LORD by being kept in seclusion as a perpetual virgin. Adam Clarke disputes the majority translation of the Hebrew and believes it should be translated as Jephthah promising a burned offering alongside the *dedication* of whatever comes out of the door of his house. There are at least two reasons why this makes more sense. First, she and her friends spend two months crying about her forgoing marriage. If she faced becoming a burned offering, then it seems strange that the fact that she would never marry should be the thing she and her friends are most upset about. Second, if she were facing death, she could have used the opportunity afforded by the two-month period of mourning away with her friends to escape her father. An

---

1. Kenneth E Bailey, Jesus Through Middle Eastern Eyes, London: SPCK, 2008 pp 29–30

objection to this might be that she would have been unwilling to bring guilt on her father by not returning and thus preventing him from carrying out his vow. But it could be replied that, just as the Israelite fathers whose daughters were taken to be the wives of Benjamites when they had vowed not to give them in marriage to them, were considered not guilty of oath-breaking because their daughters were taken without their consent,[2] so Jephthah would probably not have been thought to have been guilty of vow breaking because his daughter absconded without his permission.

Either way, it was a tragic, unnecessary and foolish vow. Like Samson and Gideon and the other judges, Jephthah was a flawed person used by God to bring deliverance to his people. Giving him victory over Israel's enemies was done as a merciful act to them, not a sign of approval for Jephthah's oath.

THE MAN TOLD TO SACRIFICE HIS SON

Let's turn our attention to the story of Abraham being told by God to sacrifice Isaac as a burnt offering. Barker says that though God intervened in the story to stop the sacrifice, the whole episode was nevertheless a cruel test. In being willing to slaughter his son, Abraham passed the test according to the Bible, but in Barker's eyes he failed it, because he put the approval of a malevolent deity over natural compassion for his son. Oddly, Barker doesn't mention any psychological damage done to Isaac as part of the indictment against God. This is certainly something which has often occurred to me in reading this passage.

The story of Abraham and Isaac contains much that is paradoxical.[3] God is the God who has everything and needs nothing. In Psalm 50 v9–11 God says

> "I have no need of a bull from your stall or of goats from your pens, for every animal of the forest in mine and the cattle on a thousand hills. I know every bird in the mountains and the creatures of the field are mine. If I were hungry I would not tell you, for the world is mine and all that is in it."

So why does God demand so much from Abraham? His own dear son, who he loves, he must offer as a sacrifice. What was God thinking of, when he tested Abraham in this way? Did God know whether Abraham was really prepared to trust and obey completely, even when the command made

---

2. Judges 21
3. See Kandiah *Paradoxology*, 7–34

no sense or was repugnant to his natural feelings of affection towards his son? Was God judging that any trauma caused to Isaac by this incident was regrettable but necessary in the grand scheme of things? Or was he factoring in to the situation that human sacrifice was a known phenomenon and that Abraham, and even Isaac, with their limited revelation as to the character of Yahweh, would have accepted that Yahweh might require it, and thus not be as morally aghast as we might be today by such a command? Was God the Father already feeling the agony of his decision to send his one and only son, who he loved, to suffer the full range of turmoil in relation to the cross?

The God of the Bible is nothing like the arbitrary and capricious gods of pagan Greece and Rome. He does not make sport of men or consider the welfare of humans as of little account. I believe that God did consider the thoughts and feelings of both Abraham and Isaac, but we also have to accept that God in his sovereign wisdom knows more about us than we do ourselves and is the ultimate source of all blessing and wellbeing, physical and psychological. So, let's think about what Abraham was being put through here and then consider Isaac.

Abraham knew God had appeared to him and had given him a clear command. Sometimes God is said to appear to him in the form of an angelic visitor, but at certain times, when Abraham is being asked to take a big faith leap, the Bible simply records God speaking directly to him. How this happened we don't know, but Abraham was always left in no doubt that the LORD had spoken. Today, we would be guilty of arrogance if we claimed with certainty that God was telling us to do something that seemed to go against his character as revealed in Scripture. If we said that we were hearing God's voice in our head calling us to sacrifice our own children the police and social services would, quite rightly, be round straight away.

But Abraham knew only of God what he had revealed up to that point. And there was no doubting what God was telling him to do. "Abraham. Take your son, your only son, Isaac, whom you love." Notice the repetition which conveys the utter clarity of the command. The LORD says his name, Isaac, and describes him as Abraham's "beloved."

So what Abraham is hearing is this. "Abraham, take your son, the one you hoped and prayed for all those years, the miracle son Sarah bore you after a lifetime of sterility. The one though whom I said your offspring is to be reckoned,[4] the one through whom I promised to give you as many descendants as stars in the sky and sand on the seashore. Isaac, the one whose name means laughter, because of the joy he has brought to you and Sarah, when you remember how she laughed with disbelief but then found all your

4. see Genesis 21

prayers and longings answered at the end of a momentous journey of faith. Isaac the one who you love very much —who is so dear—the son you adore and who has made your life complete. Go to Moriah and sacrifice him to me as a burnt offering on one of the mountains I will tell you about!" We don't need to be especially astute to know how Abraham felt when he heard this.

The text though seems to suggest not only that Abraham was in no doubt this was God's clear command, but that also, he did not delay at all. As in the previous chapter when he sent Ishmael and Hagar away, Abraham's commitment to carrying out God's will is expressed by his getting up early in the morning and starting out on his journey of obedience.

But he must of course have been in utter turmoil. His whole world was being turned upside down. It wasn't just about his affection for Isaac, the impact on his dear wife Sarah, it was his whole lifetime of ups and downs in faith leading to the final joy of miraculous childbirth according to the promise, and then, like an architect who in faith spends his lifetime building a God-ordained temple, he is being told to burn it to the ground.

Actually, Mount Moriah where Abraham bound Isaac was, unknown to Abraham, to be the site of the Temple built by Solomon. It was to be the heart of the city of Jerusalem, where God the Father would see his only beloved son sacrificed as atonement for the sins of the world. Abraham would not have known or understood all this, but in God's sovereign plan it may be that he had decided that the people to whom he would give his name and through whom the Messiah was to come must have a forefather who could see what looked like complete and utter desolation and yet still trust in the power and love of God. In the previous chapter, God allows Hagar to suffer the dread of losing everything she had hoped for. When she was expelled from Abraham's household, she and Ishmael wandered in the desert of Beersheba and she thought that they would both die of thirst. God intervened to give her and her son water and promised to make him into a great nation.

If suffering and trust was the pre-requisite for the blessing of Ishmael, born in the ordinary way, how much more should suffering and trust be necessary for the blessing of Isaac, the son born according to the promise of God?[5]

One thing Abraham would have remembered, I think, as he journeyed to Moriah, was his encounter with the mysterious Melchizedek, priest king of Salem, the forerunner of Jerusalem, described in chapter fourteen. Abraham saw him as representing God and gave him a tenth of his resources. Abraham probably reflected on how much he had been blessed, with both

---

5. Galatians 4:21–31

wealth and numbers in his camp. Maybe he thought that if God blessed him with so much in response to him giving God a tenth of the wealth he had plundered from the four kings in battle, how much more would he bless him for his obedience in not holding back his whole hope for the future? At any rate Abraham knew he could not disobey God, the source of life and of everything good that he had.

I'm sure that Abraham didn't think this at the time, but afterwards it may have been that Abraham was given a sense of renewed affirmation from God. Abraham hadn't always fully trusted God with everything in his life. From the end of chapter eleven and the beginning of chapter twelve we see that Abraham could not bring himself to fully obey God by leaving his father's household. They had together gone to Haran, but there they had stopped, until his father Terah had died.

Abraham, perhaps not trusting God to provide for him in Canaan during a famine, went to Egypt. God had promised to make him into a great nation, but even so Abraham feared for his life in Egypt and used his wife as a kind of human shield, a ploy that he used later with Abimelech the Philistine king and he was actually put to shame by the heathen king's righteous conduct. Maybe he later became grateful to God for giving him an opportunity to live up to his calling to be the father of millions of people of faith all over the world.

And Abraham did indeed pass the test. He proved that he understood God to be not only the God who tests us but the God who provides. When Isaac asked where the sacrificial lamb was, Barker says he must have lied to Isaac at this point, in saying that God would provide it. He argues that if Abraham really knew God would do this, then the test would have been a sham. But it is not necessary to charge Abraham with lying, or even telling a "white lie." Abraham, probably did not know what to say in his human wisdom and through the Spirit spoke words of prophetic faith—God himself will provide the sacrificial lamb. He didn't know how everything would work out but he maintained his faith in the God who had brought forth life out of the barren womb of his wife long past the menopause. Hebrews 11v19 says that Abraham reasoned that God could raise the dead so that if he did have to sacrifice Isaac God would still somehow honor his promise to give him offspring through Isaac. When Abraham and Isaac left the servants to go on alone, he again used words of prophetic faith—"we will worship and then *we* will come back to you."

So yes, Abraham was put through a great test, a great ordeal, but in passing this test, God poured over Abraham blessing upon blessing—and not just him but those connected to him. Even his brother Nahor is blessed with twelve sons.

To finish I want to say something about Isaac. Even if, as we know, God never intended Isaac to go under the knife, and even if Abraham came to see this episode as a faith-building test which he passed with flying colors, I imagine that many are still left troubled by thinking about the psychological trauma we imagine Isaac might have experienced, both at the time and maybe subsequently. Isaac was old enough to know what was going on, because he was old enough to carry wood and ask where the lamb was for the burnt offering, and would he not have been terrified when Abraham bound him and laid him on top the wood?

Well maybe. Perhaps he saw the knife in Abraham's hand when he reached out to take it and slay his son. If we read the passage carefully though, it may be that he didn't see the knife and he may not even have realized there was a knife. We know from verse seven that he had noticed the fire making equipment and the wood, but he doesn't mention the knife, although Abraham was carrying it. Maybe it was hidden under Abraham's clothes, and maybe Isaac had always been spared the sight of sheep having their throats cut and so did not even think a knife was necessary. I don't know.

It could be that Isaac, when he realized that *he* was the sacrifice, did not necessarily equate this with his father slitting his throat. There is no mention of a struggle, an old man trying to tie an energetic young boy down who is screaming and fighting with all his strength. It could be that Isaac knew God had commanded something very solemn concerning him and that, while perhaps somewhat fearful, his spirit was peaceful, and the emotional agony was all Abraham's.

One of the reasons why I think this might have been the case is that Isaac doesn't seem to go on to live a life marked by post-traumatic stress disorder. He marries the beautiful Rebecca. When Rebecca has difficulty conceiving, he prays to God and God answers his prayer. The problems with Isaac's character seem to have nothing to do with him seeing himself as the victim of an aborted human sacrifice. He showed favoritism to Esau over Jacob, but the dysfunctional family dynamics caused by the surrogacy arrangement his father made with Hagar was probably the chief factor here. He had no model of brothers living in harmony, equally loved by their parents. And when he felt insecure about Abimelech king of the Philistines, he repeated the sinful cycle his father Abraham had begun in passing his wife off as his sister in order to protect himself. That had nothing to do with the incident on Mount Moriah. So, Isaac may or not have been wounded psychologically. Even if he was, it seems that he grew up knowing and, for the most part, trusting God to bless him and bless his sons.

The main task of Christian parents is to bring our children up in the fear of the Lord. We're imperfect and will hurt our children through our faults and failings. Also, God may call us to do things which, at least in the short term, do bring difficulties and maybe psychological pain to our children. Godly discipline may be experienced by them as painful, even traumatic, but is necessary for their ultimate well-being. If God calls parents to move location, children may suffer the loss of friendships and the dislocation of their sense of security. I was certainly upset by the business of moving from a Staffordshire village to London when I was 13, due to my father being called to a new parish. My schoolwork and confidence temporarily suffered. But in the long term I think I was blessed spiritually, with the new church I became part of and the friends I made and new opportunities gained.

I think of my grandparents, who were called to a lifetime of mission work in South India. When my father was born to them there, he had club feet and then polio. In 1944 they sailed back to England for a six-month furlough, braving German U-boats and knowing that when they returned to India for another five year period, they would leave their little four year old boy with guardians here so he could get the medical treatment he needed. My father did suffer over this. He grew up only seeing his mother and father every five years, and yet in God's perfect plan the most important thing was that he learned to share the faith of his parents and to face the difficulties and struggles of this life trusting in the goodness and power of God.[6] Theologian Vernon Ground's wise words are relevant here.

> "An individual, quite completely free from tension, anxiety, and conflict may be only a well-adjusted sinner who is dangerously maladjusted to God; and it is infinitely better to be a neurotic saint than a healthy-minded sinner. . .. Healthy-mindedness may be a spiritual hazard that keeps an individual from turning to God precisely because he has no acute sense of God."[7]

Ultimately, all psychological wellbeing comes from knowing the love of our heavenly father and his call upon our life. If the God who has everything demands from us everything, then it is because he is God and his perfect will for us is better than anything else in this world.

---

6. See Gordon Kuhrt *Life's Not Always Easy.*

7. Vernon Grounds *Called to be Saints- Not Well-adjusted Sinners,* Christianity Today (January 17, 1986) quoted by Paul Copan in *Is God a Moral Monster?*

Chapter 15

Pestilential?

"pain is God's megaphone to rouse a deaf world"
—CS Lewis

In his chapter highlighting the God who sends judgment in the form of plagues, Barker starts with a verse quoted often by Christians when interceding for their own nation. Second Chronicles 7:14 says

> "...if my people, which are called by my name, shall humble themselves, and pray, and seek my face, and turn from their wicked ways; then I will hear from heaven, and will forgive their sin, and will heal their land."

Barker is very keen that we look at this verse in context, a concern which is not much in evidence elsewhere in his book. Nevertheless, looking at the context is of course a sound principle of biblical interpretation. It is said that if you take a text from its context you are left with a "con." Looking at the context means looking at the immediate grammatical setting and the material that comes just before and just after the passage being read. But there is always a wider context as well. What is the genre of literature and the type of situation the text addresses? What place does the passage have within the whole book, and what relevant theological principles gleaned from the whole Bible necessarily inform our understanding as we look from the general into the specific?

Barker is quite right to note that this verse is often cited as a complete sentence with the word "if" given a capital "I" as if it were the first word in the sentence. In fact, as he points out, verse thirteen provides the first clause in the sentence. The words preceding "if" go like this.

> "When I shut up the heavens so that there is no rain, or commands locusts to devour the land or send a plague among the people..."

In Barker's opinion, this negates anything merciful or majestic in verse fourteen because "the Lord Jealous" (as he refers to God) is only offering to remedy something he himself has inflicted on the people in verse thirteen because they have had the temerity to "love someone else." We are back to the assertions he made in chapter one that the biblical God is like an insecure man who feels inclined to lash out at his woman whenever someone else catches her eye. On this point, I can only refer the reader to what I said in reply in the first chapter.

Let's think more about the context of verses 13 and 14. They form part of the words spoken by God to King Solomon at the dedication of the Temple in Jerusalem. The Temple was a place where the people could come and confess their sins and through the priests offer sacrifices of atonement. However, the Temple system was not designed to give the people a license to sin. God warned Solomon that if the Israelites turned away from him and forsook his commands and went off to serve other Gods and worship them, then he would uproot Israel from the land and would reject even the magnificent, imposing Temple consecrated for his Name. Those who passed by its ruins would be appalled and ask why the LORD destroyed it and they would be told it was because of the Israelite's unfaithfulness.

The sending of plagues upon the people of Israel by God needs to be seen in the context of the overall threat to the life of the nation from the rejection of the Covenant. Israel only existed because of its relationship to its Covenant God. God was the source of its life, prosperity, unity and hope.

Ever since the Fall, humankind had been subject to spiritual alienation from God and the process of disease and death that inevitably accompanied this. Whereas in the Garden of Eden there was "ease," out of Eden there was "*dis*-ease." In his general goodness and mercy, however, God still often heals diseases and in the case of Israel, chosen for his purpose of making known his truth and glory to the nations, he undertook to continually heal them if they walked with him in faithfulness. In Exodus 15:26 God says to Moses

> "If you listen carefully to the voice of the LORD your God and do what is right in his eyes, if you pay attention to his commands

and keep all his decrees, I will not bring on you any of the diseases I brought on the Egyptians, for I am the LORD, who heals you."

When Egypt refused to let God's people go he inflicted them with pestilence and boils. This is another way of saying he withdrew his restraining hand which had hitherto kept infections at bay. When the Israelites sinned in rebellion against God, he did the same. This was not unmerciful. It *was* done in love. "Allowing" or "sending" (as the Hebrew bible puts it[1]) disease

---

1. In Hebrew/biblical culture what were regarded as secondary causes were frequently omitted and all consequences were seen in terms of the primary cause which was the action and purpose of God. In our Western culture the cause of disease is seen primarily in scientific terms. Even for Christians, God's divine activity, his "judgment" or "discipline" is very much in the background, if it features at all. But those who earnestly believe in the God of the Bible are right to consider all the spiritual questions. For example, in the 1980s, the question was raised' "is AIDS the judgment of God?" A truly biblical answer to questions like this recognises that, while things will remain mysterious, we should face the possibility that disasters might be a "judgment" of God, and not assume that the cause is a spiritually neutral one, the remedy for which lies solely in advances in healthcare and education.

However, a faithful understanding of the whole Bible, leads us to avoid the assumption that anyone suffering from AIDS (or cancer, or any other disease) is *more* sinful than anyone else. Obviously there are certain forms of behaviour which make contracting AIDS or cancer more likely, such as promiscuous unprotected sex and smoking and a repentant individual who has been involved in these things could well see that, in spiritual terms, God has "brought this upon them," along with hoping and believing in his mercy, forgiveness and healing. Also unconfessed sin and sin that is not repented of can be a block to healing. That is why the apostle James tells us to confess our sins to one another and pray for each other so that we may be healed (James 5:16). Notwithstanding this, it is wrong to say that a particular disease is necessarily a judgment of God on a particular class of people for a particular sin they have committed. It would be closer to the truth to say that AIDS and cancer are judgments on us collectively as a society. We should seek, as a society, to repent of everything which is unholy and this will result in greater health generally. We should also avoid prejudice, stigmatisation and self-righteousness and respond to people with grace and compassion. Romans 3:23 says *"All have sinned and fall short of the glory of God."*

Bible-believing Christians have been at the forefront of caring for people with AIDS. For example, Dr Patrick Dixon founded ACET (AIDS Care, Education and Training). In his work as a physician in the 1980s, Dixon began to meet patients with HIV, who had been refused care as a result of the fear and discrimination that surrounded a then largely unknown and misunderstood virus. Following the publication of his book *The Truth About AIDS*, Dixon founded ACET in 1988, as a compassionate response to the HIV pandemic. ACET grew rapidly, providing home care for HIV/AIDS patients across Greater London, as well as delivering an HIV prevention program in schools. Trained volunteers were supported by a professional team, and soon home care and schools teams developed in other parts of the UK. Independent ACET teams were also established in Uganda, Thailand, Romania and other countries. In the UK, partly as a result of campaigning by ACET, the National Health Service eventually took responsibility for the care of HIV patients.

was God's "warning system" designed to cause the Israelites to turn back to God before their nation was destroyed through its own inner corruption. Disease became part of God's sorrowful will since the Fall. His desired will is to save and heal. When Jesus came his healings were signs of that. Yet Jesus wept over Jerusalem because he knew that just as it and its Temple were destroyed by the Babylonians nearly six hundred years before he came, so it would be razed to the ground again by the Romans. Just as then, pagan swords would kill many more people than any of the diseases God sent to bring the people to their senses.

As I write we are facing the global Coronavirus pandemic. We as a family are in isolation with two of my children showing a high temperature and looking like they have the virus. Normal life is on hold. Kind parishioners are bringing us groceries and I am trying to co-ordinate pastoral care and "online church" from home. People quite justifiably ask questions like "Is this from God?" or "Why is God allowing this?" or "What is God saying to us in all this?" "Is this God's judgment?"

DISEASE AS GOD'S JUDGMENT?

It is good to define what we mean by "judgment." The biblical witness indicates that God's judgment has to do with his moral evaluation of our condition and his sentence of punishment upon sin. Judgment in the Old Testament is mainly seen in terms of God's action in this age, particularly upon the nation of Israel for its idolatry and wickedness, although his judgment comes upon other nations as well and in the case of the Flood, the whole world.

In the New Testament, judgment is mainly focused on what happens at the end of this age when Christ returns. Every knee will bow before him and recognize his authority to judge, and he will bring everyone's actions to light, making us all accountable to him. Those whose sins have not been washed away by him will receive due justice. The Greek word translated "judgment" is *krisis*, indicating that the last judgment will be the archetypal crisis for humanity.

Before then, some crises that human beings go through could be God allowing or giving us a foretaste of judgment, warning us to repent and reminding us that we are not independent masters of our destiny and the future of the universe. These crises are opportunities for us to re-evaluate what is important and return to God in humble repentance, seeking his kingdom which is an everlasting one that will not be shaken. Disasters should be seen as a wake up call to all humanity. As CS Lewis said

> "We can ignore even pleasure. But pain insists upon being attended to. God whispers to us in our pleasures, speaks in our conscience, but shouts in our pains: it is his megaphone to rouse a deaf world."

Furthermore, in the Gospels, Jesus taught that when disasters happen, whether caused directly by human beings or not, we should not assume or even speculate that those affected are more guilty of sin than anyone else.

> "Now there were some present at that time who told Jesus about the Galileans whose blood Pilate had mixed with their sacrifices. Jesus answered, 'Do you think that these Galileans were worse sinners than all the other Galileans because they suffered this way? I tell you, no! But unless you repent, you too will all perish. Or those eighteen who died when the tower in Siloam fell on them—do you think they were more guilty than all the others living in Jerusalem? I tell you, no! But unless you repent, you too will all perish."

Jesus said the two "disasters" referred to here, one an act of brutal violence and the other perhaps caused by an earthquake, were not judgments of God in the sense that they were punishments on people guilty of exceptional sinfulness. But they were judgments of God in the sense that they highlighted the fate that will befall all humanity unless we repent and turn to him. They were a foretaste of judgment for everyone, calling for radical re-evaluation of our lives on earth.

In August 1854, there was a cholera outbreak in London. Having admired the Puritan ministers who tended to the dying in the great plague of 1665, a young pastor, Charles Spurgeon, decided to curtail his many engagements in the country in order to stay and minister to the neighborhood of New Park Street Chapel. He tirelessly visited the sick and dying and his ministry had a profound impact. He later recalled,

> "In the year 1854, when I had scarcely been in London twelve months, the neighborhood in which I labored was visited by Asiatic cholera, and my congregation suffered from its inroads. Family after family summoned me to the bedside of the smitten, and almost every day I was called to visit the grave."[2]

He was more than willing to risk his own life, as were his fellow ministers.

> "All day, and sometimes all night long, I went about from house to house, and. saw men and women dying, and, oh, how glad

---

2. Charles Spurgeon, *Autobiography*, 1:371

they were to see my face! When many were afraid to enter their houses lest they should catch the deadly disease, we who had no fear about such things found ourselves most gladly listened to when we spoke of Christ and of things Divine."[3]

Alongside deep sorrow, his message of Gospel hope had this kind of effect.

"I went home, and was soon called away again; that time, to see a young woman. She also was in the last extremity, but it was a fair, fair sight. She was singing,—though she knew she was dying,—and talking to those round about her, telling her brothers and sisters to follow her to Heaven, bidding goodbye to her father, and all the while smiling as if it had been her marriage day. She was happy and blessed."[4]

In a sermon preached on 18 February 1855 Spurgeon spoke of the fear of death:

"Who is the man that does not fear to die? I will tell you. The man that is a believer. Fear to die! Thank God, I do not. The cholera may come again next summer—I pray God it may not; but if it does, it matters not to me: I will toil and visit the sick by night and by day, until I drop; and if it takes me, sudden death is sudden glory."[5]

On 12 August 1856, after another outbreak, Spurgeon preached a sermon on Amos 3:3–6:

"Do two walk together unless they have agreed to do so? Does a lion roar in the thicket when it has no prey? Does it growl in its den when it has caught nothing? Does a bird swoop down to a trap on the ground when no bait is there. Does a trap spring up from the ground if it has not caught anything? When a trumpet sounds in a city, do not the people tremble? When disaster comes to a city, has not the Lord caused it?"

The sermon was entitled "The Voice of Cholera." Spurgeon praised advances in cleanliness, better dwellings for the poor, and scientific research which had successfully mitigated the spread of cholera. He criticized those who thought that the disease should be left to its own devices. In a representative section, he says:

3. Ibid.
4. Ibid. 373
5. https://www.spurgeon.org/resource-library/sermons/spiritual-liberty#flipbook/

> "It seems to me that this disease is to a great extent in our own hands, and that if all men would take scrupulous care as to cleanliness, and if better dwellings were provided for the poor, and if overcrowding were effectually prevented, and if the water-supply could be larger, and other sanitary improvements could be carried out, the disease, most probably, would not occur; or, if it did visit us occasionally, as the result of filth in other countries, it would be in a very mitigated form. . . .The gospel has no quarrel with ventilation, and the doctrines of grace have no dispute with chloride of lime. We preach repentance and faith, but we do not denounce whitewash; and much as we advocate holiness, we always have a good word for cleanliness and sobriety."[6]

But then he goes on to say:

> "On the other hand, it is even more common for those who look to natural causes alone to sneer at believers who view the disease as a mysterious scourge from the hand of God. It is admitted that it would be most foolish to neglect the appointed means of averting sickness; but sneer who may, we believe it to be equally an act of folly to forget that the hand of the Lord is in all this. . .
>
> "If you ask me what I think to be the design, I believe it to be this—to waken up our indifferent population, to make them remember that there is a God, to render them susceptible of the influences of the gospel, to drive them to the house of prayer, to influence their minds to receive the Word, and moreover to startle Christians into energy and earnestness, that they may work while it is called to-day.
>
> "Already I have been told by Christian brethren laboring in the east of London, that there is a greater willingness to listen to gospel truth, and that if there be a religious service it is more acceptable to the people now than it was; for which I thank God as an indication that affliction is answering its purpose."[7]

On 18 January 1857 Spurgeon spoke of the conviction that the cholera epidemic brought, but then how many had subsequently turned away from God.

> "How many of the same sort of confessions, too, have we seen in times of cholera, and fever, and pestilence! Then our churches have been crammed with hearers, who, because so many funerals have passed their doors, or so many have died in the street, could not refrain from going up to God's house to confess their sins.

---

6. https://www.spurgeon.org/resource-library/sermons/the-voice-of-the-cholera#flipbook/

7. Ibid.

And under that visitation, when one, two, and three have been lying dead in the house, or next door, how many have thought they would really turn to God! But, alas! when the pestilence had done its work, conviction ceased; and when the bell had tolled the last time for a death caused by cholera, then their hearts ceased to beat with penitence, and their tears did flow no more."[8]

I believe, like Spurgeon, God is sovereign over pathogenic viruses just as he is sovereign over everything else. If a pandemic happens it is not God's desired will, but it is his sorrowful, permissive, will. We do all we can to limit the spread of harmful viruses but if we want to know why an all-loving, all powerful God has allowed our defenses to be breached, it must be to further his purposes in bringing people to salvation. The greatest virus is the sin virus, which affects all and is transmitted by all, and which causes not only death but the fearful dread of death. The only antidote to this dread is faith and trust in the Lord Jesus Christ, the one to whom the whole Bible points.

---

8. https://www.spurgeon.org/resource-library/sermons/confession-of-sin-a-sermon-with-seven-texts#flipbook/

Chapter 16

Megalomaniacal?

megalomania (noun): *a mental disorder producing delusions of grandeur*

—Oxford English Dictionary

A megalomaniac is someone who believes they are much more powerful or important than they really are.

If God is an eternal and infinite being, the one who created the universe and sustains it by his power; if he is omnipotent and omniscient, the fountain of wisdom and love as the Bible claims, then his grandeur is beyond our imagination. Words cannot fully express his glory and magnificence. It is obviously ludicrous to say God is deluded about his greatness when he really is as great as it is possible to be and when he is also the source of all sanity and right judgment.

Barker tries to prove his point (or more accurately, Dawkins's point) by listing numerous verses where God is praised for his glory and suggests that because these are part of Scripture, God must be keen on all this "flattery." Barker is doing here what he does throughout his book. He takes a characteristic that we would rightly deplore in a human being and projects this on to the biblical God and says, in effect, "we don't like people who enjoy taking all the glory, so why should we respect a God who seeks glory from his people and from all the nations of the earth?" What he fails to notice is that the verses he cites are freely given and natural outbursts of praise from those who know and love God and enjoy praising him. It is true that the biblical God does have a concern for the glory of his Name, but does this necessarily mean that God is an unpleasant character? It could indicate that he is zealous for what is rightfully his and what is good for human beings to appreciate. (See chapter one).

In human beings, creatures made by God to reflect his glory, humility is an important virtue. Humility is not, however, an emotionally unhealthy belief that we are useless and incapable of achieving anything of significance. If it were, it would be as wrong as megalomania. True humility is the virtue of knowing who we are in relation to God. We are his creatures, capable of amazing things, but also dangerously flawed. A humble person is responsive to the views and opinions of others because they realize that they need the perspective of others to see things that they themselves may not be able to see. A humble person recognizes their limitations, even when they are aware that they have unique gifts and capabilities. They recognize the truth of Jesus' teaching that true greatness lies in serving others. A person of humility has the inner peace and security of knowing that they are loved, accepted and deeply significant for who they are and do not have to prove it by demonstrating their superiority over others. A humble person makes others around them feel good about themselves, even as those others recognize and celebrate the humble person's gifts and achievements.

Is humility a quality we could possibly see in the God of the universe? If humility meant denying one's own attributes, then of course God could not be humble. But if humility includes being secure in who you are, valuing the perspective of others, being willing to think of others before ourselves, and being a person around whom people flourish and are able to express themselves, then the God of the Old Testament could indeed be said to be humble.

God was under no obligation to create human beings but did so out of a desire to love and be loved. He used to walk with Adam and Eve in the garden of Eden "in the cool of the day," suggesting that he, the God of everything, enjoyed their company.[1] God delegated Adam and Eve to exercise stewardship over the earth.[2] He allows us freedom. He does not micro-manage. God enters into frank conversations with those he chooses. He confides in Abraham and permits Abraham to question him over his justice,[3] He allows Jacob to wrestle with him and indeed names his chosen people Israel which means "he who struggles with God."[4] Throughout the

1. Genesis 3:8
2. Ibid. 1:28
3. Ibid. 18:16–33
4. Ibid. 32:22–32

psalms God clearly values the honest expression of views and emotions directed to himself.[5] The biblical God loves his people, rejoicing over them with singing,[6] planning good things for them.[7] He even invites them all to a banquet of choice meat and fine wine[8] and "prepares a table for them" in the way a servant would.[9] Jesus of course showed the humble love of God throughout his ministry on earth, but the humility of God is there in the Old Testament too.

---

5. E.g., Psalms, 10:1; 13:1–3; 22; 64:1; 74:10
6. Zephaniah 3:17
7. Jeremiah 29:11
8. Isaiah 25:6
9. Psalm 23:5

Chapter 17

Sadomasochistic?

Sadist (Noun): *"a person who takes pleasure in inflicting pain, punishment, or humiliation on others"*

—Merriam-Webster Dictionary

As I said in the introduction, Dawkins alleges that the crucifixion of Christ shows God's masochistic nature. If Jesus is God incarnate, why should torturing himself to death be necessary for him to forgive our sins? I will deal with this claim in the final chapter of this book. In his seventeenth chapter Barker does cite Isaiah 53:10 "Yet it was the LORD's will to crush him and cause him to suffer." However, he does not explicitly link this to the cross of Jesus. Throughout this chapter he concentrates on the charge that God is a sadist. He alleges first that the God of the Bible liked to threaten *sexual violence* against the people of Israel and secondly, that he is said in several places in Scripture to want us to *fear* him.

The accusation of sexual abuse would be a startling one, were we not used by now to the kind of misrepresentations made about the God of the Bible. We have already seen the accusation that God is an insecure lover, unable to countenance any freedom of choice for his beloved. In chapter one we answered the "jealous and proud of it" slur and in chapter nine we saw how God is not misogynistic. Feminine imagery is used in speaking of beauty, purity and glory as well as shame and infidelity. We've also seen that in Scripture when God warns his people that he will inflict disaster upon them if they refuse to repent of their wickedness, and he must follow through with this, he does so with a heavy heart. The terrors of his judgment are part of his sorrowful will. The disasters that befall his people are of their own making, but even then, God in his mercy and faithfulness works for their ultimate redemption.

An honest and open reading of Isaiah chapter one is enough to put to shame the insinuations of people like Barker and Dawkins. It is worth setting out the bulk of this chapter below so that the reader can have the chance to hear God speak.

> "Hear me, you heavens! Listen, earth! For the Lord has spoken: 'I reared children and brought them up, but they have rebelled against me. The ox knows its master, the donkey its owner's manger, but Israel does not know, my people do not understand.' Woe to the sinful nation, a people whose guilt is great, a brood of evildoers, children given to corruption! They have forsaken the LORD; they have spurned the Holy One of Israel and turned their backs on him.
>
> "Why should you be beaten anymore? Why do you persist in rebellion? Your whole head is injured, your whole heart afflicted. From the sole of your foot to the top of your head, there is no soundness— only wounds and welts and open sores, not cleansed or bandaged or soothed with olive oil.
>
> "Your country is desolate, your cities burned with fire; your fields are being stripped by foreigners right before you, laid waste as when overthrown by strangers. The Daughter Zion is left like a shelter in a vineyard, like a hut in a cucumber field, like a city under siege. Unless the Lord Almighty had left us some survivors we would have become like Sodom, we would have been like Gomorrah.
>
> "Your hands are full of blood! Wash and make yourselves clean. Take your evil deeds out of my sight; stop doing wrong. Learn to do right; seek justice. Defend the oppressed. Take up the cause of the fatherless; plead the case of the widow. Come now, let us settle the matter', says the Lord. 'Though your sins are like scarlet, they shall be as white as snow; though they are red as crimson, they shall be like wool. If you are willing and obedient, you will eat the good things of the land; but if you resist and rebel, you will be devoured by the sword.' For the mouth of the Lord has spoken. See how the faithful city has become a prostitute! She once was full of justice; righteousness used to dwell in her— but now murderers! Your silver has become dross, your choice wine is diluted with water.

"Your rulers are rebels, partners with thieves, they all love bribes and chase after gifts. They do not defend the cause of the fatherless; the widow's case does not come before them. Therefore, the Lord, the Lord Almighty, the Mighty One of Israel, declares: 'Ah! I will vent my wrath on my foes and avenge myself on my enemies. I will turn my hand against you; I will thoroughly purge away your dross and remove all your impurities. I will restore your leaders as in days of old, your rulers as at the beginning. Afterward you will be called the City of Righteousness, the Faithful City.'

"Zion will be delivered with justice, her penitent ones with righteousness. But rebels and sinners will both be broken, and those who forsake the LORD will perish. You will be ashamed because of the sacred oaks in which you have delighted; you will be disgraced because of the gardens that you have chosen. You will be like an oak with fading leaves, like a garden without water. The mighty man will become tinder and his work a spark; both will burn together, with no one to quench the fire."[1]

Isaiah prophesied to the southern kingdom of Judah during the eighth and seventh centuries before Christ. The cruel Assyrian Empire was the dominant force in this period of history. In 722 BC it invaded the northern kingdom of Israel, whose capital was Samaria and deported and scattered its population, replacing them with others from around its Empire. Judah and Jerusalem, protected by God, were spared a similar fate, but Isaiah warned that unless there was true repentance disaster would eventually come to them as well.

As if the passionate call from Isaiah for the nation to come to its senses was not enough, God later sent another prophet, Jeremiah, to urge the people to turn back to him as time was running out. Jeremiah suffered greatly for his calling. He was arrested and beaten, thrown down a well, mocked and continually resisted by the false prophets and rulers who hated his message. Yet he had God's heart for the people and carried on despite all this hateful opposition.

So this makes its all the more iniquitous that Barker claims the message of this courageous and sensitive man, who deeply loved his God and his people, and who served them at deep personal cost, was one of divine molestation and abuse.

In sorrow Jeremiah prophesies that pain will grip the nation as suddenly as labor comes on a pregnant woman. Like a woman who is humiliated and raped, the people of Judah will suffer at the hands of the Babylonians.

1. Isaiah 1:2–9, 16–31

God takes no perverted sexual pleasure in this. It is abhorrent to him, but it was the consequence that a proud and rebellious people had to face through the outworking of their sinful choices. Barker particularly homes in, out of context on Jeremiah 13:26 saying this shows that God is a rapist. This verse *is* a terrible one, as are many others throughout the prophets. Verses thirteen and fourteen together say this

> "I will pull up your skirts over your face that your shame may be seen—your adulteries and lustful neighings, your shameless prostitution."

What God is warning the people of here is that their shame will be exposed. The human and animal imagery used is feminine but as even Barker manages to realize (although he descends to smuttiness as regards the *Song of Songs*) that is because throughout Scripture masculine to feminine imagery is used of his relationship with Israel. Although rape was (and still is in most cases) a consequence of war and invasion, you have to approach this passage with a wooden literalism to think that God is guilty of the kind of things Barker accuses him of. Ever since the Fall from grace in the garden of Eden, humankind, both men and women, have had a sense of shame, reflected in our need to cover up our bodies. Most of the time our shameful thoughts, words and deeds are hidden from others by our skill in doing this or by God's mercy, but there are times in Scripture when God's judgment breaks through and all is laid bare. Jesus issued a similar warning in Luke 12:2–3,

> "There is nothing concealed that will not be disclosed, or hidden that will not be made known. What you have said in the dark will be heard in the daylight, and what you have whispered in the ear in the inner rooms will be proclaimed from the roofs."

Does God want us to fear him? The answer is "no" if by "fear" we mean any emotion caused by a lack of understanding as to his true character. He doesn't want us to fear him because of how he is portrayed by Dawkins and Barker. We have no reason to fear that God is a cruel, unforgiving, unjust, vindictive, tyrannical monster. But if we understand the word "fear" to mean, in the biblical context, the showing of appropriate respect and reverence, yes indeed we should "fear" him. His light penetrates all the dark and sordid areas of our lives. His purity burns hotter than the blazing sun. His love is such that to shut ourselves off from it is unimaginably lonely and hellish. His truth destroys all the comfortable lies in which we clothe ourselves. In this sense we should fear him. Only the most foolish of fools would not.

Chapter 18

Capriciously Malevolent?

"Surely I spoke of things I did not understand, things too wonderful for me to know"
—Job 42:3

Barker sees little of value in the book of Job and says, "it makes the God of the Old Testament the most malevolent creature in all fiction."
His summary of the book is this caricature:

GOD: "Job is a good man. I will torture him to see if he stays good."

JOB: "Why is God punishing me?"

JOB'S FRIENDS: "It must be your own fault."

JOB: "I am undeserving, but it's not my fault."

ELIHU: "God is greater than all of us."

GOD: "Yes, I am greater than all of you."

JOB: "You are powerful. I'm sorry."

GOD: "Correct answer. I'll stop torturing you now."

Barker continues, "that's it. There is no moral lesson in those forty-two chapters. No answer to suffering. No reasons, no redeeming social value to the graphic violence. The point of the book is simply: "The Lord is powerful.

He can make you suffer. Don't ask why. Be faithful. Might makes right. God can do whatever he wants."

For Barker, the salient points are that this book has God boasting to Satan about his "poster boy" Job, who is blameless and upright, a man who fears God and shuns evil. Satan retorts that he is only good because God has enabled him to prosper. God then says that Satan can take away everything he has, but not directly attack him. That is what happens. Job loses everything. His sons, daughters, servants, cattle, sheep and camels—all killed or stolen. But despite this he does not sin by charging God with wrongdoing.

Barker then seizes on chapter two verse three as the most damning verse in the Old Testament.

> "Then the LORD said to Satan, 'have you considered my servant Job? There is no-one on earth like him; he is blameless and upright, a man who fears God and shuns evil. And he still maintains his integrity, *though you incited me against him to ruin him without any reason*.'"

Satan then raises the stakes with another proposed wager with God. He says that Job only really cared for *himself* and that if God strikes Job's own flesh and bones he would curse God to his face.

> God replies. "Very well, then, he is in your hands, but you must spare his life."

With that Satan goes out from the presence of the LORD and inflicts loathsome sores all over Job's body, and he scrapes himself with broken pottery as he sits among the ashes. Even his wife tells him to curse God and die.

So, there we have it. God unnecessarily exposes Job to Satan's attention by pointing him out boastfully. When Satan is unimpressed, God enters into what looks like a wager over bragging rights. Job suffers enormously because of this but even when his own wife wants him to charge God with being evil, he refuses and says, "shall we accept good from God and not trouble?"

The seventeenth century *Authorized Version* of the Bible (also called the *King James* version) which Barker likes to quote a lot, translates this last statement "shall we accept good from God and not *evil*." Near the end of the story, when a vindicated Job prays for his friends, the KJV says that they comforted him over all the "evil" which the LORD had brought upon him.

Throughout the book, Job is aware that all that is happening to him is from God. He does not take refuge in the argument that Satan is operating without God's license.

"For he [God] crushes me with a tempest, and multiplies my wounds without cause.[1] You made me and now you turn and destroy me.[2] The arrows of the Almighty are in me, my spirit drinks their poison, the terrors of God are arrayed against me."[3]

Although at the end of the story, God gives Job a new family and restores his health and wealth and blesses the latter part of his life more than the first, Barker still triumphantly concludes that God is evil because he sent evil on Job for no good reason. He even says that Dawkins understated it when he called God a capriciously malevolent bully. God is actually "an evil terrorist." Can this interpretation of the book of Job be answered?

I recently officiated at the burial of a young victim of a road traffic accident, caused by the careless driving of another person. Not long ago I took the funeral of a young mother who died of cancer. In Mozambique, as I write, a cyclone has devastated communities. Most of the pain and suffering in the world, including traffic accidents, is easily traceable to the actions of human beings, but cancer and cyclones are less straightforwardly accounted for. Even things for which we clearly bear responsibility for like road deaths often seem to affect the innocent as much as the guilty. So why doesn't God intervene more to make the world a safer and more just place? Where is God when it hurts? Doesn't God care or understand? Are some things beyond his reach? Is God sympathetic but powerless in some situations?

The book of Job confronts this question without giving easy answers. But would we *want* simplistic answers to the question of suffering? Job's friends come to comfort him, and they start well by identifying with his pain and sitting in silence with him for seven days. When Job starts to pour out his perplexed anguish however, the friends start to enter a theological debate with him as to why he is suffering—a debate that doesn't end well. God basically reprimands them at the end of the book for misrepresenting him and only forgives them after a sacrifice and a prayer from Job himself. This alone should lead us to be reticent about commenting on what might lie behind other people's suffering.

---

1. Job 9:17
2. Ibid. 10:8
3. Ibid. 6:4

WHAT NON-BIBLICAL BELIEF SYSTEMS SAY ABOUT SUFFERING

Krish Kandiah in his book *Paradoxology*[4] outlines the ways some religious and philosophical traditions approach the question of the cause of suffering. The simplest answer is given by the "new atheists" like Dawkins. For Dawkins it is just silly and pointless to ask the question "why is there suffering?" There is nothing beyond the materialist universe and the world of atoms, molecules, genes and physical laws operates with "blind, pitiless indifference." In a random world some are unlucky, that's all. It is interesting that Dawkins uses emotive language for the outworking of unguided fate. We suspect he might recognize that it is wrong for someone to walk past another human being in need and respond with "blind, pitiless indifference," but if that is what the universe is essentially like, from where do we get the sense that blindness, pitilessness and indifference are bad things?

Some people say things like "the universe seems so cruel and unjust, I just can't believe in a God who lets it be that way." CS Lewis admitted that this was his rationale until his conversion. But then the thought occurred to him that ultimately, atheism removes any basis for judging things as cruel and unjust. He realized that if there is no God, then where could he have got the feeling that things could and should be better? Intellectually consistent atheists are few because the logical consequences are so bleak. "Blind, pitiless, indifference" is not a great strapline for world that wants hope, meaning and purpose.

A more popular philosophy about what causes suffering comes from Hinduism. The doctrine of Karma has as its basis the pantheistic belief that the highest form of God is not a deity separate and distinct from creation but is one with everything. The presence of the divine spirit is in everyone—you, me, Jesus, Buddha, the trees, the stars, and the great white whale migrating north. The answers to suffering lie in the concept of the divine cycle of life. We are immortal souls temporarily inhabiting various bodies, human and animal. All our actions, good and bad, produce karma. Good karma blesses us in our future lives while bad karma affects us negatively, reducing our wellbeing and status. The idea of karma has been incorporated into various New Age beliefs, popular today with those who like to think of themselves as "spiritual" but not affiliated to a particular religion. In February 1999, the England football (soccer) manager, Glenn Hoddle, a man influenced by such spiritual beliefs, was sacked by the Football Association. A journalist reported that he had told him that for disabled children, as

---

4. Kandiah, *Paradoxology*, 88–93

opposed to people with "half-decent brains" like themselves, "the karma was working from a different lifetime."

The doctrine of *karma* is most enshrined on the Indian subcontinent, where Hindus absorb the belief that those in lower caste poverty deserve their lot because of their sins in previous lives and it is their own responsibility to generate better karma for themselves for the future. Compassion towards orphans and widows has to come from the committed Christians (themselves now persecuted by emboldened Hindu nationalists) who believe in a compassionate, personal God and has revealed in Scriptures like Job that there is no simplistic link between suffering and sin. Furthermore, the doctrine of reincarnation is clearly refuted in the Bible. We have one life to live in this age and then we die and face judgment.[5]

Buddhism is another belief system people in the West superficially endorse without really understanding. This teaches that pain and suffering is caused by the cultivation of earthly desires. An important goal of Buddhism is to cultivate, through meditation, a detachment from the world. The more detachment we succeed in, the less we will be troubled by our own pain and suffering and that of others. Ultimate bliss is *Nirvana*—the final absorption into the "divine reality" where all desires and attachments cease.

So broadly, the answers of atheism, Hinduism and Buddhism to the cause of suffering are bad luck, bad karma and bad desires. The remedy according to atheism is to promote science over superstition. The solution in Hinduism is to live purer lives in our current station. The answer for the Buddhist is to detach ourselves from desire. New Age pantheists combine the latter two ideas and say we must realize the divine within us.

HOW THE BOOK OF JOB RESPONDS TO A PROBLEM UNIQUE TO BIBLICAL FAITH

All this is very different from the Bible's teaching. The Bible reveals that God is omnipotent, separate and distinct from his creation. His essential nature is love. Desire is a good thing if it is channeled towards the source of all truth and goodness i.e., him. God is all-knowing. He is personal. He thinks and feels. He acts in human history. So, if God is all-powerful and all-loving, then the question "why do bad things happen to good people?" is a particularly Judeo-Christian one. Our natural cry is to echo the psalmist by asking "what is going on?"

How does the book of Job help? Those who think they are sophisticated are full of indignation at the idea of God literally making a wager

5. Hebrews 9:27

with Satan in the courts of Heaven about how well his boy will stand up under pressure, but if they really were being sophisticated they would recognize the kind of poetic wisdom genre of literature this book belongs to. Understanding something in a deeper way than the crudely literal, does not automatically remove theological problems, but it does help us to take a more nuanced and intelligent approach to certain Scriptures. Also, there is the concept of divine accommodation. Scripture uses myth, metaphor, parable and anthropomorphisms to convey what is necessary to reveal the character and purposes of God and provide for our salvation. Calvin said that, just as adults "lisp" when speaking to children, God puts things in the words of Scripture that we able to comprehend.

One of the central principles of the book of Job is that there is hidden wisdom in the counsels of God that we do not have access to. However, in chapters one and two we are given some insight, but in a way that it is possible for us to relate to on some level. God chose to do this whilst no doubt knowing that some would, culpably, mistake divine accommodation for a depiction of a crude and worldly way of operating.

What I think God wants us to learn from the opening scene of the book is that he is all-powerful in relation to Job's life. Satan cannot do anything to Job without God's permission. God is a personal being who knows what is going on and is in overall control. This speaks against the idea of a dualistic universe where God and Satan, good and evil are equally matched and doggedly slog it out with each other for eternity. But the fact that God is all-powerful does not, contra Barker, mean that "might is right." Throughout the book God allows Job to question his justice and a humble Job is vindicated before his friends at the end.

We see also that suffering is not always deserved. Obviously bad decisions often lead to bad outcomes. If I'm lazy and thoughtless, I'm not likely to get far in life. If I'm violent and unstable, I'm likely to come to a sticky end. If I'm selfish and cruel I'm likely to end up friendless and alone. But the reverse is not always true. Bad things do sometimes happen to *relatively* good people—even people known personally to God. God declared Job innocent of the things his friends assumed he must be guilty of. Job and his friends believed that God was good and all-powerful, but the issue that throws them into forty chapters of tormented debate is "can a great and a good God allow the innocent to suffer?" The friends don't see how he can. However they wrap it up, they have to claim that Job must in some way deserve what he got. They say he should find refuge in admitting his wrongdoing and becoming respectable again, submitting to their wisdom, as others had learned from his in times gone by. They say much that is true in itself and in line with lots of the Old Testament, about God's justice, wisdom, rewards to the righteous, his condemnation of the wicked, but they fail to factor in the possibility that innocent, undeserved suffering might be within the mysterious purposes of God.

For Job, this adds insult to injury because he is convinced that he has been true to his reputation as a godly, righteous person. He could find within himself nothing to merit the extreme disasters which had befallen him. All he has left is his integrity. He will not concede that the world works the way his friends think. He knows there must be some other answer which, if only he could present his case before God, would come to light.

As Job becomes increasingly desperate as his strength ebbs away, he still refuses to go along with the conventional wisdom. One of the testaments to Job's heroism is that God honored him with an insight into an eternal hope. If Job's only hope lay in restoration in this life, unjust suffering lasting a lifetime and ending in death presented even more of an agonizing problem to a believer in a great and good God. As he cried out for pity from his friends he exclaims "O that my words were recorded, that they were written on a scroll, that they were inscribed with an iron tool on lead or engraved on rock forever. I know that my redeemer lives and that in the end he will stand upon the earth. And after my skin has been destroyed, yet in my flesh I will see God. I will see him with my own eyes—I, and not another."[6]

Job's words have been enshrined in Scripture for all time for us to read. And furthermore, Job spoke prophetically of the bodily resurrection, that he, Job would rise to see God with his identity intact, honored and vindicated into eternity. Very few people in the Old Testament got this insight.

In chapter thirty-eight God finally speaks to Job out of the storm, out of the turmoil of his circumstances. At first sight it looks as if God is speaking to him harshly, considering all he has been through. "Who is this that darkens my counsel with words without knowledge? Brace yourself like a man; I will question you and you shall answer me."

God doesn't tell Job about his wager with Satan, perhaps because the scene in the courts of heaven represents, in a simple and striking way, something about the reasons God allows suffering only those who know the full resurrection story can grasp. God always acts to promote his own glory, which is good for us because it means he will always act with justice, integrity and in a way that will cause us to praise, worship and adore him. If God appears to allow things that diminish his glory like the suffering of his faithful servants like Job and the prophets and ultimately his son Jesus on the cross, it is only then to double-trump Satan by showing his resurrection power. The resulting end game brings even more glory to God because, seen

---

6. Job 19:25–27

in the light of the resurrection, innocent suffering becomes an eternal badge of honor for those who trust in God.

Job might not know the full story and receive an intellectual answer to all his questions, just as we don't get all the specific, detailed answers to our own struggles, even if we know the resurrection hope, but he did get an encounter with the living God, who spoke to him. God knows what we need more than we do. He revealed himself to Job in just the way he needed. Job's struggle to present his case arose out of the question burning in his heart. "God, what is going on? It doesn't make sense to me. Do you really know what you are doing? Have you forgotten me? Has something gone wrong? Where are you? I need you. Turn up, in Heaven's name."

When God does turn up, it is not with point by point explanations, but in a way that reminds Job that he is, after all, Almighty God. God's speech is designed to reach Job on a deeply emotional and therapeutic level rather than on an intellectual and philosophical one. God gave Job a blast of awe. Maybe he gave him a pictorial display of his creative majesty while he was talking to him. Far from being harsh, God is playfully and maybe even humorously showing Job he really does know what he is doing. The God who made billions of galaxies and designed subatomic particles smiled at Job "Are you really going to doubt my competence Job?"

A few years ago, I went on a retreat to Aberdeenshire in Scotland and stayed at a place called Blairmore House. During the Second World War it was used as a training base for members of the Special Operations Executive (SOE). This consisted of civilians who volunteered to go behind enemy lines in the occupied territories of Europe and work with partisans, harrying Nazi forces, blowing up strategic railways, bridges, factories and causing as much disruption as they could. Although there were heroic successes, there were also many failures. Many SOE operatives were captured, tortured and shot and many more resistance nationals were tortured and killed too. Reprisals on communities were harsh. If there was a successful operation, local civilians were often rounded up and executed by the Gestapo. MI6, the intelligence service, did not particularly like the SOE. They thought it was too amateurish and although the individuals in the SOE were brave, they caused too much trouble for too little gain. But Churchill believed that, although their actions resulted in many failures and many allied deaths, their overall effect, in terms of raising the morale of the resistance groups and showing that Britain hadn't given up on Europe, was worth the cost. Churchill even borrowed a phrase from Tertullian, a second century church father, and reminded MI6 that "the blood of the martyrs is the seed of the church." In other words, he judged that the suffering was not in vain and would eventually help the cause of victory.

Well if human leaders can make these kinds of judgments in which valiant people seeking to serve can be horribly tortured and ordinary civilians can be shot or hung, how much more can God be competent in doing so? In Dostoyevski's novel *The Brothers Karamasov*, Alyosha a young novice monk faces the hostile argument from his brother Ivan that God could not be all-powerful and all-loving because he should have foreseen that giving us free will would result in terrible suffering for children and other innocents. He said that no good person could go ahead and create a universe which allowed the inevitability of child torture.

But the message of Job is that God can be trusted to be God. He is competent to weigh up whether creating the universe in the way he has brings him a glory and results in a human joy which outweighs the pain and suffering. The resurrection of Christ tells us that God can reverse the cruelty and destruction of sin and triumph over it. The cross and the last judgment tells us that all suffering due to human wickedness will be avenged. The book of Job tells us that God is God and knows what he is doing.

At the end of the book Job is blessed with a deeper knowledge of God. He says "my ears had heard of you but now my eyes have seen you."[7] God vindicates Job and tells his three friends that they have spoken falsely whereas Job had been true. The three friends had to offer a sacrifice and God forgave them when Job prayed for them. After this God restored to Job twice as much wealth as he had before. He had another seven sons and three daughters.

This is a kind of resurrection, as much as the Old Testament could know. The innocent suffering of Job points forward to the innocent suffering of Jesus on the cross. When we suffer and maintain faith, we are not further away from God but closer to him. Philippians 3:10 speaks of having intimate friendship with Christ through sharing his sufferings. We who live this side of the cross have even more reason than Job to trust that when God seems to be absent, he is in fact working things out for the good of those who love him.[8] As Krish Kandiah says "we worship a God who acted decisively to deal with suffering, and a God skillful, reliable and wise enough to be trusted in the darkest times."[9]

---

7. Job 42:5
8. Romans 8:28
9. Kandiah, *Paradoxology*, 111

Chapter 19

Bully?

bully (noun): *"one who is habitually cruel, insulting, or threatening to others who are weaker, smaller, or in some way vulnerable"*

MERRIAM-WEBSTER DICTIONARY

We've reached the final word in Dawkins' tirade. Barker applauds the choice of the noun "bully" to follow the sixteen nasty adjectives and two other pejorative nouns. He says that using the word "tyrant" or "dictator" would be to give God too much respect, since they are words more fitting to describe real people like Hitler and Genghis Khan. God, he says, is more like a fictional villain such as Cruella de Vil, or a playground brat who enjoys throwing his weight around till an adult arrives on the scene. We are the grown up, he claims, and before our mature gaze God withers, like a typical school bully.

So what is the main source material Barker reaches for to justify the culmination of Dawkins's indignant charge sheet? It is God's sending of ten plagues upon Egypt when Pharaoh refused to let Moses and the Israelites go as recorded in the book of Exodus!

When Dawkins first wrote *The God Delusion* his paragraph about the Old Testament God came to the notice of the Chief Rabbi in England who called it anti-Semitic.[1] Dawkins assures us in his new introduction

---

1. I prefer the term "anti-Jewish" to "anti-Semitic." The Semitic peoples (descendants of Shem) include not just Jews but Arabs. What is often described as "anti-Semitism" is

to the tenth anniversary edition that he then got a "gracious and charming apology" after he had told the Chief Rabbi he was not just singling out the Jewish Old Testament God for vitriol but also thought the central doctrine of the atonement regarding the New Testament "Christian" God was obnoxious too.[2] If this is indeed what happened, then I think the Chief Rabbi apologized too quickly. His first instincts were not far off. Generally speaking, Dawkins is more scathing about the Old Testament than the New. Furthermore, the Hebrew Scriptures provide the basis for the Christian faith regarding the need for atonement. So an attack on the concept of the atonement is a further, indirect, attack on those Scriptures. Reading Barker's chapter in support of Dawkins's "bully" accusation, one can feel the hatred he exudes to Jewish people because of his spiritual antipathy to the God of their Bible.

Barker describes the Passover festival as a celebration of the murder of Egyptian children by the God of the Old Testament. He says the lamb's blood they smeared on their door frames was "apparently. . . the only way God's Angel of Death could tell the difference between the bad innocent children and the good innocent children. Jews all over the world annually rejoice over that non-difference, happy that *they* [sic] are the good chosen people."[3]

Barker says the infliction of this plague was "unnecessarily cruel and unfair" but says a "perverse case" could be made for its utility in allowing the Jews to escape. But he then questions the point of first nine plagues. He says "the God of the Old Testament, being omniscient, would have known

---

specifically hatred of Jewish people, and Arabs are often at the forefront of this enmity. There are certainly links between racism and anti-Jewish attitudes, but anti-Jewishness has a much longer history than relatively modern racist ideas. Much of it is theological and spiritual. The New Testament recognizes that Jewish people who do not accept Jesus as the Messiah are "enemies" of Christians in one sense (Romans 11:28) There was strong persecution of believers in Jesus by Jewish authorities in the first two centuries after Christ and to this day in many orthodox Jewish communities a believer in Jesus will be ostracized. However the Bible (Romans 9–11) also says that Christians must respect Jewish people as the original elect people of God, love them, pray for them, and understand that God has not finished with them as an entity, but will one day bring a great many of them into a saving relationship with Christ, with huge blessing for the whole world. Tragically, Christians throughout history have frequently ignored the New Testament teaching about this and have allowed a spirit of anti-Jewish hatred to get a foothold, with terribly evil consequences such as blood libels, legal oppression, pogroms and of course the Holocaust. Anti-Jewishness is alive and well today all over the world. The antidote is to love Jesus, the Jewish Son of God, by trusting and obeying God's Word in both Testaments.

2. Dawkins *The God Delusion*, 118

3. In fact the suffering of the Egyptians *is* acknowledged by Jewish people when they observe the Passover, even though they rightly celebrate the freedom God brought them.

that the first nine plagues would have had no effect. In fact he "hardened Pharaoh's heart" so that he would resist. Why? If the final plague was the clincher, why did God bother with the first nine?" He answers his own question by saying that those plagues were just the wanton violence of a bully.

So is this claim justified by the Exodus story? According to Genesis, Jacob's favorite son Joseph was, under the providential hand of God, sold into slavery in Egypt by his jealous brothers. In Egypt, after some ups and downs, God enabled him to become Pharaoh's prime minister because of his wisdom in interpreting dreams and preparing Egypt to survive and prosper during an international famine. Joseph's brothers came to Egypt to beg for food and Joseph revealed himself to them. He forgave them and invited them all and his aged father to come and live in Egypt with him. The Egyptians welcomed them initially but a few hundred years later, when the Israelites had multiplied from seventy people to thousands, and there was a Pharaoh on the throne who knew nothing of what Joseph the Israelite had done for them, the Egyptians considered them as unwelcome immigrants and a security threat. They put them to forced labor and treated them cruelly. They even put to death the baby boys by throwing them into the Nile, to limit their population expansion.

Under God's plan, one Hebrew boy hidden in the bulrushes, Moses, survived and was brought up in the palace as the adopted son of a princess. When he grew to manhood, he saw the oppression of his people but didn't know how to help. His attempt at intervening failed and he fled Egypt to spend forty years in the desert. During this time though God was preparing him to return to Egypt and confront Pharaoh in his strength with the demand to "let God's people go." When Pharaoh refused to be impressed with the miraculous signs Moses gave of his commission from God, the plagues began.[4]

The Exodus account does indeed say that God "hardened Pharaoh's heart" so that, as the plagues made life in Egypt progressively worse, this did not result in him letting the Israelites go. I discussed this point in chapter twelve. It is the Bible's way of saying that God withdrew his grace from Pharaoh leaving him to the stubborn devices of his own sinful nature. The nine plagues were judgments upon Pharaoh, the cruel slave-drivers and the gods and people of Egypt. Barker makes out that the situation is one of a bully unfairly targeting an undeserving victim. Egypt was hardly that. It was a world superpower. The Bible emphasizes the ruthlessness with which the Egyptians oppressed the Israelites. They were made to build cities and

---

4. The first nine plagues were blood, frogs, gnats, flies, livestock disease, boils, hail, locusts and darkness.

work the fields. When they continued to multiply, the Egyptians threw baby Hebrew boys into the Nile.

Egypt was thoroughly deserving of the plagues and Pharaoh was fully culpable for the necessity of the final plague, which was qualitatively different to the others. It was indeed terrible. God was to send the Angel of Death to kill the firstborn son of every household. Was this just? Well Egypt had killed the baby sons of Israel (and not just the firstborn) and it was enslaving and abusing a nation God regarded as his first-born son.[5] Furthermore, it was defying the will of God despite the warnings which the earlier plagues represented.

However, the final act of judgment was not just more terrible than the ones beforehand, it was also different in that the Israelites had to carefully follow divine instructions in order to be spared the same judgment coming upon themselves. This might seem strange. The Israelites had been spared some or all of the other plagues with the LORD showing a distinction between the Egyptians and the Israelites.[6] Wasn't God's issue just with the Egyptians? Why was the Israelites' escape now conditional on obeying a ritual command?

This is where we see that when it comes to the most serious and dreadful kind of judgment, God's holy and just nature means that he cannot simply overlook the evil committed by some, even if they are his chosen people. Ezekiel 20:1–12 tells us that God revealed himself to the Israelites while they were still in Egypt, promised that he would rescue them and lead them to a beautiful land, flowing with milk and honey, and told them to get rid of the vile Egyptian images and idols they had set their eyes upon. They disobeyed and did not do this. It was for the sake of his name that God did not pour out his wrath on them and leave them languishing in slavery.

So how did God both satisfy his righteous wrath upon sin *and* show mercy to the Israelites? How did he combine justice and grace (unmerited favor) in this situation? The answer was a sacrifice of atonement that foreshadowed the greater saving act of Christ on the cross. God told the Israelites that every household must take part in a sacrificial meal. They must slaughter a year-old male lamb without defect at twilight and before they eat the roasted meat with bitter herbs and unleavened bread in a state of readiness to leave, they must take some of the blood and daub it on the top and sides of their door frames. When the Angel of Death came from midnight onwards, he would see the blood and *pass over* the house, sparing the firstborn son.

5. Exodus 4:22
6. Ibid. 9:4

Every year thereafter, the Israelites were to commemorate the Passover festival. Centuries later Jesus came, heralded by John the Baptist as the "Lamb of God who takes away the sin of the world."[7] He was crucified on the very day of the Passover[8]. God presented him as a sacrifice of atonement,[9] dying in our place, for our sins, the death that we deserved.[10] All those who are in Christ are thus saved from the righteous and deserved wrath of God.[11] The just penalty, curse and consequence of sin was borne by Jesus rather than by us.[12] He died in our place—a substitutionary sacrifice, just as the lamb died in place of the firstborn Israelite sons. The lamb had to be a male without defect, symbolizing the fact that Jesus had to be a sinless male for atonement to be made for us.

I will deal more with the question of the propitiatory aspect of the atonement in chapter twenty-one.

7. John 1:29

8. Jesus celebrated the Passover the night before he was crucified but the Jewish day runs from evening to evening

9. Romans 3:25

10. First Peter 2:24

11. Romans 8:1

12. Isaiah 53:5–6

Chapter 20

Pyromaniacal?

"The LORD is gracious and compassionate, slow to anger and abounding in steadfast love"

—Psalm 103:8

A pyromaniac is someone with an obsessive desire to set fire to things and who can't control their impulse to do so. In the Bible though God is not portrayed as a starter of fires but as one who is himself "a consuming fire" and sends fire from heaven as an expression of his wrath and judgment on sin and his vindication of the righteous. Also, far from having impulse control disorder, God always acts in a just and measured way and never in an arbitrary or capricious way (See chapter eighteen).

God appears to Abraham as a blazing torch in Genesis 15. He rains down fire and sulfur on Sodom and Gomorrah in Genesis 19. He appears to Moses as a burning bush in Exodus 3. In Exodus 19 the LORD descended on Mount Sinai in fire and the mountain was covered in smoke and in Exodus 40 he appeared by night as pillar of fire above the Tabernacle in the desert. When the Aaronic priests begin their ministry in Leviticus chapter nine, fire comes out from the presence of the LORD and consumes the burnt offering and fat portions on the altar. In the next chapter fire again comes out from the presence of the LORD and consumes two of the sons of Aaron for disrespecting God's holiness.

A similar fate befell two hundred and fifty rebels against Moses in Numbers chapter sixteen. In Deuteronomy 4:24 Moses tells the people that God is a "consuming fire" and this is linked to his jealousy regarding the tendency of the Israelites to run after idols. (see chapter one of this book.) God sends fire to consume the sacrificial offering of Elijah in the contest with the prophets of Baal on Mount Carmel in First Samuel 18 and on the soldiers sent to arrest Elijah in Second Samuel 1. He was taken up to heaven in a chariot of fire and when his successor Elisha was surrounded by Aramean soldiers, he prayed for his terrified servant, who then saw the hills full of horses and chariots of fire all round Elisha. These references are the inspiration behind William Blake's line in the hymn *Jerusalem* "bring me my chariot of fire" and the film of that title about Eric Liddell, missionary and Olympic sprinter.

The connection between God and fire is apparent in the New Testament too, when at Pentecost, the Holy Spirit came on the disciples in what seemed like "tongues of fire." Hebrews 12:29, in urging Christians to worship God acceptably with reverence and awe, confirms that "our God is a consuming fire." In Revelation 19:11–12 John sees Christ as the "Faithful and True" rider of a white horse, who with justice judges and makes war. "His eyes are like blazing fire." His robe is dipped in blood and out of his mouth comes a sharp sword and he rules with an iron scepter, treading the winepress of the fury of God. (see the next chapter for God's anger or wrath).

It might be argued that because in Luke 9:51–56, Jesus rebuked James and John for suggesting they ask God to call down fire on a Samaritan village that had not welcomed them, that he was showing his repudiation of the concept of God as "a consuming fire." However, Jesus reprimanded the "sons of thunder" as he called them, because they were eager to take pleasure in the destruction of a people against whom they were already prejudiced (something not characteristic of the God of the Old Testament[1]). They had failed to grasp that Jesus' mission was to die in Jerusalem an atoning death in order to provide the opportunity for repentance and new life for all those who believed in him, including Samaritans. Judgment would come at his second coming, and it would start with Israel.

So why is God revealed as a "consuming fire"? Fire speaks of purity, passion and power. First, Scripture testifies to the *purity* and holiness of God. This means he is perfect in truth, goodness and love. He is completely distinct from his creation, which is fallen and infected with sin. With God, there is no compromise with evil. The prophet Habbakuk says "Your eyes are too pure to look on evil and you cannot tolerate wrong."[1] This is why God

---

1. Ezekiel 18:23

warned the people of Israel that they were not to approach him in worship without his divine permission and in compliance with all his instructions about observing holy boundaries. This is the reason he instituted the rituals laws around sacrificial worship and the concepts of ritual purity. When people treated these warnings with contempt they were consumed by fire.

The interesting thing about fire is that it refines some materials but destroys others. Indeed, the reason that it refines precious metals like gold and silver is that it consumes the impurities which attach themselves to those metals. Although fire is so destructive of the flesh, in spiritual terms the fire of God never harmed anyone. God is the one who purifies our souls so that we are transformed more into the likeness of Christ and made fit for heaven. In First Corinthians 3:12–15 the day of judgment when Christ returns is pictured as a day of fire which will test the quality of the work we have done in this life. All that is of no eternal value will burn away but that which is of God will endure and result in reward and glory.

Secondly, fire speaks of *passion*. The heart of God is revealed as a heart that longs for his people with a passionate love, even when they reject him and rebel against him. A particular low point in Judah's history was when God sent Jeremiah to earnestly plead with the people to repent and avert the coming catastrophe of Babylonian invasion and exile. Jeremiah had the thankless task of imploring the people and at great cost to himself. He faced ridicule and mocking. He was continually tempted to disobey God and give up warning of violence and destruction, but whenever he said to himself he would not speak any more in God's name, he found that the word of God was in his heart like a fire, "a fire shut up in my bones,"[2] a fire he could not contain. We all find fire frightening to a degree. We also find it attractive. We can stare at a fire for ages, enjoying its warmth and glow. God's passion is not to be trifled with, but it is enormously comforting to know that the heart of God burns with such love for his people.

Thirdly, fire is *powerful*. The chain reaction which occurs when flammable material combusts and rapidly oxidizes is a wonder to behold. In Scripture this is used as an example of the deadly danger of the damage that can be done by our tongues.[3] A great forest can be destroyed by a fire started by a small spark. The nature of God is that he is powerful. God is not slow, cumbersome and dilatory in carrying out his judgment, once he decides to act. If he delays in sending judgment, it is because he is merciful, and wants all men not to perish, but come to repentance.[4] When we are

2. Jeremiah 20:9
3. James 3:5
4. Second Peter 3:9

faced with problems and enemies all around us that seek us harm, do we want a God who is tame and ineffectual, or do we want a God of power? I'd rather have the latter. There is no point in praying for deliverance from evil if our God cannot deal with it with fearsome might.

Chapter 21

Angry?

"Anybody can become angry—that is easy, but to be angry with the right person and to the right degree and at the right time and for the right purpose, and in the right way—that is not within everybody's power and is not easy."

—ARISTOTLE

Barker says that the emotion most commonly expressed by the God of the Old Testament is not love, mercy, empathy or joy, but *anger*. He seems to be confused about the nature of an emotional feeling. Love, mercy, empathy and joy are more than mere emotions. They are *qualities* or *virtues*.

He is also in two minds about whether anger is something you can choose to turn on or off. He concedes that anger may be a good or appropriate spontaneous emotion in some situations, as when a parent is motivated to protect a child. But later in the relevant chapter he approvingly relays his mother's homespun teaching that "no one can make you angry" and that if you are angry, it is because you choose to be. Barker however then says that this is not true for everyone and that God, like other short-fused people, has little control over his anger because it arises "from his own indignant impulses."

Anger, like all emotions, is not necessarily inappropriate or something we can always choose to avoid, initially at any rate. Certainly, it can flare up in some people more than others through character faults like impatience, pride, insecurity and judgmentalism. It can sometimes be based on a mistake or a misunderstanding. But it also can arise as a reaction to being wronged or observing wrongdoing towards others. In this case owning our anger is emotionally healthy even though its initial presence is not something we necessarily choose. However, we do have a choice in how we *deal* with the anger. A person who is being true to Christ will let this anger out to God in prayer,[1] trusting in the God who has promised just retribution for all wrongs,[2] and will seek grace to forgive,[3] always bearing in mind our own faults and failings[4] and God's mercy in Christ to ourselves.[5] A person who sins when they are angry, however, makes their own addition to the evil in this world, which in turn leads to anger in others.[6] A vicious cycle indeed.

However, if we never get angry at anything in this world this is not a noble thing but proof of a selfish lack of empathy. I once watched an episode of *Rogue Traders* on BBC television, where a man was secretly filmed boasting about the way he ripped off vulnerable pensioners by fraudulently convincing them their house was in danger without his expensive brick coating product. He joked he would "burn in hell" for the way he operated. Clearly, he thought the idea of the wrath of God was not to be taken seriously, probably because our culture treats the idea of God being angry with us as a primitive pre-enlightenment belief. In a town I used to live in, I found a twelve-inch pick-axe blade stuck in the grassy bank of a children's play area. It had been placed in the ground, sharp side up, ready to pierce the vital organs of any toddler unfortunate enough to fall on it while rolling down the slope. Anyone who is not angered by this has no love for children.

We live in a world where people who are already rich, seek to gain more luxuries knowing they are causing suffering to others. People abuse others to satisfy their lusts. People steal, cheat, lie, bully, manipulate, slander and take pleasure in cruelty. Those who are in a position to uphold truth and justice fail to do so because of corruption or cowardice. A God who didn't get angry at these things would be a God who didn't care about justice or about us.

However, Barker contends that God's anger is almost always provoked because he is *jealous*, rather than because he has a protective concern about his people doing morally harmful things. In chapter one we saw that the

---

1. Many of the psalms contain expressions of anger regarding others which are addressed to God.
2. Romans 12:19
3. Ephesians 4:32
4. Matthew 7:3–5
5. Ibid. 18:21–35
6. James 1:20

biblical God is certainly a jealous God, but we explored what is meant by that. God has a rightful concern that his people acknowledge him as the creator of all things and the source of all that is good and all that blesses them. There is an appropriate kind of jealousy, when something which is rightfully yours and important to you is threatened.

Thus, although Barker is right that much of God's anger is linked to God's jealousy in the Bible, he is wrong to deduce that God's anger is therefore of the wrong kind, and unconnected with concern about the welfare of his people and all those on the earth. Idolatry among God's people both aroused God's jealous anger, *and* always resulted in spiritual, moral, social and physical harm to the people of Israel.

TWO EXTREMES

Is Barker right though about anger being the God of the Bible's most commonly expressed emotion? There are certainly numerous verses in the Bible about God's anger, or *wrath*. (Too many to cite, although Barker makes a good stab at it![7]) Many of these are warnings given by God not to provoke his wrath, sometimes by looking back to instances of this happening in the life of Israel. However, the Bible of course does not portray God as being angry *all the time*. On the contrary, he is described as "slow to anger" and "not harboring his anger forever."[8] On the other hand, God's *loving faithfulness* to Israel is often cited as a permanent characteristic.[9] The God of the Old Testament is regarded by the apostle John (a Jew steeped in the Hebrew Scriptures of course) as being, *in his very nature*, love.[10] He is not always angry, but he *is* always love. Even if we are talking simply on the level of emotions, there are multitudes of verses where God speaks of his happy delight in his people (again too many to list). But love, mercy, empathy and joy are virtuous qualities which are not dependent on circumstances. Whereas the God of the Bible is only angry at certain times and for certain reasons, his love expresses a defining quality as to who he is, *all the time*.

At this point I must acknowledge that some Christians go to the opposite extreme to Dawkins and Barker and resist the concept of God *ever* being angry. There are those who simply deny that sin incurs God's wrath. Despite the wealth of biblical evidence (as outlined by Barker in chapter twenty-one of his book) they attempt to justify this denial by saying one

7. Barker, *God: The Most Unpleasant Character in all History* 235–255
8. Psalm 103:8–9
9. Ibid.
10. First John 4:8,16

of two things. First, those without much knowledge of the Bible are happy to go along with the idea that the Old Testament "God of Wrath" evolved through human progress to become the New Testament "God of Love." A man called Marcion in the second century AD made a theological case that the God of the Old Testament was a completely different being from the God of the New Testament, revealed as the Father of the Lord Jesus Christ. He believed and taught that the God portrayed in the Old Testament was a wicked creator demi-god whereas the Father of Christ was pure light and uninvolved in the messy business of creating and relating to the world. This was officially rejected as heresy by the church but similar ideas to Marcion's persist among some Christians today.

Secondly, those who know full well that the New Testament also talks of God's wrath say that today this should be understood by children of the Enlightenment to mean no more than that we face the "natural" working out of the consequences of wrongful behavior. There is no *personal* "anger" in God at human sin and it has never provoked wrathful indignation within his being. New Testament talk of God's wrath is merely a way of saying that sin inevitably leads to an unhappy or unfulfilled life. God's wrath is simply a "metaphorical" term for this impersonal spiritual law. Practically speaking, this leaves us with something akin to the Hindu / Buddhist doctrine of impersonal karma. Put in popular terms, what goes around, comes around, in this life or any subsequent ones. That is all.

Why are some Christians reluctant to accept that God's wrath is real and personal? There are a mix of interrelated reasons, which include the belief that divine wrath is incompatible with divine love and the worry that to countenance God acting in anger might be to promote or encourage violence in human beings or nation states. More troublingly there may simply be a lack of submissiveness to biblical authority, and prideful resistance to the message of the cross of Christ. I will consider these last two factors in chapter twenty-eight.

Let us consider the first two reasons. First, is it true that love and wrath cannot be both attributed to God without fear of contradiction? The difficulty here is that our understanding of wrath and anger is so conditioned by our experience of sinful expressions of it. "Anger" or "wrath" is listed among the traditional seven deadly sins. Expressed explosively, it can do untold damage in seconds. Repressed, it can lead to years of bitterness, depression and physical infirmity. It is the "fever and frenzy' of the soul. A feeling of intoxicating power one moment gives rise to the hellish regret the "morning after." Henry Drummond said,

> "no form of vice, not worldliness, not greed of gold, not drunkenness itself, does more to un-Christianize society than evil temper. For embittering life, for breaking up communities, for destroying the most sacred relationships, for devastating homes, for withering up men and women, for taking the bloom off childhood, in short for sheer, gratuitous misery-producing power, this influence stands alone."

Little wonder the Bible repeatedly warns us of the danger of anger and urges us to cultivate peaceable self-control.

We may agree that anger can, *in theory*, be understandable or even justified in certain situations but because angry thoughts are so often steeped in sin or become so quickly defiled in human experience, there is emotional and psychological reluctance to attribute anger to God. Even the example given by Barker of parental anger towards a child in the context of loving protection, is tainted by the painful awareness we have of parental anger sometimes either not being justified or leading to abusive behavior. In fact, I suspect that those who have most difficulty in accepting the theological truth of the "wrath of God" are those whose struggle to know the Father heart of love for themselves after their own experiences of sinful anger in their upbringing.

However, this is where a strong belief in the holiness of God can help us to see how different God's wrath is from human anger or bad-temperedness. John Stott wrote

> "God's wrath in the words of Leon Morris is his 'personal divine revulsion to evil' and his 'personal vigorous opposition' to it. To speak thus of God's anger is a legitimate anthropomorphism, provided that we recognize it as no more than a rough and ready parallel, since God's anger is absolutely pure, and uncontaminated by those elements which render human anger sinful. Human anger is usually arbitrary and uninhibited; divine anger is always principled and controlled. Our anger tends to be a spasmodic outburst, aroused by pique and seeking revenge; God's is a continuous, settled antagonism, aroused only by evil, and expressed in its condemnation."[11]

Once we appreciate this, then it is easier to see that divine love and wrath are not mutually exclusive attributes and the Bible does not contradict itself when it proclaims the God of love who is also angered by sinful rebellion. God's anger is not merely "metaphorical" any more than his love can be said to be "metaphorical." If human words are adequate, in God-breathed

---

11. Stott, *The Cross of Christ*, 105–6

Scripture, to convey the essentials of knowing God then we must pay heed to the full range of biblical words used to describe what God is like and what he does. Barker and Dawkins are at least right in this, in a way that some Christians are not. We cannot ignore, gloss over, play down or "demythologize" the huge amount of biblical material attesting to the wrath of God.

What about the idea that belief in a God of Wrath promotes or condones violence? Theologians Walter Wink and Rene Girard are exponents of this view which has been adopted by popular writers such as Steve Chalke and Alan Mann. They attack the doctrine of penal substitutionary atonement, which is the belief that God gave himself in the person of his Son to suffer instead of us the death, punishment and curse due to fallen humanity as the penalty for sin,[12] because they think that it perpetuates what they call "the myth of redemptive violence." If God's wrath was experienced violently by Jesus on the cross and the result was that those in Christ are now no longer under that wrath then they say this would be contradictory to Jesus' message of peace and love and sanction violent and punitive behavior which in human experience they claim always contributes to the problem rather than providing a solution.

However, these objectors again fail to see that the divine expression of wrath is, just like everything else, of a different order from sinful human expressions of wrath. They are right that violence that is man-centered is always evil and productive of evil (although the sovereign hand of God brings good even from this, as is shown most supremely by the day of the crucifixion now being referred to as "*Good* Friday.") Force, even lethal force, that comes from God or is authorized by him accomplishes his divine purposes of justice *and mercy* and is a blessing to the world. Thus we should not be embarrassed by the expression of God's wrath in the Old Testament (or New).

It was *good* that God destroyed a world that was full of irredeemable evil in the Flood. It was *good* for the Israelites (and for us) when God visited his wrath on the Egyptians because it was both just and the means by which they were released from slavery and this furthered his plan of salvation for those in Christ. It was good that Canaanite religious practice was stamped out in Israel, and *bad* that some remained through the Israelites disobedience. It was even good for the Israelites (though they experienced it as misery for a time) that they came under God's severe judgment for idolatry because this brought true Israel to repentance. It is good for us that the state

---

12. Jeffery, Ovey and Sach, *Pierced For Our Transgressions*. I will consider further the biblical doctrine of substitutionary atonement and examine why Dawkins and Barker think it is so outrageous in chapter 28.

is "an agent of God's wrath" and "wields the sword" to punish wrongdoing and maintain law and order, as God ordains.[13] It is good that one day God will destroy all who are irredeemably wedded to evil.

In summary, although God cannot be described as "angry" in the same way as he can be described as "love," the God of the Bible is certainly provoked to anger by human behavior. However, his anger is completely distinct from human anger in that it is untainted by sin. Expressions of divine anger are always just and result in blessing for those who he is drawing to himself through Christ.

I think it would be good to end this chapter with the insights of theologian Miroslav Volf, who was born in Croatia and lived through the nightmare years of ethnic strife in the former Yugoslavia that included many atrocities.

> "I used to think that wrath was unworthy of God. Isn't God love? Shouldn't divine love be beyond wrath? God is love, and God loves every person and every creature. That's exactly why God is wrathful against some of them. My last resistance to the idea of God's wrath was a casualty of the war in the former Yugoslavia, the region from which I come. According to some estimates, 200,000 people were killed and over 300,000 people displaced. My villages and cities were destroyed, my people shelled day in and day out, some of them brutalized beyond imagination, and I could not imagine God not being angry. Or think of Rwanda in the last decade of the past century, where 800,000 people were hacked to death in one hundred days! How did God react to the carnage? By doting on the perpetrators in grandfatherly fashion? By refusing to condemn the bloodbath but instead affirming the perpetrators' basic goodness? Wasn't God fiercely angry with them? Though I used to complain about the indecency of the idea of God's wrath, I came to think I would have to rebel against a God who wasn't wrathful at the sight of the world's evil. God isn't wrathful in spite of being love. God is wrathful *because* [my emphasis] God is love."[14]

---

13. Romans 13:4

14. Miroslav Volf *Free of Charge, Giving and Forgiving in a culture Stripped of Grace* Grand Rapids: Zondervan, 2006 138–139 quoted by Paul Hogan in *Is God a Moral Monster?* Grand Rapids: Baker Books, 2011

Chapter 22

Merciless?

Merciless—synonyms: *"callous, hard-hearted, inhumane, pitiless"*

Barker says that when the psalmist speaks praise to God for his mercy he is like a nervous wife trying to calm an abusive husband, telling him what he wants to hear. In reality, he claims, God's actions in Scripture are impetuous and violent. He argues that even the psalmist gives the game away in by saying that God's mercy extends only to those who *fear* him,[1] which Barker interprets as those who cower before him.

> "The mercy of the Lord Jealous was conditional and selfish, based not on his love for the people, but on the people's love for *him*."[2]

In the previous chapter we saw how a God of love can be angry in a way that is not inconsistent with his divine nature of love. God is described as merciful and "rich in mercy" but this does not mean he is constrained to always show mercy in every situation. Mercy is a quality which God often chooses to demonstrate because it reflects something of the goodness of his heart, but the Bible includes many passages, some of which are cited by Barker, where God explicitly says he will *not* show mercy.

1. Psalm 103:11
2. Barker, *God: the Most Unpleasant Character in all Fiction*, 257

Mercy is like the biblical virtue grace. Grace can be understood as God giving us wonderful blessings which we do not have a right to. Grace is when God gives us what we don't deserve. Mercy, on the other hand, is when God does *not* give us what we *do* deserve, in terms of punishment. There is of course a tension between mercy and justice. A God of justice un-tempered by mercy would always give us exactly what we deserved. But because God *is* merciful, he so often in the Bible withholds judgment, softens punishment, or allows time for repentance and forgives.

How does he show mercy without compromising his justice? The answer is the atoning death of Christ which gave full expression to his justice while enabling us to benefit from his mercy. God's forbearance to humanity during the time of the Old Testament was because of his eternal plan in Christ. Romans 3:25 says

> "God presented him as a sacrifice of atonement, through faith in his blood. He did this to demonstrate his justice, because in his forbearance he had left the sins committed beforehand unpunished."

To say that God *must* always show mercy robs mercy of an essential quality which is the free willingness to forgo inflicting just retribution. If God did not or does not show mercy in any situation no one would have any right to complain. Mercy that someone has a right to is not mercy. It is the same with grace. The point about grace is that it is undeserved. No one has a right to expect it from God. We cannot presume on it, in the way that we *can* presume on God's holiness and justice. God tells *us* to be gracious and merciful because he has shown grace and mercy to us. But with God, no one has shown *him* grace and mercy, so there is nothing external to himself by which he should rightfully be constrained.

I have already discussed in chapter seventeen what the Bible means by "the fear of the LORD." It is not necessarily craven terror (although that might sometimes be appropriate!) but the respect and reverence for God due to his divine majesty, holiness and almighty power. Therefore, it is entirely appropriate for the psalmist to laud God's mercy towards those who fear him. If we did not fear God in the right, biblical sense, then we would be presuming on his mercy in a way that he will not allow us to do for very long. Nor should he, because this would be such an affront to his holiness and justice.

The worship songs of Israel, the psalms, constantly proclaim God's mercy to his people. His mercy is something to be trusted in and celebrated for those whose hearts are genuinely turned towards him in reverent fear. It endures forever to the faithful. However, mercy to those who God calls into a relationship with him does not mean that there is not final judgment for those who remain God's enemies. His judgment is held back to give people time to repent but ultimately God's love for his people requires acts of judgment on those who are oppressing them. We see this in Psalm 136 where the constant refrain "His mercy endures for ever" follows not only his acts of creation and provision, but also the recounting of God's judgment falling on Pharaoh and the Egyptians and the heathen kings who opposed the Israelites coming into their land of inheritance.

In Revelation chapter six the apostle John sees a vision of the souls of the Christian martyrs under the altar in heaven calling out in a loud voice

> "How long, sovereign Lord, holy and true, until you judge the inhabitants of the earth and avenge our blood? Then each of them was given a white robe, and they were told to wait a little longer, until the number of their fellow servants and brothers who were to be killed as they had been was completed."

So we see here that the delay in God's judgment does cause anguish among the saints and more suffering for God's people. His mercy to those who have not yet repented prolongs the wait for justice for those who already have. But ultimately God's everlasting love necessitates the establishment of that justice.

Chapter 23

Curse Hurling?

"We like the idea of blessings but not the idea of curses, but the two are but different sides of the same coin"

—Anon

To accuse God of hurling curses at people is to suggest that God curses irrationally and in fits of foul temper rather like when Saul suddenly flew into a jealous rage and threw a spear at David while he was playing the harp.[1]

However, the Bible reveals a God for whom a curse is a solemn enacting of divine judgment in response to deep seated iniquity. A curse is not a short-term lashing out. It is long term feature of divine punishment but is restorative in intent. When humanity rebelled in the Garden of Eden God cursed both people and land. Why did God do this? It was not because he is merciless and unforgiving, but because humankind needed to see the effect of sin and be driven back to God in humble contrition. Had the curse not operated upon childbirth[2] human sin along with unlimited procreation would have wreaked havoc on the planet. Had it not operated on the world of work, turning it to painful toil,[3] men everywhere would have become rich and proud, spurning God in an orgy of materialism. Not needing to work as

1. First Samuel 18:10–11
2. Genesis 3:16
3. Ibid. 3:17–19

hard, idle hands would have been given more work to do by the Devil. Had not the flaming cherubim with swords closed off access to the tree of life[4] then mankind would have lived forever in a fallen state—and this would have been literally hell on earth.

On the eve of their entry into the Promised Land, the Israelites were reminded by Moses of the terms of the covenant God had made with them. The blessings and curses were part of this covenant. The people needed to know that their health, prosperity, security and future lay in faithfully worshipping the one true God who had made himself known to them, living in trust that he would provide for them and obeying the law he had given them.

If, on the other hand, they went after the gods of the pagan nations, put their trust in political maneuvering, and neglected God's law, then they would not only receive the consequences of their own folly but God would describe himself as actively cursing them. He could have said he would simply withdraw his blessing because this amounts to the same thing. But Hebrew modes of expression are more direct and visceral. It is similar to God being described as jealous. When the Israelites committed idolatry they ascribed to material objects (and the demons behind them) the honor and glory that belonged to God and this always resulted in ethical depravity and dehumanization. Whether they were then said to be disciplined because of God's jealousy or because they were simply reaping what they had sown is a matter of semantics.

The terrible curses outlined by Moses in Deuteronomy 28:15–68 are not evidence that God sat light to his covenant or that God loaded a contract with his people with unfair conditions that would then void his responsibilities. No, the curses were an integral part of the covenant. Had God chosen to give up completely on the people of Israel they would have experienced no more curses than any other people for their sin. But then neither would they have received so much mercy, forgiveness and renewed hope from God when their periods of suffering came to an end. The curses were devastating but their ultimate purpose was restorative. God showed his faithfulness to the covenant by continuing to have regard to the Jewish people, bringing a remnant back from exile in Babylon and sending the Messiah to begin the process of Israel's true restoration.

---

4. Ibid. 3:24

Chapter 24

Vaccicidal?

"God made the wild animals according to their kinds, the livestock according to their kinds, and all the creatures that move along the ground according to their kinds. And God saw that it was good."

—Genesis 1:25

The word *vaccicidal* literally means a killer of cows, but because there is no general term for the killing of animals, Barker elected to co-opt this word. After all the other things he charges God with, this seems tame. It suggests that Barker is just trying to "throw the kitchen sink" at God.

Of course, God did afflict the livestock of Egypt with plague as part of his judgment upon Pharaoh and his gods.[1] But human beings have always been more important to God than animals and the Bible is not apologetic about that fact. That is not to say that God does not have concern for all of his creation. He does. In God's eyes *all* his creation was good.[2] Every species was saved in the Ark. The prophetic glimpses of the future reign of God over his creation include visions of harmony in the animal world.[3] When the prophet Jonah was sulking because God did not destroy the capital city of the Assyrian Empire, due to its repentance at his preaching, God said to

---

1. Exodus 9:1–7
2. Genesis 1:25
3. Isaiah 11:6–9

him "Nineveh has more than a hundred and twenty thousand[4] people who cannot tell their right hand from the left , *and many cattle as well.* Should I not be concerned about that great city?"[5]

The humorous story of Balaam and his donkey portrays the mercenary prophet in a poor light compared to his faithful animal.[6] Balaam is on his way to curse the Israelites, having been hired by Balak, king of Moab. Riding his donkey, his way is barred by an angel of the LORD with a drawn sword. He doesn't have the spiritual insight to see the angel, but his donkey does, and turns aside. Balaam beats his donkey into carrying on. This happens a second time, injuring Balaam's foot against a stone wall in a narrow passageway. Again Balaam beats the poor donkey. This time it speaks to him and the two have a discussion in which Balaam claims he is being made a fool of. The reader is being invited to see that he is doing a good job of that himself. His eyes are then opened to the angel, who tells him that the donkey had saved his life, because if he had continued on his way, the angel would have killed him.

Some may be troubled by Joshua 11, where God enables Joshua to defeat an alliance of kings, burn their chariots and hamstring their horses. To hamstring a horse might seem a very cruel thing to do. It means disabling the horse from being able to run. But the horse can still walk. Horses were not pets, they were fearsome weapons, especially when harnessed to a chariot. Hamstringing warrior horses and burning chariots was about destroying aggressive military technology, used to crush the opposition. It was the equivalent of "beating swords into ploughshares."[7]

It is true that God ordered animals to be used in sacrificial worship. However, this does not indicate a lack of value for them—quite the opposite. Bulls, goats and lambs were to be sacrificed as a way for the Israelites to show their devotion to God. They were offering something of significant importance and expense to them. The meat of most of the sacrificial offerings was eaten by the priests and people, and this ceremonial feasting was not unlike the enjoyment of meat today. Of course, the animal sacrifices had a serious spiritual function—they were part of the making of atonement for the people. Atonement is about the people becoming "at-one" with God again, remedying the alienation brought about with God through sin. Sin

---

4. On this large number see chapter 3 footnote 11
5. Jonah 4:11
6. Numbers 22
7. Micah 4:3 See Paynter, *God of Violence Yesterday, God of Love Today* 88–90

causes estrangement from God because of its offensiveness to God and our inability to overcome it.[8]

Many of the sacrifices had a penal substitutionary element to them, such as the burned offerings and sin offerings. The Passover lambs were sacrificed in memory of the time when each family in Egypt slaughtered a lamb and put its blood on their doorposts so that the angel of death would "pass over" the house and not kill the first-born son inside. The lamb was killed in place of the Israelite firstborn, who, like the Egyptians would otherwise also have come under God's wrathful judgment. Jesus was hailed by John the Baptist as the Passover lamb, who takes away the sin of the world.[9]

A passage from Josephus says that at least 256,500 lambs were killed in the Temple for a Passover in one year between 66–70 AD.[10] This is a huge number, yet the Temple mount area, covering an area of about fourteen football pitches would have been up to the task. The sheer scale of the animal sacrifice and the amount of blood that would have flowed is testament to the vast reservoir of human sin that needed to be atoned for and the plentiful supply of forgiveness through the cross of Christ, which fulfilled all this and abrogated the need for the continuation of such bloody sacrifice.

---

8. Illustrated Bible Dictionary (Leicester: IVP, 1980) 147
9. John 1:29
10. Josephus (*Jewish Wars* 6.9.3)

Chapter 25

Aborticidal?

"You knit me together in my mother's womb."
—Psalm 139:13

This accusation is as much a travesty as any other made by Barker or Dawkins. The nations which have over the years had the most appalling abortion statistics are the former countries of the atheistic Soviet Union. In Russia, in the fifty years from 1957 to 2007, abortions outstripped live births by up to two to one, with some 137 million abortions taking place during this time.[1] The rate has slowed down in recent years with the collapse of communism and efforts by pro-life politicians and the Russian Orthodox Church to change the long-established abortion culture.[2] The history of Russia shows godlessness is no friend of babies in the womb.

With the rejection of our Christian heritage in the West, the abortion culture is now firmly established and those driving it are seeking to crush all conscientious opposition. The European Court of Human Rights ruled in March 2020 that two Swedish midwives who entered the profession to help bring children into the world were not protected from having to be involved in abortion.

1. http://www.johnstonsarchive.net/policy/abortion/ab-russia.html
2. https://en.wikipedia.org/wiki/Abortion_in_Russia

In America there have been roughly sixty million abortions since the notorious 1973 Supreme Court ruling in *Roe v Wade* that Americans had a constitutional right to them.

In Israel, had there not been so many abortions, both illegal and legal since the modern state was founded in 1948, the demographic of the country today would be very different. There would be enough Jewish people to safeguard the Jewish character of the state while incorporating the so-called "West Bank" (biblical Judea and Samaria) into Israel and giving the non-Jewish residents there full civil and political rights. Abortion has prevented a possible route to peace with the Palestinians.

In Britain there have been over eight million "terminations" since the 1967 Abortion Act which opened the door for the UK, with the noble exception until recently of Northern Ireland, to become the country most hostile to the right to life of ante-natal children throughout Western Europe. So tenaciously is the de facto "abortion on demand" system guarded in the UK that doctors who were found agreeing to perform "sex selective" abortions were protected from prosecution by the Crown Prosecution Service.

In 2012, undercover reporters from *The Daily Telegraph* secretly filmed two doctors agreeing to sign off abortions simply because the babies were girls. A police investigation followed and the Crown Prosecution Service (CPS) considered prosecution. However, the CPS concluded that, whilst there was sufficient evidence to provide a realistic prospect of conviction, it would "not be in the public interest" to bring such a prosecution.

Following the CPS's decision, a courageous young woman called Aisling Hubert launched private prosecutions against the two doctors. The CPS intervened, took over the cases as it has the power to do, but then dropped them. Aisling was then ordered to pay £36,000 in costs to the doctors. Further costs of £11,000 were awarded against her, after she challenged the costs order and the CPS's decision to intervene in the prosecutions.[3]

In 2019, while the UK was obsessing about Brexit few noticed that the abortion rate was running at two hundred thousand per year. It is not really surprising that the Hubert case was dealt with as it was, because ever since the passing of the Abortion Act which Parliament intended to allow abortions in limited circumstances, there has been a demonically inspired campaign to apply this loophole in the most permissive way possible to open the floodgates and promote abortion on demand. The powerful abortion industry, together with socially liberal politicians, do not want a light to be shone on the way the system is now operated to permit abortions in almost any circumstances.

3. https://www.christianconcern.com/gender-abortion

Late term abortions (up to birth) are happening in the UK for fetal abnormalities such as club feet, hare lip, and cleft palate. The Department of Health tries to hide the figures because of the likelihood of adverse public reaction. Recently the UK government used the opportunity of there being no sitting Northern Ireland assembly to impose on the province this kind of extreme abortion regime against the will of the people there.

Ann Furedi is the highly paid head of the innocuous sounding "charity" BPAS (British Pregnancy Advisory Service). It is the UK's chief abortion provider on behalf of the National Health Service which funds it. She has stated publicly she would like to see zero legal restrictions on abortion so it can happen for any or no reason *up to birth*. On 22 November 2019 she received an honorary doctorate from Kent University, for "services to society." The venue for the award ceremony was, of all places, Canterbury Cathedral.[4]

By comparison with the historical and worldwide number of babies in the womb killed illegally or with the connivance of state authorities, the number killed by actions described as being the outworking of God's judgment in Scripture is tiny. The death of women and the babies they carried was never part of God's desired will, only his sorrowful will, when, under his just and ultimately merciful sovereign purposes, judgment had to fall on people in certain situations. God repeatedly warned his people, as in Hosea 13:16, that their idolatry would lead to invasion by hostile powers who would "dash their little ones to the ground" and "rip open pregnant women." I have covered the issues surrounding this in chapters seven, eight, twelve and thirteen.

---

4. https://righttolife.org.uk/news/abortion-giant-boss-who-is-campaigning-for-abortion-up-to-birth-awarded-honorary-doctorate-by-kent-university/

Chapter 26

Cannibalistic?

An unbelieving American sailor during WW2 was washed up on a Pacific island. An islander looked after him and proudly showed him his Bible. "Where I come from," he said dismissively, "we've learned to have no time for such nonsense." "It's a good thing for you that we've had time," replied the islander, "or you would have been a meal by now."

—ANON

Barker is really scraping the barrel with this one, so this will be the shortest chapter in the book.

There are certainly dreadful predictions in Scripture about what will happen to people who trust in their fortified cities rather than the living God. God warns the Israelites with great sadness through the prophets that following the ways of the world, making and breaking alliances with ungodly nations, pursuing deals with pagan powers, and rejecting his presence and protection will mean that they too will suffer at some point all the terrible exigencies of siege warfare. When human beings are starving, they will eat anything—even human flesh.[1] This is of course something that God never wanted to happen and greatly distressed him. This was why he sent

---

1. Leviticus 26:27–29; Deuteronomy 28:47–57; Isaiah 9:19–20, 49:25–26; Jeremiah 19:7–9; Ezekiel 5:8–10

prophet after prophet to warn his people. But his prophets were insulted, beaten and killed.

As for Barker's cheap shot that Christians today who heed Christ's words, "This is my body, this is my blood" when partaking of Holy Communion, are themselves practicing cannibalism under divine instruction, this is precisely what the early Christians were accused of by the pagan authorities. In reply to someone, like Barker, who has been a Christian minister, who willfully promotes such a crude libel, I can only refer the reader to Jesus' words about blasphemy against the Holy Spirit.[2]

Also, Hebrews 6:4–6 says "it is impossible for those who have once been enlightened, who have tasted the heavenly gift, who have shared in the Holy Spirit, who have tasted the goodness of the word of God and the powers of the coming age, if they fall away, to be brought back to repentance, because to their loss they are crucifying the Son of God all over again and subjecting him to public disgrace."

---

2. Matthew 12:30–32; Mark 3:28–30; Luke 12:8–10

Chapter 27

Slavemonger?

"Do not deprive the foreigner or the fatherless of justice, or take the cloak of the widow as a pledge. Remember that you were slaves in Egypt and the Lord your God redeemed you from there. That is why I command you to do this."

—Deuteronomy 24:17–18

The belief that the God of the Bible approved the practice of slavery, *as slavery is commonly understood today*, is widespread. There are two main reasons for this. One is that there is a lack of understanding about what life really was like in ancient Israel and in later Roman times. Many do not appreciate the differences between

1. the kind of working relationships God regulated in ancient Israel,
2. slavery in the New Testament era,
3. the transatlantic slavery Britain and other Western nations were involved in up to its abolition in the nineteenth century, and
4. the various forms of people-trafficking and modern slavery today.

The second reason is that there are many people who bring an ungodly, spiritually rebellious agenda to this subject. Their reasoning is that if it can become a common assumption that the God of the Bible was happy with a practice which decent people today now know to be evil, then this provides a trump card to play whenever the Bible appears to challenge their values. So, the Bible's apparent justification of slavery is continually brought up in the debates about sexual ethics. "Why should we follow the Bible?" the cry goes. "The Bible supports slavery but we all now know slavery is wrong! Therefore, it is irrelevant that the dusty old Bible texts might have a negative view towards certain sexual practices."[1]

So what was meant by the term "slavery" in the context of the Old Testament law of Moses? The Hebrew word *ebed* can be translated as servant or slave. Much of what is misleadingly described in English translations as slavery was similar to what we would call domestic service. There were indentured and bonded servants who were, through their service, offering legally recognized labor. There was a distinction between foreigners acquired by Israelites, normally through the capture of enemy peoples after war,[2] and Hebrew "bondservants" who had sold themselves to escape poverty,[3] defaulted on debts,[4] or been unable to make restitution for criminal acts.[5]

Paul Copan, in chapter twelve of *Is God a Moral Monster?* page 125, explains the mistake people make in associating this bonded or indentured service with slavery in the antebellum (pre civil war) southern states of the USA. Hebrew servanthood was much more akin to another situation in colonial America. Paying fares for passage to America was too costly for many individuals to afford. So they would contract themselves out, working in households, often in apprentice-type positions, until they paid back their debts. One half to two thirds of white immigrants to Britain's colonies were indentured servants.[6]

---

1. It is true that, because people read the Bible through their own cultural lenses, some Christians living in slave-owning societies mistakenly read the Bible as supporting the case against abolition. Therefore we today should be open to the possibility that our own interpretation of the Bible may be culturally prejudiced, and we may be missing what the Bible really says or reading into it what it does not say. In connection with homosexual practice, the relevant point is that we should be willing to look afresh at texts that we thought we understood, in order to avoid a similar mistake. I completely agree with this providing it is a genuine plea to do serious exegetical biblical work. This is, however, very different to saying "we rightly ignore the Bible with regard to slavery, so we can rightly ignore it with regard to sex too." I have heard campaigners within the Church of England say in nationally organized diocesan "shared conversations" that biblical study and debate on sexuality is not a priority because the LGBT+ agenda will prevail, as did the movement for the abolition of slavery (they claim), by political maneuvering and unstoppable cultural pressure rather than an appeal to biblical truth.

2. Leviticus 25:39–43

3. Deuteronomy 21:10

4. Second Kings 4:1

5. Exodus 22:3

6. David W Galenson, "Indentured Servitude" in The Oxford Companion to American History (New York: Oxford University Press, 2001) 368–9

Even Barker recognizes that because these Hebrew bondservants had the right to marry,[7] be redeemed by relatives,[8] and were to be freed from their bonded labor every seventh year,[9] their status was much higher than the term "slave" would indicate. Indeed, God said they were to be regarded as hired workers rather than slaves.[10] When they were released from service, Moses in Deuteronomy 15:12–15 commanded they were to be provided with a generous amount of livestock, wheat and wine. The Hebrews were to remember that they had all been forced laborers in Egypt and God had redeemed them. A righteous man was one who listened and responded to any complaints their bondservants might have. Job accepts that had he mistreated any of them, he would be subject to God's judgment.

> "If I have denied justice to any of my [ebed] servants, whether male or female, when they had a grievance against me, what will I do when God confronts me? What will I answer when called to account? Did not he who made me in the womb make them? Did not the same one form us both within our mothers?"[11]

It should be understood that it was not God's desired will that there was any poverty in Israel and therefore the need for people to become bondservants to make ends meet. In Deuteronomy 15:4 God said through Moses that if they obeyed his laws and were faithful to him there should be no poor among them. There were laws to provide a safety net for the widow, orphans, and refugees such as the command to reapers not to harvest right to the edges of the fields or go back to collect the grain or grapes they missed the first time, so that the vulnerable could come and glean what remained.[12] Also the people were forbidden to profit on loans to their poor countrymen.[13] Of course these laws were not always followed and the poor were sometimes exploited and abused rather than helped out of poverty. However, this was because of the idolatry, greed and selfishness which infected Israel. God hated all this and the prophets inveighed against those who behaved in this way.

Foreign bondservants, unlike Hebrew ones, could be "owned" for life and passed on through inheritance to children and so the term "slave" could

---

7. Ibid. 21:2–11
8. Leviticus 25:48
9. Ibid. 25:39–43
10. Ibid. 25:39
11. Job 31:13
12. Leviticus 19:9–10, 23:22
13. Deuteronomy 23:19

be applied to them.[14] However even these people were not to be treated as people without rights. True they could be subject to corporal punishment that left no lasting physical effect,[15] but they were not to be killed[16] or misused sexually.[17] If permanently injured by a master they were to be set free in compensation.[18] Slaves were to enjoy the Sabbath rest[19] and, after circumcision, could participate in the festivals as well as freemen.[20] Scripture never suggests God condoned the treatment of people as mere chattels to be abused at the whim of the master.

It is true that when Israel had kings like Solomon who aped the ways of pagan kings and forced large numbers of people into conscripted labor, these people could fairly be described as slaves, whether Hebrew or foreign. But this was not intended by God to be the way things were in Israel and he specifically forbade it. The writer of Kings draws attention to Solomon's worldly pursuit of riches and grand schemes which depended on the toil and sweat of oppressed workers.

Genesis 1 and 2 reveals that God created man to enjoy stewarding his creation, not to be slaves. This was different to the pagan understanding of what the gods had intended. In the Akkadian / Babylonian creation myth *Atrahasis*, humans were indeed created to be the slaves of the gods, who had tired of the work they needed to do.

> "When the gods instead of man
> Did the work, bore the loads,
> The gods load was too great;
> The work too hard, the trouble too much. . .
> Belet Ili the womb goddess is present—
> Let her create primeval man
> So that he may bear the yoke."[21]

Clearly, no kind of forced labor was part of God's original plan for mankind where work was meant to be a joy. Painful toil came in with the Fall.[22] The great saving act of God which was the foundation of God's rela-

---

14. Leviticus 25:44–46
15. Exodus 21:21
16. Ibid. 21:20
17. Deuteronomy 21:10–14
18. Exodus 21:26–27
19. Ibid. 20:10
20. Ibid. 12:44
21. Dalley, Stephanie. *Myths From Mesopotamia*, https://geha.paginas.ufsc.br/files/2017/04/Atrahasis.pdf
22. Genesis 3:17–19

tionship with his covenant people was deliverance *from* slavery in Egypt and the long march to freedom in the Promised Land. The vision of a redeemed earth sees every man peacefully 'sitting under his own vine and fig tree" (enjoying his own time and property).[23] There is nothing about slavery which is declared good in itself, although God used the Israelite's time as slaves in Egypt to increase their population size and forge their identity as a people.

Having said this, the Old Testament God is one who relates to the world as it is. In ancient times, forced servitude as practiced then was better than the alternatives of being tortured and killed in the aftermath of a battle by a victorious army, or living in destitution or grinding poverty. God decreed just laws and all just laws must be realistic as well as humane, in order to be effective. Being realistic meant recognizing enforced labor and regulating it, mitigating its harsher features and constraining any evil that is likely to be promulgated when there is an established power imbalance between human beings. Thus the treatment of bonded workers under God's law was far more just and compassionate than their treatment in pagan nations, although even in those societies slaves were not necessarily treated with harshness or brutality and could gain education, influence, social standing, and a large measure of freedom.[24]

SLAVERY IN NEW TESTAMENT TIMES

In the New Testament, the Greek word *doulos* should always be translated "slave," whether it refers to people being slaves of Christ, slaves of sin, or slaves of Roman masters. The fact that *doulos* is sometimes translated "servant" represents embarrassment at the shame implied in the word "slave" when translators began to translate the Greek into the vernacular in the sixteenth century. But the New Testament writers themselves were living in a world where Roman law gave masters absolute rights in law over their slaves. Until slave-owners became Christians, restraints on cruelty were limited only to the self-interest of masters in having healthy, well-motivated and useful people to do their will. Those who were treated the worst were criminals and rebels who if not executed were sent to be galley slaves on warships or to work in the mines or fields.

However, domestic slaves, despite their lack of legal rights were often treated well and could be allowed by their masters to marry, get educated and enjoy a good standard of living, sometimes earning their freedom or even being adopted into their master's family as sons. Greek slaves were

23. Micah 4:4
24. See the story of Joseph in Genesis 39:1–6a

often what we would see as skilled professionals like doctors. This is the context in which we should view New Testament teaching, which encouraged slaves (and they were definitely slaves in the sense of being completely under the legal authority of their masters for life), to serve well,[25] and continue to respect their masters even (or especially) if they shared brotherhood in Christ.[26] Christian slave owners were instructed not to threaten their slaves[27] and were to provide them with what was right and fair.[28] Slave *traders*, on the other hand, were regarded as ungodly and unholy sinners whose behavior was contrary to the Gospel[29] (probably because of incvitable cruelty and perhaps illegality in their operations).

Paul urged a Christian slave owner to consider granting freedom to his runaway slave Onesimus who had, like his master, become a believer and who Paul had sent back to him.[30] The fellowship and equal standing of those in Christ before God set in train a new way of viewing human relationships and provided a trajectory of thought which was always going to undermine any socio-economic system which was inherently oppressive or cruel.

Nowhere does the New Testament give theological justification for slavery. It simply recognizes it as a fact in the Roman world and the apostles give pastoral advice to slaves and masters as to how them both being "slaves of Christ" should affect their working relationships.

THE TRANSATLANTIC SLAVE TRADE

The transatlantic slave trade in the seventeenth and eighteenth centuries involved people from Christian nations going to West Africa and purchasing tribal people captured or purchased by their enemies and transporting them in the most appalling conditions to the Americas to work on sugar and cotton plantations for the benefit of industrial entrepreneurs and landowners. Although there were some prominent Bible-believing Christians, like George Whitefield in the eighteenth century and Charles Hodge in the nineteenth who owned slaves and argued on scriptural grounds that, provided they were well treated, owning slaves was not sinful *per se*, the evils that the commercial trade entailed, particularly The Middle Passage were increasingly seen as being indefensible. Most non-conformist Christians

25. Ephesians 6:5–8, Colossians 3:22–25
26. First Timothy 6:1–2
27. Ephesians 6:9
28. Colossians 4:1
29. First Timothy 1:10–11
30. Philemon

and Evangelical Anglicans, as opposed to the worldly Church of England establishment, supported the abolitionist movement, including prominent figures such as John Wesley, Charles Simeon, Charles Spurgeon, Charles Finney, Harriet Beecher-Stowe (author of *Uncle Tom's Cabin*), John Newton (author of *Amazing Grace* and former captain of slave ships), and of course William Wilberforce and his circle of fellow Evangelicals. They were the driving force behind the abolition of the British slave trade in 1807, followed by abolition of ownership of slaves in British colonies in 1833. It was their efforts that resulted in the Royal Navy changing from being the primary enabler of transatlantic slavery to it primary opponent around the globe.

Even Hodge in America saw abolition as eventually desirable because of the persistence of evils associated with slavery in the Deep South, such as physical cruelty, the denial of the right to marry and enjoy family life and gain an education. American and European enslavement of Africans also had a pseudo-scientific racist dimension with the subsequent bitter legacy we see today, a factor which we saw in chapter eleven was not present in biblical times, let alone supported by Scripture.

I would agree with Whitefield and Hodge that if the Bible (Old Testament or New) sanctioned something intrinsically evil then this implicates God in wrongdoing and undermines biblical credibility in the area of ethics and in fact all other areas too, such as salvation and kingdom values. Our view of whether it does or not will depend on what we understand by the term "slavery."

LEGALLY ENFORCED LABOR

If slavery is defined as legally enforced labor for a period of time (in some cases for life, as a better alternative to death) under the direction of a private individual or the state, which is the kind of slavery recognized by God in Old Testament Israel, then I would say that this is not necessarily evil. In fact, it is similar to the basis on which most people are employed today. When we are "at work" we are legally obliged to follow the directions of our superiors. True, we today prize the element of individual choice which means we *could* choose to leave our job but we might be inhibited by legal or practical considerations (such as having to give contractual notice, or finding that without the job we could not support ourselves or those we love financially, or pay our debts).

The practice of negotiating short-term contracts of employment, while appealing to some, puts others at a disadvantage to those who are employed on a long-term basis in a manner more akin to the definition of slavery given above. In fact, in the harsh reality of the world we live in, the polar opposite to slavery as understood in the paternalistic full-time sense is the neo-liberal "zero hours contract" which leaves many people worse off and not enjoying the freedom they might want because of lack of employment rights, inconsistency of employment availability and difficulty in planning their lives.

There are indeed some cases where a reluctance to impose a kind of "slavery" (under the strict definition given above) causes harm and denies people possible rehabilitative possibilities. People who are convicted of offences would be more likely to become reformed, productive citizens if they were subject to constructive forced labor for a period of time rather than left to rot in their prison cells for twenty-three hours a day while taking drugs and watching a screen. Also allowing people who *can* work to lead an idle life, drip-fed by welfare payments may mean we pride ourselves as a "tolerant" and "progressive" society, but our rejection of the "if you don't work you don't eat" principle (a *New Testament* rule[31]) does nothing to instill a dignified work ethic, enable personal self-respect or help people help themselves.

WHAT DOES IT MEAN TO "OWN" SOMEONE?

If slavery is defined as the illegal and/or cruel trafficking of people for abusive exploitation, which is what most of us today would understand by the term "slavery," then of course this is inherently evil and any truth in the charge that the God of the Bible approved of it would indeed make him the unpleasant character Barker and Dawkins allege he is. However, slavery as understood like this is certainly not desired or condoned by the God of the Bible and will result in his severe judgment on those guilty of having a hand in it.[32] Kidnapping, for example, was a capital offence under the law of Moses.[33] Had Western nations been subject to Old Testament law, there would have been no transatlantic slave trade.

Some might argue though that while the Bible might not directly support that kind of slavery or the underground modern day slavery that happens in Britain when vulnerable people are lured here with promises of good jobs and then held hostage and forced into prostitution or unpaid backbreaking field labor, it does nevertheless countenance the "ownership"

---

31. Second Thessalonians 3:10
32. Deuteronomy 24:7
33. Exodus 21:16, Deuteronomy 24:7

of human beings, and therefore bears some responsibility for the persistence of all the various kinds of slavery in the last two thousand years.

Well the first thing to say in reply to this is that not only does the Bible not directly support cruel behavior, it directly condemns it. God is the all-seeing, totally just God who calls to account everyone in their treatment of others. People who have no knowledge of the living God or reject him are more likely to feel they can treat others with impunity than those who fear him.

The second thing to say is that while the Old Testament does countenance and regulate the "ownership" by Hebrews of foreign workers, the concept of "ownership" is more complex that might be recognized at first. To "own" something does not necessarily imply that we have the right and the power to deal with it in any way we choose. In *some* instances it does. Admittedly I could, for example, buy and own a book and then abuse it or burn it in my back garden without any legal repercussions (unless perhaps it was a copy of the Qu'ran and I filmed what I was doing and put it out on social media). However, there are things we can be said to "own" over which we do not enjoy absolute rights. Ownership of land and animals is subject to many restrictions. To "own" something implies some responsibility for it. "Ownership" of a full-time employee is only different in degree from "ownership" of the time of someone you employ to do some work. It need not imply cruelty or injustice, it may be regulated by legal codes as to what is permissible and it may be preferable to alternatives, which is why the biblical God allowed it at a certain time in history.

Nothing said above should mean the work of abolitionist Evangelicals in the eighteenth and nineteenth century or the *Stop the Traffik* campaigners of today should be considered unbiblical. The Bible has no problem with the right of a state to outlaw practices which have come to facilitate evil, or for people to campaign for that. Indeed, the Bible provides the theological groundwork for the establishment of God's kingdom values in all areas of relationships, including laws to protect the vulnerable, and the offering of pastoral guidance to people who are subject to the legal authority of others or have authority over others.

Chapter 28

Jesus and the Cross

"God was in Christ reconciling the world to himself."
—2 Corinthians 5:19

Dawkins and Barker rightly dismiss all misguided attempts to disassociate the Jesus of the New Testament from the God of the Old Testament. They understand, much more than some woolly Christians who are hazy about their Christology, that Jesus claimed to be the Son of God, and that he was totally loyal to his Father in accepting his authority and perfect will. Barker knows enough about the Bible to refer us straight to John's Gospel where Jesus says "the Father and I are one,"[1] "whoever has seen me has seen the Father."[2] John describes Jesus as "the Word who was God."[3] John tells us that what made the Jewish religious leaders angry enough to stone Jesus was that he said things like "whoever keeps my word will never see death" and "before Abraham was born, I am," deliberately assigning to himself the sacred name of their God, Yahweh.[4]

Barker speculates that there may have been a Jesus other than the Jesus of the New Testament, a simple man who was humbler and nicer than him who didn't claim to be God and whose "original message of peace and

1. John 10:30
2. Ibid. 14:9
3. Ibid. 1:1
4. Ibid. 8:51–59

love" has been lost. But the Jesus of Scripture stands four-square behind the God of Scripture. In the Gospels Jesus saw all the Hebrew Scriptures as the inspired, authoritative Word of God.

> "For truly I tell you, until heaven and earth disappear, not the smallest letter, not the least stroke of a pen, will by any means disappear from the Law until everything is accomplished."[5]
>
> ". . .Scripture cannot be broken."[6]

"IT IS WRITTEN"

For Jesus, what the Scripture said was what God said. For example, when tempted by the Devil in the desert, Jesus responded each time with the words "*It is written. . .*" The verses he quotes are recorded in the Old Testament as being God's words, so Jesus might have said to the Devil "*God says. . ..*" But he didn't need to expressly invoke God to make the quotes authoritative in the face of the Devil, because that was clearly implied when he said, "it is written."[7]

Some people, in arguing for discontinuity between the Old and the New Testaments claim that Jesus rejected the retributive "eye for an eye" principle of the Old Testament, and took a much softer line on sin, but this view shows a deep misunderstanding. Jesus said,

> "*You have heard that it was said* 'eye for eye, tooth for tooth,' but I tell you. . If someone strikes you on the right cheek, turn to him the other also."[8]

However, what he was countermanding was not the original commandment by God. He did not say "*It is written. . .* but I tell you something else." He said, "*You have heard it was said. . .*" So, he was challenging the current understanding or faulty memory of the command as it had become distorted by Jesus' day. The "eye for an eye" legal principle was an important Old Testament law which provided just compensation for injurious acts and prevented the escalation of blood feuds. It was also not necessarily meant to be applied literally. If a master, for instance, struck his slave and damaged his eye, the law specified that rather than have his own eye put out, the

---

5. Matthew 5:18
6. John 10:35
7. Matthew 4 and Luke 4
8. Matthew 5:38–39

master had to grant the slave's freedom.[9] Jesus was in no way undermining this just and wise Old Testament law which was the best kind of protection for the vulnerable against the detrimental actions of those more powerful than them and provides the basis for recompense in civil law claims today. What he was challenging was the assumption in his day that the principle justified a personally bitter and vindictive spirit towards anyone who upset or hurt you. The Old Testament itself explicitly warns against a desire for personal revenge.

> "Do not say, 'I'll do to him as he has done to me; I'll pay that man back for what he did.'"[10]

The difference between Jesus saying "it is written" and "you have heard it was said" is also clearly demonstrated when Jesus says in Matthew 5:43 "you have heard it was said, 'love your neighbor and hate your enemy.'" It is assuredly *not written anywhere* in the Old Testament that you should "hate your enemy." So, this proves that when Jesus said "you have heard it was said" he was sometimes referring to extra-biblical ideas.

At other times he was referring to what Scripture *did* say, but was correcting a misunderstanding of it, as with the "eye for an eye" principle. Other times he was intensifying the ethical demands, as when he says in Matthew 5:27 "you have heard that it was said, 'do not commit adultery,' but I tell you that anyone who looks at a woman lustfully has already committed adultery with her in his heart."

On other occasions he was calling back the people to God's original desired, perfect and holy will, as when he said "it has been said, 'anyone who divorces his wife must give her a certificate of divorce,' but I tell you that anyone who divorces his wife, except for marital unfaithfulness, causes her to become an adulteress." (Matthew 5:31). In Matthew 19:7–9, Jesus said Moses permitted divorce because of their hardness of heart, "but it was not that way from the beginning." A Pharisee who might be tempted to claim he was complying scrupulously with Torah by legally divorcing his wife to marry the new object of his desire, was told by Jesus that, according to the spirit of the Torah, he was behaving in an adulterous way.[11] The important point is that Jesus never corrected, qualified, extended or deepened anything he had prefaced with "it is written."

---

9. Exodus 21:26–27
10. Proverbs 24:29
11. Mark 10:2–12

DID JESUS THINK THE OLD TESTAMENT REVELATION OF GOD TOO SEVERE?

In the area of sexual sin, the story of the woman caught in adultery is often cited with the intention of showing that Jesus thought adultery was less serious than made out in the Hebrew scriptures. But if we look at the story closely in John chapter eight, we see that that is not what Jesus said at all. The Old Testament penalty for adultery was stoning for the man and the woman. Harsh, we might think, but since adultery destroys community and causes misery and injustice, who has the right to say God got it wrong in the particular context in which he gave that law?

In the Gospel story, the scribes and Pharisees drag the woman into the Temple courts. They have the *woman only,* even though if she had been caught in the very act, as they had claimed, they could have apprehended the man as well. The law of Moses stipulated death for the man involved too, but *he* hadn't been dragged to the Temple courts. The whole thing reeked of misogyny and hypocrisy and even under scribal tradition, so often unfair and demeaning to women (unlike the Torah, the Old Testament Mosaic law—see chapter nine) the evidence probably would not have been admissible under Jewish due process. Two witnesses had to be provided to prove adultery and these witnesses had to show they could not have prevented the adulterous act from happening.

"Moses commanded us to stone her," the Pharisees and teachers of the law say; "what do *you* say Jesus?" After some writing on the ground, Jesus straightened up and said, "let the one who is without sin throw the first stone." It is important to note that Jesus did not criticize the law of Moses but said that the Mosaic punishment had to be initiated by someone who had the right to do so. In Jesus time, the moral state of Israel was utterly compromised. The Pharisees and "teachers of the law" asking Jesus if the woman should be stoned knew they were not acting in a properly legal way under Jewish procedures and the Romans had taken away their right to impose capital punishment anyway. The Gospel writer John tells us that their motive was not to honor the Torah but to trap Jesus. If he had said "stone her" then this would have been against Roman law and they sensed rightly he would have been perceived as heartless and misogynistic by the common people, especially the women. If he had said "don't stone her," he could have been accused of disrespecting the law of Moses given by God in the sacred Scriptures and being "soft on sin."

Jesus says the punishment can go ahead, the one who was morally perfect throwing the first stone. In other words he upholds the seriousness of the sin and the punishment, as long as it is initiated by someone who is without stain themselves and who therefore had the moral standing in that corrupt and hypocritical society to carry out this solemn act of judgment on behalf of God—and in the Temple courts of all places! He writes on the ground, and as he does so, the would-be executioners leave one by one, the eldest first. Many have wondered what Jesus was writing in the sand. Was it something to do with the sins (possibly sexual sins) of each individual, causing them to flee in terror? The eldest would have a longer list of sins (or more awareness of them) and be the keenest to get away.

Jesus was the only one who could have carried out the death penalty on this woman. His was the divine law the woman had broken. But his mission at his incarnation was to save, not to condemn. He was initiating a new (or *re*newed) covenant and forming a new kingdom on earth in which the civil penalties of the Torah were not to be directly translated, but which not only retained all the moral principles of the Torah but *intensified* them. Not only the act of adultery but lust in the heart should be repented of. And so he firmly but lovingly told the woman to "go and leave your life of sin." There was nothing ambiguous about this. It was a strong command to her to end her sinful behavior so that, apart from anything else, she would not be eternally condemned along with all those who refuse to repent of sin, sexual or otherwise.

Some point out that when, in Luke chapter four, Jesus went to Nazareth and preached in the synagogue and quoted from Isaiah chapter sixty-one he only quoted verse one and part of verse two, which spoke about the "good news to the poor"; the "binding up of the broken-hearted"; "freedom for captives"; and the "year of the Lord's favor." Jesus did not finish quoting verse two in which Isaiah speaks of the "day of vengeance of our God." This means, they argue, that Jesus was abrogating the idea of God's wrath. If this were true then it would make a nonsense of all Jesus' warnings about judgment. It is also a wrong assumption because it does not allow for the difference between Jesus' first and second coming. His first coming was to "proclaim the year of the Lord's favor." He heralded the opportunity to repent and believe the good news. He was not, as some hoped, during his earthly ministry, going to unleash God's judgment on the ungodly. Quoting that bit of Isaiah about the day of vengeance might have confirmed that mistaken idea to his hearers. But that time will come. There is plenty about that in the New Testament, both from Jesus own words and those of the apostles.

Another passage which might be used to claim that Jesus was *unlike* the God of the Old Testament is Luke 9:51–55. Jesus is resolutely "setting his face" to Jerusalem and the cross. Going through Samaria, he and his disciples were refused hospitality in a Samaritan village because they were heading for Jerusalem, and the Samaritans and Jews generally despised each other. James and John, called by Jesus the "Sons of Thunder" said "Lord, do you want us to call down fire from heaven to destroy them?" Some manuscripts add the words ". . .even as Elijah did." Jesus, the passage says, simply turned and rebuked them and they went on to another village.

So, in the eyes of some, this proves the disconnect between the fire-breathing Old Testament God with his vindictive prophets and a Jesus who would not countenance such a severe expression of divine power. But if the situation of Jesus and his disciples here is being compared to the incident in Second Kings chapter one involving Elijah and fire from heaven consuming two groups of fifty soldiers, then there are significant differences. Elijah was a single, vulnerable prophet "speaking truth to power." The king of Israel, based in Samaria, and referred to "as the king of Samaria" had been injured in an accident, but instead of turning to the LORD he sent messengers to a pagan god to see if he would recover. Elijah was told by God to confront the messengers and tell them to return to the king to ask why he was acting as if there were no God in Israel. They were to tell him that he would therefore not leave his deathbed. The king sent a captain with a detachment of fifty men to arrest Elijah, who was sitting at the top of a hill. The captain said, "man of God, come down." Elijah replied, "if I am a man of God may fire come down from heaven and consume you and your fifty men." Then this is what happened. The king sent another captain with fifty men and he took the same approach and the same thing happened.

The third captain had the spiritual insight to beg Elijah to spare his and his men's lives and to come voluntarily, which he did, after an angel of the LORD told him to go and not be afraid. So, we see that Elijah was not acting in a spiteful, vindictive way towards the previous two detachments of soldiers from Samaria who had come for him, but, as God's prophet, was appealing to his just intervention. The scenario in Luke chapter nine, hundreds of years later was very different. It happened in Samaria, but that is where the similarity ends. James and John, as Jewish zealots, had been influenced by generations of prejudice and antagonism towards Samaritans. In their anger at not being given lodgings, this hatred towards the Samaritans spilled over into a desire to see these ordinary civilians, who were unsurprisingly not pre-disposed to want to welcome Jews, suffer. Jesus knew the hearts of James and John and that is why he rebuked them. It was not a case of a humble appeal to God's protection and vindication, as per Elijah, but more like a case of smug one-upmanship and a desire to see premature fireworks of judgment. Furthermore, Jesus had told them he was on his way to Jerusalem to suffer and die for the sins of the world, not blast his enemies.

JESUS BELIEVED IN ALL THE HEBREW SCRIPTURES AND WAS HIS FATHER'S SON

The New Testament makes clear that for Jesus, what the Scriptures said about God was true and he believed every word. He told his disciples "everything written about me in the law of Moses, the prophets and the psalms must be fulfilled."[12] When asked by a lawyer to name the greatest commandment, he quoted the words of the Old Testament God from Deuteronomy 6:4 "You shall love the LORD your God with all your heart, and with all your soul, and with all your mind."[13] This is the book, essentially a sermon by Moses on the eve the Israelite invasion of Canaan, which contains many of the passages Barker cites to claim that God is the most unpleasant character in history.

Barker, though of course he does not believe in Jesus or God, correctly points out that Jesus constantly referred to the Hebrew Scriptures. He did this when in conflict with the Devil,[14] in argument with the Pharisees,[15] and when teaching his disciples.[16] The demands he made on his followers were every bit as uncompromising as the demands of Israel's God.[17]

However, Barker says that the New Testament is "one colossal missed opportunity."[18] The writers of it could have used the chance to develop a religion that moved on from all the jealousy, anger and misogyny. They could have invented a Jesus who denounced the God of Israel as being all the things he and Dawkins accuse him of being and proclaimed a new, loving God. Jesus could have apologized for the genocidal crimes of his father but instead he tells parables which suggest the enemies of God will be slaughtered in front of him.[19] He should have been horrified by his father's inhumane treatment of animals but instead sent a legion of demons into a herd of pigs, causing them all to drown.[20] Far from condemning his Father's pyromania, Jesus pours petrol on the flames by warning of fiery judgment for all who reject him and do evil.[21] Amputation would be better than the

---

12. Luke 24:44
13. Matthew 22:36–40
14. Ibid. 4:1–11
15. Mark 7:9
16. Luke 24:44
17. Luke 9:23; Matthew 10:34–37
18. Barker, *God, the Most Unpleasant Character in all Fiction*, 295
19. Luke 19:27
20. Matthew 8:28–34
21. Ibid. 13:42

fires of hell, he says.[22] Far from repenting of anger and cursing, Jesus was angry with the Pharisees, attacked Temple tradesmen with a whip[23] and cursed a harmless fig-tree.[24] He was his father's Son. He did not retreat from his Father's megalomania but said he was "greater than the Temple," greater than Jonah and Solomon[25] and behaved like a "paranoid warlord" when he said, "he who is not with me is against me."[26]

Jesus continued his Father's misogyny by appointing only male apostles and failed to condemn slavery. He told people they had to put himself so far above their wives and children, father and mothers, brothers and sisters, and their own lives as to "hate" them.[27] Rather than encourage expensive perfume to be sold to feed the poor, he commended a woman who lavished it on his feet.[28]

Barker just about brings himself to acknowledge Jesus did away with the need for animal sacrifice and healed some people. But he says Jesus did it not out of true compassion, but as signs of his deity and power. He refused to heal the sick child of a foreigner till pressured by the mother.[29] The "tiny handful" he healed ended up dying anyway. He could have helped millions if he'd taught us about microbes, parasites, water-borne diseases, earthquake preparedness, skin cancer and mosquito nets. Yes, he offered something that sounds nice—"eternal life" but this is cancelled out by all the horrible stuff he said about hell. His moral advice was unrealistic. Any good advice was copied from others. "Love your neighbor" meant only "love your fellow Israelites," Barker says. The Beatitudes contain some useful ethical principles and suggest a gentler faith than we find in the Old Testament but were predicated on receiving a reward rather than doing right for right's sake. He pours scorn on the idea of Jesus as a great ethical thinker, mainly because he was identical with "the Lord Jealous" of the Old Testament.

I am glad to be nearing the end of this book, because it means I will soon no longer have to read and think about the evil, slanderous things this man has said about the Lord Jesus and our heavenly Father. If Barker had a remaining shred of interest in the truth then he would acknowledge that if the Jesus of the Gospels is of the same character as the God revealed in

22. Ibid. 5:29–30
23. John 2:15
24. Matthew 21:19
25. Ibid. 12:6, 12:41–42
26. Matthew 12:30
27. Luke 14:26
28. Matthew 26:6–13
29. Ibid. 15:21–28

the Old Testament, then the qualities of the God Christians believe in have been admired by millions across the centuries. Jesus reveals the Father to be beautiful, humble, faithful, gracious. full of integrity, honest, self-controlled, merciful, compassionate, kind, patient, and willing to serve and suffer to the utmost degree out of love for friend and enemy alike.

Jesus *did* heal people out of compassion and without ulterior motive.[30] Healing people often meant great inconvenience because of the pressure of people flocking to him all the more.[31] He often told people to keep his healing work quiet so Jewish crowds would not be whipped up into misguided messianic fervor. He did not court publicity in Israel through his healings. Jesus felt compassion for those he knew would endure pain. When Jesus envisaged judgment and suffering for the people of Jerusalem, he wept,[32] as he did at the tomb of his friend Lazarus.[33] When Jesus highlighted the Old Testament command to "love your neighbor as yourself" and a lawyer wanted him to define "neighbor" he told *the parable of the Good Samaritan*, teaching that a neighbor was someone who needed your compassion whoever they were.[34]

Jesus welcomed little children at a time when they were unsentimentally viewed as a nuisance to be looked after only by women.[35] He did not ingratiate himself with high ranking people or despise lowly people. He treated every woman he met with dignity and respect, whether respectable or not in the eyes of society.[36] The foreign woman whose daughter, Barker says, Jesus was pressured into healing against his will, was a Syro-Phonecian woman whose people were steeped in demonic idol worship. Jesus was not asked to heal her daughter from a medical condition but to perform an *exorcism* on her. He was initially reluctant because he always deferred to his Father's will which was that in his earthly ministry he should concentrate on the "lost house of Israel." Exorcising an evil spirit from a child (which atheists like Barker would say is, by definition, child abuse) must be done in the context of humble, loving faith, otherwise the child is liable to suffer more harm. It was only when the girl's mother demonstrated this kind of faith that Jesus felt he had the Father's blessing to cast the demon out of her daughter.[37]

30. Matthew 9:36
31. Mark 6:30–31
32. Luke 19:41–44
33. John 11:35
34. Luke 10:25–37
35. Matthew 19:14
36. John 4:1–42
37. Mark 7:24–30

Jesus' character was so compelling and attractive that people left everything to follow him.[38] He used his power and authority to serve others.[39] When harried by crowds he did not have "compassion fatigue" but ministered to their physical and spiritual needs.[40] Jesus' moral teaching was revolutionary, not because it contradicted Old Testament law but because he revealed the full extent of God's commands as they were to be lived out. His authority and wisdom astounded friend and foe alike.[41]

Jesus' unselfishness and concern for others is shown by the fact that even when he knew his terrible death was near, he comforted his disciples.[42] While in agony on the cross, Jesus prayed for the forgiveness of those "who knew not what they were doing"[43] and made provision for the care of his mother Mary by the apostle John.[44]

THE CROSS OF CHRIST

Of course, the cross is the supreme example of Jesus' selfless love. However, Richard Dawkins has only contempt for the doctrine of the atonement.

In his foreword to Barker's book, Dawkins refers to the Chief Rabbi's accusation of anti-Semitism against him (withdrawn on reflection) which came about, Dawkins insists, because the Jewish leader initially misread the line "The God of the Old Testament is. . ." to mean *"as opposed to the God of the New Testament."* He says,

> "Of course that was not my intention. Indeed I gave reasons, elsewhere in *The God Delusion* for regarding the God of the New Testament as almost equally bad. There's little in the Old Testament to match the horror of St Paul's version of the ancient principle of the scapegoat: the Creator of the Universe and Inventor of the Laws of Physics couldn't think of a better way to forgive our sins. . . than to have himself hideously tortured and executed in human form as vicarious punishment. As Paul's [sic] epistle to the Hebrews (9:22) puts it, 'without the shedding of blood there is no forgiveness.' To be fair, Paul's authorship of

---

38. Matthew 19:27
39. John 13:1–17
40. Luke 9:10–11
41. Luke 4:32, Matthew 22:22
42. John 14:1–4
43. Luke 23:34
44. John 19:26–27

this epistle is disputed, but it is fully in the spirit of his often-expressed doctrine of atonement."[45]

The authorship of Hebrews is not an important issue because the Church recognizes the epistle as part of the canon of Holy Scripture. Hebrews, like the rest of the New Testament does indeed teach that God gave himself in the person of his Son to suffer, instead of us, the death, punishment and curse due to fallen humanity as the just penalty for sin. What is particular to Hebrews is the in-depth teaching of how the Old Testament sacrificial system was fulfilled in Christ and how that system taught the necessity of blood sacrifice to atone for sin. Atonement is about enabling sinful people, alienated from a holy God to be "at-one" with him again.

Sadly, it must be admitted that some Christians are confused about the cross of Christ and some even cease to be faithful to the message of the cross out of pride or fear of the kind of worldly scorn Dawkins shows. Some argue the message that Christ died in our place the death we deserved and turned aside God's wrath from us is no longer "saleable" in today's culture and therefore to be rejected or downplayed. It is true that there are aspects to atonement other than propitiation of wrath. There is the redemption and reconciliation which flows from propitiation. There is the truth that God showed us the full extent of his love and the full horror of sin, in a way that can move our hearts to thankful faith. The powers of evil did their worst and Jesus still won the victory. The memory of his sacrifice acts a focal point for sacramental fellowship and the healing love of the Christian community.

However, a key part of the way that atonement works is based on the truths revealed about God in the Old Testament which have come under so much attack from scornful writers. It is views like those of Dawkins and Barker about the Old Testament which undermine belief in the Gospel message. These views are that sin is not really such a big issue to God and was not central to what Jesus underwent on the cross. God's hostility to sin is not personal. The need for propitiation is a primitive human instinct, unworthy of the kind of God "enlightened" people can believe in.

There are Christians who even say that in effect we don't need Old Testament concepts of holiness, sin and judgement. They like to cite the story of the Prodigal Son to say that this proves there is no need for atonement for sin. God will be there to forgive us and shower us with blessing whenever we get tired of sin and its consequences. This is a serious mishandling of a wonderful parable Jesus told about the Father heart of God and his grace and mercy to his beloved children. It shows us the Father, longing for his errant son to return, scanning the horizon day after day and seeing him in the

---

45. Barker, *God the Most Unpleasant Character in all Fiction*, p ix foreword

distance and running out to meet him and embrace him. The father doesn't need to hear a repentance speech because the son's return and humbled attitude of heart is itself a sufficient act of repentance. He is not accepted back as a slave but as a son, with the full dignity and position of a son in his father's household.

What this parable does not do is to explain how we become a son of God nor does it deal explicitly with the price paid for our forgiveness. That is why there is no mention of an atoning sacrifice. The relationship the son has to the father is already a given in the parable. Those who deny the seriousness of sin say that everyone is a son of God, like the prodigal was a son of his father. This is not what the Bible teaches. The only way to become a son of God is to be given that spiritual privilege by God and he only gives it to those who are united with Christ—those who have faith in the living Word of God.[46] Faith in this Word is faith in Christ, and in his atoning death for our sins. If we genuinely believe Jesus is the Son of God who died for our sins and rose again and sincerely submit to him as Lord, then, and *only* then, do we have the right and status of sonship with Almighty God. It is only in this light that we can know the real Father heart of God as demonstrated in the parable of the prodigal son.

The Old Testament teaches that spiritual alienation from God through sin is mankind's chief problem.[47] Sin brings God's wrath and condemnation.[48] This wrath has to be *propitiated*, turned aside, made atonement for,[49] by some expression of sincere contrition connected to the ultimate sentence of death for sin.[50] God's justice must be upheld, not because of some impersonal or arbitrary law external to himself but because in his very nature he is holy.[51] However, God in his forbearance delayed his just punishment for the sin of humanity,[52] putting into operation a plan of salvation that involved calling into being a holy nation, from which, at the right time, would come a Savior to justify and vindicate his people, be they near or far, and put the whole world to rights.[53] Jesus, in both his first coming, and

---

46. John 1:12–13
47. Genesis 2:17
48. See chapter 21. Just to give three references from just one of the prophets—Jeremiah 21:5–6, 23:19–20, 30:23–24
49. Exodus 12:1–30, Leviticus 16, Numbers 16:46–50, 25:1–13
50. See chapter 7
51. See chapter 20
52. Romans 3:23–26
53. Matthew 3:2, First Corinthians 15:20–28

crucifixion, resurrection, ascension and his coming again, is the fulfilment of everything promised in the Old Testament.[54]

In particular, his death at Passover enabled our deliverance from God's just wrath and rightful condemnation. He was the lamb who was sacrificed so that we might go free.[55] He bore our sins on the tree by becoming a curse for us.[56] The punishment for our sin was inflicted on Christ.

> "He was pierced for our transgressions, crushed for our iniquities; the punishment that brought us peace was upon him, and by his wounds we are healed. We all like sheep have gone astray, each one of us has turned to his own way, and the LORD has laid on him the iniquity of us all."[57]

In Mark chapter ten, when Jesus was challenging the presumption of James and John in asking "to sit at his right and left" when he came into his kingdom, he asked them if they would be willing to undergo the baptism that he was to undergo (meaning his crucifixion). He said also "can you drink the cup I drink?" Drinking a cup is an allusion to "drinking the cup of God's wrath" as referred to in Psalm 71:8, Isaiah 51:17, Jeremiah 25:15-16, and 17-28, Ezekiel 23:32-34, and Habbakuk 2:16. The darkness that came over the land when Jesus was crucified symbolized the Day of the Lord's wrath in Isaiah 13:9-11 where it says "the sun will be darkened." Jesus cried out "why have you forsaken me?"[58] The forsakenness that Jesus experienced was a consequence of the wrath of God which his voluntary sacrifice was propitiating.

54. Second Corinthians 1:20

55. John 1:29. First Peter 1:18-19

Some question why, if substitutionary atonement was a central part of the crucifixion, Jesus did not die on the Day of Atonement rather than at Passover. This fails to understand that the motif of substitutionary atonement was at the heart of the Passover festival. The lamb without defect was sacrificed and its blood put on the door posts to turn aside God's wrath which would otherwise have fallen on the Israelite firstborn as well as the Egyptian firstborn. The Passover commemorations celebrated not only propitiation of just wrath however, but also everything which flowed from that—redemption from enslavement, victory over the powers of evil, and the trusting and obedient response of the people in following God's instructions for the new life of God's kingdom. The Bible does indeed teach there is more to the cross of Christ than the doctrine of penal substitutionary atonement, but this aspect is essential and cannot be denied. The connection between Christ's death and the Day of Atonement is clearly demonstrated by the curtain in the Temple being torn from top to bottom on the day of Christ's crucifixion (Matt. 27:51) providing access to all to the "Holy of Holies." Before this, only the High Priest could enter the Most Holy Place after the requisite sacrifice once a year—on the Day of Atonement.

56. First Peter 2:24

57. Isaiah 53:5-6, Acts 8:26-35

58. Matthew 27:46

Jesus said in John 3:14–15 "just as Moses lifted up the snake in the desert, so the Son of Man must be lifted up, that everyone who believes in him may have eternal life." This refers to when God's wrath, provoked by their rebellious spirit, was upon the Israelites in the form of venomous snakes. God mercifully provided a means by which the people could escape his wrath. All who looked to a bronze snake lifted up on a pole were healed from poisonous snake bite. To atone for all the sins of the world required more than a bronze snake however, it required the sending of God's one and only Son. But, as the famous next verse says, God so loved the world that he did indeed send his only Son into the world, so that all who believe in him should not perish but have eternal life.

Those who are united to Christ through faith "have been crucified with him."[59] We have "died to sin"[60] and are no longer under God's wrath and condemnation, which we would be if we were among those who reject the Son.[61] We are united with Christ also in his resurrection,[62] having eternal life guaranteed by his Spirit within us.[63] We share in the glorious future of the restoration of all creation.[64] Consequently our lives have meaning and purpose and we are destined for eternal joy with our loving heavenly father and the Lord Jesus Christ.[65]

This is the glorious Gospel. A faithful response to it is not a matter of mere cerebral assent to a legalistic formula for salvation, but a real relationship of trust and obedience to the Lord Jesus Christ. We show our love for him by obeying his commands.[66] When we submit to him as Lord his kingdom comes. His will is done on earth as it is in heaven.[67] And one day every knee will bow and confess he is Lord[68] and heaven and earth will come together in a glorious consummation of every truly human hope and dream.[69]

---

59. Galatians 2:20
60. Romans 6:2
61. Romans 8:1 cf. John 3:18, 36
62. Romans 6:5
63. Ephesians 1:14
64. Romans 8:18–25
65. Psalm 16:11, 1 Corinthians 2:9
66. John 14:15, 21, 23
67. Matthew 6:9–13
68. Philippians 2:10–11
69. Revelation 21, 22

Chapter 29

The Integrity and Authority of Scripture

"All Scripture is God-breathed and useful for teaching, rebuking, correcting and training in righteousness, so that the man of God may be thoroughly equipped for every good work"

—2 Timothy 3:16

We have seen in the introduction to this book and in the previous chapter that it is a mistake to see the Bible as a "game of two halves" with the first "half," the Old Testament, depicting a nasty, tribal, sectarian Jewish God, and the second "half," the New Testament, portraying a nice, universal, inclusive "Christian" God.

OLD VERSUS NEW?

Many also fall into the mistake of seeing the Old Testament as all about law, judgment, and vengeance while the New Testament is all about grace, mercy, forgiveness, restorative justice and faith. The New Testament itself testifies that this is a travesty of understanding. With regard to the supposed dichotomy between Old Testament law and New Testament faith, Hebrews chapter eleven tells us to follow the example of all the people of faith in the Old Testament, who lived both before and after the giving of the Law to the People of Israel on Mount Sinai. When the apostle Paul is at great pains in his letters to the Galatians and Romans to say that believers no longer have to be circumcised and obey all the Mosaic laws, he argues that the father of all who relate to God through faith, independently of law, was Abraham, who lived two thousand years before Christ came.[1] Faith has always been the primary requirement.

> "Without faith it is impossible to please God, because anyone who comes to him must believe that he exists and that he rewards those who earnestly seek him."[2]

God never wanted merely legalistic adherence to a set of religious rules. He wanted his people to love and trust him and reflect his character in their treatment of others. The Old Testament prophets, foreshadowing Jesus, inveighed against outward legal compliance hiding inner moral corruption.[3]

So why did God give "the Law" to Moses and the people of Israel after he delivered them from slavery in Egypt? The New Testament gives us the following reasons:

1. It was a temporary means of teaching and disciplining the Israelites, who were very prone to transgression, about holiness and moral behavior.[4] At that stage in salvation history the people of God were identified with the nation state of Israel and therefore civil and criminal codes had to ensure Israel lived in a noticeably different way from the surrounding nations.

2. It held the Israelites in a kind of "protective custody" while they were immature and lacking in godly wisdom and discernment, until the new life given by faith in Christ was revealed. The law was "put in charge to lead us to Christ," when that supervision was no longer needed.[5]

3. The law brought knowledge of God's standards of righteousness and convicted the spiritually aware of their need for God's mercy in Christ to take them from "the body of death" to life.[6]

The New Testament says the Old Testament law was holy, righteous, and good (Romans 7:12). The only problem for sinful human beings was that it showed up our sin but could not empower us to overcome our deep-rooted sinful nature. In terms of salvation, it was the diagnosis of the problem rather

1. Galatians 3
2. Hebrews 11:6
3. E.g., Amos 5:21–24
4. Galatians 3:19
5. Galatians 3:23–25
6. Romans 7:7–25

than the solution, which it was never designed to be. In terms of a deep inner change, the law was weak and powerless.[7] If a law had been given that *could* have imparted life, then this would have been it.[8] But law itself is not capable of changing human beings deep on the inside. Trying to rely on the law for salvation would only result in us being cursed when we fail to keep it.[9] So the law cannot justify us in God's sight or make our hearts pure.[10] Legalism is a form of idolatry, which is when we take something good that God has made or given us and put it above a genuine, trusting relationship with the living God.

The Old Testament itself recognizes the problem with the Old Covenant, of which the Law was a part, and Jeremiah prophesied.

> "Behold, the days are coming, declares the LORD, when I will make a new covenant with the house of Israel and with the house of Judah. It will not be like the covenant I made with their fathers when I took them by the hand to lead them out of the land of Egypt—a covenant they broke, though I was a husband to them, " declares the LORD. "But this is the covenant I will make with the house of Israel after those days, declares the LORD. I will put my law in their minds and inscribe it on their hearts. And I will be their God, and they will be my people. No longer will each man teach his neighbor or his brother, saying, 'Know the LORD,' because they will all know me, from the least of them to the greatest, declares the LORD. For I will forgive their iniquities and will remember their sins no more."[11]

So the necessity of faith, grace, mercy, forgiveness, and the promise of a new covenant is all there in the Old Testament.

Professor John Goldingay, an Old Testament scholar, provocatively then asks the question "do we need the *New* Testament?"[12] With a twinkle in his eye, he reverses the usual question of "do we need the *Old* Testament?" and asks what the New Testament gives us that the Old Testament doesn't. I would answer that it gives the following:

1. It reveals the fulfilment of all the Old Testament promises, such as the Jeremiah prophecy above. There are hundreds of prophecies which

---

7. Hebrews 7:18
8. Galatians 3:21
9. Ibid. 3:10
10. Hebrews 7:19
11. Jeremiah 31:31–34
12. Goldingay *Do We Need the New Testament?*

find their fulfilment in Christ, whether in his first coming or second regarding the coming of God's kingdom rule, the establishment of justice and mercy and the renewal of all things. Those Jewish people who do not recognize Jesus as their Messiah say that Jesus did not accomplish all the things the Messiah was supposed to do e.g., bring world peace. But the New Testament does announce the inauguration of God's kingdom[13] and says that Jesus will complete his reign[14] and bring world peace at his second coming.[15]

2. The New Testament reveals the full extent of God's incarnational love. God honored humanity by coming in the flesh in the person of his Son Jesus and demonstrated in a human life in a Jewish context what God is like.

3. Jesus provided the basis for an "enlargement theology"[16] which extends the covenant to all Gentiles who respond in faith to him. Believing Gentiles can now be grafted on to the olive tree of faith to join faithful Jewish people, without having to become circumcised, kosher compliant Jews.[17] The only qualification for belonging to the people of God is now faith in Christ. Circumcision and adherence to legal boundary markers are no longer necessary since faith in Christ supersedes them. Gone is the ritual distinction between "clean" and "unclean" symbolizing clean Jews and unclean Gentiles.

4. Jesus provided full atonement for sins and therefore abrogated the need for continuing blood sacrifices. No-one need any longer fear God's wrath and condemnation as we can be united with Christ through faith.[18] We have full reconciliation with God.[19] Jesus became the guarantee of a better covenant, because the old covenant had priests who died, but Jesus is our high priest who ever lives to intercede for us before the throne of God above.[20]

5. Through the resurrection of Jesus, the New Testament teaches an eternal perspective which was only hinted at in places in the Old. This

13. Matthew 11:4–5
14. Ibid. 25:31–32
15. Revelation 21:1–8
16. See Jacob *Enlargement Theology*. Jacob shows how the Bible rejects both "dual-covenant theology" (which claims Jews don't need Jesus) and "replacement theology" (which claims God no longer has any purpose or special concern for ethnic Israel).
17. Romans 11:17–21
18. Ibid. 8:1
19. Second Corinthians 5:18–19
20. Hebrews 7:22–25

makes a radical difference to the attitude we can have to those who currently reject God. We now have full confidence that those who refuse to repent and continue to defy God and oppress others will be judged eternally. In this life we can endure suffering with patience, forgiving those who hurt us and leaving it in God's hands to judge the wicked on the day of his wrath.[21] We have eternal life[22] and the New Testament tells us how we can live in the light of the resurrection hope.

6. Jesus ascension and God's gift of the Holy Spirit to all who believe in Christ enables us to know him and have the law of Christ written on our hearts (in fulfilment of Jeremiah 31:31–34) and so we want to live to please him, serving him in the power of the Spirit and displaying the fruit of the Spirit in our lives.

What the New Testament does not do is provide evidence that the Old Testament misrepresents God's character. It does not undermine it or correct it or suggest any of it is unworthy of being part of the whole Scriptural witness.

However, I do empathize with those who find themselves wincing at parts of the Old Testament, or who are embarrassed or perplexed by some passages. I have experienced these feelings too. The longer I have been a Christian though and the more passages I have studied in preparation for preaching and teaching from them, the more I realize that much wrestling is needed when we, who "see through a glass darkly,"[23] encounter the whole breadth and depth of God's holy Word.

TRUSTING AND OBEYING THE WORD

I have though found myself unsettled and perplexed by difficult passages throughout the whole of Scripture, not just the Old Testament "texts of terror." In the New Testament, the teaching about the seriousness of sin and the exclusive demands of Christ are as much a challenge as anything in the Old Testament. I know however that something is fatal to this necessary wrestling with God's Word. That is any lessening in our commitment to recognizing the *whole of Scripture as God's Word*.

It is possible, by subtle and sophisticated intellectual means, to undermine the impact of the severe accounts of God's holy and just wrath in action, or the "hard sayings" of Jesus or the propitiatory nature of the atonement. Because biblical interpretation is not easy and straightforward,

---

21. Romans 12:19, Deuteronomy 32:35
22. John 3:16
23. First Corinthians 13:12

many question whether the notion of "biblical authority" has any meaning. They argue that it is too simplistic to say "The Bible says" about anything and they maintain that biblical diversity means the Bible does not speak a coherent, clear and consistent message and it cannot therefore have the kind of authority that requires humble submission.

N.T. Wright in *The Authority of God in Scripture* says that it only makes sense to use the phrase "the authority of Scripture" if it is shorthand for "the authority of the triune God exercised somehow *through* [sic] Scripture."[24] I do not think this is true and it leaves the door open for a wedge to be driven between God and his Word. It is axiomatic that God has authority. He wouldn't be God otherwise. What is not axiomatic is whether a particular collection of writing has any authority. But it does if God authorizes it.

A king who issues a proclamation puts his authority into it. If one of his subjects says that he submits to the king's authority but not the authority of the proclamation, he is separating the king from his proclamation in a way that would undermine the king's effective governance. Of course, the subject might argue that the proclamation is a forgery or has been mistakenly copied down or mischievously "edited" by those who have their own agenda or has been otherwise "lost in translation." People say this about the Bible. But we cannot simultaneously say that the Bible is "God-breathed" or that it is "God's Word" on the one hand *and* that it does not possess authority, albeit authority derived from God, on the other. If it were merely an *unauthoritative* repository in which, through human ingenuity or spiritual enlightenment, the authority of God might be found somewhere, then there would be little if anything to distinguish it from any other writing.

A human being who is given authority by someone able to delegate authority *carries* the degree of authority which is delegated. A man who speaks the truth is recognized as having authority in his communication because he is reflecting the authoritative God of truth. The Bible has both types of authority. Therefore, it is right and necessary to talk about the Bible's authority if we are to believe that its purpose is to conveying to us the truth of the character, deeds and purposes of God.[25]

24. Wright *Scripture and the Authority of God*, 17–18

25. I have learned a lot from Tom Wright and his prolific output of scholarly work (particularly in the 1990s) in explaining how the New Testament holds together in itself and he has helped to further biblical understanding among so many. He has done much great work in countering the sceptics who claim the "historical Jesus" was different to the Jesus of the Gospels, has demonstrated the biblical witness to the historicity of the bodily resurrection, and has skillfully demolished the inadequate understanding of the Christian hope as a vague disembodied afterlife in the clouds. Like other "New Perspective on Paul" theologians he rightly argues against the false dichotomy of Old Testament "Law' versus New Testament "Grace." I slightly tremble at having to disagree

Just as the incarnate Jesus is fully man and fully God, so Jesus attested to Scripture's status as both fully the word of man and fully the Word of God. If God through his Holy Spirit "authored" Scripture (through various human beings with their distinctive backgrounds, personalities, and experiences) then he "authorized" it and it carries his authority. In practice this means, among other things, that when we are seeking to maintain a pattern of sound teaching in the Church, remaining faithful to the one true Gospel into which we have been baptized, we appeal to Scripture when there is debate as to what this means.

Old Testament Scripture has authority not because it contains commands which are all directly transferable to today, or absolutely everything in it can or should be expressed in the form of propositional truth, but because the faithful and humble reader can trust it to make us "wise unto salvation through faith in Christ Jesus."[26] Chris Wright says that the Old Testament Scriptures are described as "God-breathed" in Second Timothy 3:16 and because of this divine origin,

> "they are both savingly effective and ethically relevant. This New Testament text agrees with the unselfconscious affirmation of dual authorship of the law (human and divine) found in Ezra 7:6—'the law of Moses, which the LORD, the God of Israel, had given.' The question therefore is not *whether* the Old Testament law has authority and relevance for us as Christians, but *how* that given authority is to be earthed and that relevance applied."

There is some sterility in the "biblical inerrancy" debate because of a misunderstanding as to the issues at stake. I prefer not to use the term "inerrancy" because it conjures up an image of the Bible as too much like a telephone directory in which it is vital for its credibility that there is not one digit out of place.[27]

A better way of describing the Bible's authority is to say that it is completely trustworthy in revealing God's character and saving purposes and activity in the world. If the biblical writers in the Old Testament misrepresent the character of God by claiming that God did and said things which he did not do or say (and which are immoral, unjust or cruel), then this undermines the trustworthiness of Scripture and hence its authority.

---

with him about biblical authority.

26. Second Timothy 3:15

27. The discipline of textual criticism is necessary where there are divergencies in the surviving manuscripts. There will always be difficult questions of translation from the Hebrew and Greek. Mention has been made of the difficulty in translating the numerical units given for the population and armies of Israel.

THE INTEGRITY AND AUTHORITY OF SCRIPTURE   269

A few years ago, I attended a conference for all the clergy in the diocese of Salisbury. One of the keynote speakers, the author and theologian, James Alison, invited by the Bishop of Salisbury, gave a good example of the connection between rejecting the authority of the Old Testament (in the way I have described its authority above) and de-constructing the New Testament's teaching about the propitiatory nature of the atonement.

Alison, a disciple of René Girard, who dismisses all ideas of propitiation as promoting the "myth of redemptive violence" referred to Joshua 7 where, after the successful battle of Jericho, the whole city was to be "devoted to the LORD" by the Israelites, which meant that every living thing was to be killed and all gold, silver, bronze and iron placed in the LORD'S sanctuary. There was to be no plundering for private gain. This chapter says that a man called Achan broke this solemn command and took for himself a beautiful robe, and some gold and silver and hid them in the ground inside his tent. It is written that "the LORD'S anger burned against Israel" because of this, and the Israelites then suffered what was for them a perplexing military setback, resulting in a catastrophic loss of spiritual confidence and anguished prayer to God as to why he seemed to have left them. God then revealed to Joshua the reason for their defeat and his anger with them. Israel had lied and stolen some of the devoted things. God supernaturally revealed the culprit to be Achan, who admitted his sin. He and his family were all stoned to death and all his possessions burned and over Achan was heaped a large pile of rocks. Joshua 7:26b says, "Then the LORD turned from his fierce anger." The invasion of Canaan then proceeded in chapter eight with the LORD giving the city of Ai into Israel's hands.

Alison's take on the story was a masterclass in beguiling de-construction, designed to enable him to radically re-shape what the New Testament says about the cross and, significantly for him, as a self-identified gay man, sexuality. He says that after destroying Jericho, Israel suffered a minor military defeat and its leaders were thrown into a moral panic. Everyone had been plundering things for themselves from the city, and the leaders of Israel needed to find a scapegoat for their shame, so by means of a lottery system of "justice" they picked on poor Achan. He was just an ordinary Israelite, just like them all, no more guilty or less guilty than anyone else, but the wrath of the community needed to find a focus in order to draw the boundary line between who was "in" and who "out" and renew their feeling of social cohesion.

By inflicting their wrath on Achan and his family in a "classic lynch murder" they restored their sense of peaceful equilibrium. At both ends of the story, being primitive fundamentalists, they projected their feelings onto God. So, when they suffered a collapse in morale, they attributed their shame and confusion to the "wrath of God" being upon them. When they had vented their fury (claiming it was God's wrath) on the unfortunate victim, they projected their sense of self-satisfaction onto God and described his wrath as being propitiated—turned away from them. The Old Testament thus does not reveal the character of God, but the warped projections of men onto God. It becomes anthropology, not theology.

Not being enlightened of course, these Israelites did not realize that there is no wrath in God. The Old Testament becomes for Alison simply the dark backdrop of numerous vindictive sacrificial murders which evolved from human sacrifice to liturgical animal sacrifice but with the same mindset of redemptive violence, as against the light of the New Testament. He then deftly evaded the problem though that the New Testament also speaks of the wrath of God upon sin. Having unashamedly deconstructed the Hebrew scriptures, Alison went on to apply a similar, but more subtle, technique to the New. He contended that Jesus died on the cross, an innocent victim, in order to show the scapegoat system itself to be the essence of all that is wrong in the world. Speaking of the wrath of God becomes a way of describing the mindset that is a leftover from the way God was perceived in the dark days of the Old Testament. Wrath is in fact simply the consequences of living with the old belief that it is necessary for us to inflict some kind of justified wrath on others. Wrath is what rebounds on us when we attempt to play the game of excluding people—the Achans of this world, such as gay people.

So we see the connection between rejecting the revelation of God's character in the Old Testament, as the false teacher Marcion did in the second century AD, and the sophisticated skewing of the nature of Christ's atonement and the life we are called to live in the light of the Gospel. Wrath, whether mistaken or cynical, is not the only sin which disfigures humanity but Alison's schema holds that the only real sinners and recipients of "wrath" are those who believe the limits of Christian diversity exclude those who willfully and persistently refuse to put to death the things that belong to our sinful nature. But the New Testament says,

> "Put to death, therefore, whatever belongs to your earthly nature: sexual immorality, impurity, lust, evil desires and greed, which is idolatry. Because of these, the wrath of God is coming."[28]
>
> "For of this you can be sure: No immoral, impure or greedy person—such a person is an idolater—has any inheritance in the kingdom of Christ and of God. Let no one deceive you with empty words, for because of such things God's wrath comes on those who are disobedient. Therefore do not be partners with them."[29]

28. Colossians 3:5–6
29. Ephesians 5:5–6

The New Testament's authority would be similarly undermined if the Gospel writers claim Jesus did or said things which he did not do or say, or if the epistle writers wrote prophetic teaching and pastoral instruction which was flawed because of their own sinfulness or ignorance. In this sense the Bible, as the original authors wrote it, unlike the Pope, or the bishops and the General Synod of the Church of England, has to be infallible or it is not fit for the purpose of instructing us in the ways of an infallible God and his righteousness. It is no good saying, "well it's not perfect but it's all we have." Whenever anyone wants to reject anything the Bible says they can then say that they are merely dispensing with the "imperfect" bits, one of the verses or passages or even books, which does not, in their opinion, sit comfortably with the kind of God they want to believe in. Just as it would be fatal to Jesus' status as the divine Son of God come in the flesh (the living Word) were he in fact to have been a sinful, flawed or fallible human being *in any respect*, so it would be similarly fatal to Scripture's status as the written Word of God for its message[30] to have been corrupted by *any* flawed revelation of the character of God.

HOW DOES GOD SPEAK THROUGH AUTHORITATIVE SCRIPTURE?

Of course the Bible is not written as an easy step by step instruction manual addressed directly to us in our world today. To read the Bible for ourselves and discern what God is saying to us is to become, to some extent, a theologian. We read the text, coming to it with all our experience, knowledge, pre-suppositions, emotions and spiritual understanding. Some things we will immediately understand, or think we understand, about the truth the biblical writer or narrator is saying. In order to understand well however, we must try to enter the world of the writer and appreciate the genre of literature being used, the historical, cultural and linguistic context and the way the writer has chosen to present his material. This will reveal how the writer,

---

30. There are those who say that because we don't have the original Bible manuscripts it is meaningless to say they were without error in revealing theological truth. But the many thousands of ancient surviving copied manuscripts we have make it possible, through the discipline of textual criticism, to attest to the reliability of the Hebrew and Greek content we have. See *Does God believe in Atheists?* Blanchard, 389–407. There is no body of ancient literature in the world that comes anywhere near the wealth of textual attestation of the Bible. Tiny differences have occasionally been found, but not as to question anything of significance as to what it says. The idea that the text we have today was formed by copyists who made things up, added and changed things over time is easily disprovable by anyone with any knowledge in this area.

inspired by God, relates to God and sees God's character and his interaction with the world. God accommodates himself into the world of the writer, so that transcendent truth can be earthed in human experience. Because this accommodation had to take place at a particular time and place in history, we, who live in a different period of history, have to somehow "travel" to that time and place to see how God accommodated himself.

For example, to understand the narrative parts of the Old Testament, we need to "time travel" to the world of the ancient near east and appreciate that culture and worldview. To really "get" the psalms we must understand both this and the poetic conventions the psalmists used to express his feelings. These conventions include very passionate, visceral language.

To understand the wisdom book of Job, we have to see that God, through the compiler(s) of the book, somehow speaks through the conflicting (and contradictory) dialogue of the actors in the drama as well as his recorded intervention at the end of the book. To learn what Paul was saying in his letter to the Corinthians we must "travel to Corinth" in the first century AD to see what specific issues Paul was addressing in the light of the unchanging Gospel.

The technical word for all of this is "exegesis." It is the discipline of ascertaining the meaning of the text in its original context. I believe this should be the foundation of "hermeneutics," which is the wider process of applying Scripture to today's world. Some fall into the temptation of going straight to a process of distinguishing "now" from "then" in a way that gives them a lot of room for "creative re-interpretation."

Some people do this because it is easier than doing serious exegetical work and it flatters us by allowing us to start from the position of feeling superior to the writer because of our modern knowledge. It feeds into what C.S. Lewis called "chronological snobbery."

I suspect others avoid thorough exegesis because they don't want to be confronted with any exegetical findings that might alleviate some of the perceived problems *and* challenge the current *zeitgeist*. So, regarding the sexuality debate, it is quite convenient for revisionists who claim to be biblically rooted to take an exegetically simplistic approach to what Paul says about women (as some conservatives do), readily believing he commanded their literal silence in the congregation and forbade them to exercise any form of leadership. They know they can then safely use a form of hermeneutics to allow a departure from it—e.g. "Paul's worldview was one of male hegemony, but we now understand God to be more egalitarian and inclusive," A similar hermeneutic is used to breezily sidestep the clearly negative passages about homosexual acts. E.g. "Paul was ignorant about loving, stable, faithful same-sex relationships, therefore we should now interpret the Bible as not having a problem with homosexuality today. For example, Steve Chalke does this.[31]

And when it comes to the Old Testament, the withering of exegetical muscles through disuse and the diet of hermeneutical "fast-food," means little challenge is raised to the view that the Bible claims God commanded an indefensible genocide against the Canaanites. Why bother learning about God's overarching purposes, the debased and corrupting nature of Canaanite religion, the writer's use of hyperbolic military language, the composition of the resisting Canaanite fortified towns, and the incorporation of Canaanites into the believing community of Israel, when so-called hermeneutics offers the easy solution of saying that the backward people in those days had a perverted idea of what loyalty to God required, but we can extract from it some message about being fully committed to the LORD in the fight against evil. Today, the argument goes, we are much more ethically advanced and can critique the biblical witness, using a hermeneutic which can throw out what is bad and keep the good, which we can then use to shape our own spirituality. The effect of all this, however, is certainly not to increase zeal to obey the Word of God. A reasonable person would think "if being zealous for the LORD can result in the kind of atrocities spoken of in the Bible, then I don't want to be that committed."

DOES BELIEVING IN THE INTEGRITY AND AUTHORITY OF THE BIBLE MEAN "TAKING IT LITERALLY"?

It is impossible to answer this question properly without examining what we mean by "taking it literally." If it means that we read the Bible with zero intelligence, or mistakenly thinking it was dictated directly by God in the way Muslims believe the Qu'ran to have been, paying no attention to the genre of literature that a particular passage is part of, applying a crude and simplistic interpretation of biblical material, failing to appreciate nuance, metaphor and truth other than the obviously propositional, and failing to see how Jesus is the fulfilment of all Scripture, then absolutely we should *not* "take the Bible literally."[32]

---

31. https://www.premierchristianity.com/Featured-Topics/Homosexuality/The-Bible-and-Homosexuality-Part-One

32. A historical example of "taking the Bible literally" in a wrong way was the use by some sixteenth century authorities of Psalm 93:1b to refute Galileo's insistence that the earth orbited the sun. "The world is firmly established. It cannot be moved." The psalm is a poetic tribute to God's power and majesty and ability to give us a secure earth to live on, not astronomical science.

But it must be said that even those who are mocked as "literalistic fundamentalists" are generally people who do not seek to worship the book, but the God of the book. Nobody thinks God directly engraved the whole Bible on tablets (like the Ten Commandments on Mount Sinai) rather than inspiring the different authors with the Holy Spirit. Nobody is an absolute literalist. No one I know reads the account of Jesus saying "Go tell that fox. . ."[33] and thinks Jesus was saying that his disciples should convey a message to a creature with pointy ears and a bushy tail. Everyone knows from the context he was talking about King Herod.

As with the phrase "taking it literally," talking about "Fundamentalists" is fruitless unless the term is defined. I would say that for me the main things associated with the category Christian "Fundamentalist" would be:[34]

1. An insistence on reading Genesis chapter one as teaching creation in six, twenty-four-hour periods, a belief known as "young earth creationism."

2. A general suspicion of *all* modern biblical scholarship and an instinctive anti-intellectualism.

3. The belief that the King James Bible (Authorized Version) is quasi-inspired and the only acceptable English translation.

4. The placing of a such a high emphasis on cultural separation from "the godless" that this sometimes means isolated and deeply embedded cultural traditions influence beliefs and practices more than the ongoing reformation and renewal which comes from spiritual openness to the fullness of biblical truth. This "cultural imprisonment" can lead to suspicion of outsiders, and even support for ethnic segregation, such as in South Africa and the Southern States of America. It can also lead to equating right-wing political views with Christianity, in a mirror image of those who claim Christianity should be on the side of left-wing or liberal political agendas.

5. A simplistic espousal of Zionism and an uncritical, political support for all the actions of the nation state of Israel as against Arabs and Muslims.

6. A tendency to interpret over-literally the kind of pictorial language used in eschatological and apocalyptic biblical literature such as

---

33. Luke 13:32

34. See Edwards and Stott, *Evangelical Essentials*, 90–91 for a slightly fuller list of things associated with Christian fundamentalism. It is important to say (as Stott does) that some who are characterized by one or more of these beliefs or attitudes may not be characterized by others

Daniel and Revelation, leading to dogmatic assertion of beliefs around the millennial reign of Christ and the rapture.

Of course, the term "fundamentalist" is also used derogatively, not just to describe people who are considered on the lunatic fringe of Christianity, but adherents of other faiths who are regarded as "extremist" or "militant." It is worth, however, thinking about what we mean by the term, whoever it is applied to. If we build a framework of belief or practice on a foundation that is wholly good and true, such as Christians believe the God and Father of our Lord Jesus Christ to be, then holding to the foundations (fundamentals) will be a very good thing. If however, the foundation is even slightly awry, this will lead to all manner of problems. The resulting superstructure will be unstable and dangerous.

Jesus could be described as a "radical Fundamentalist" or a "fundamentalist Radical" because his understanding of who he was and what he had come to do was rooted in and based on his Father's revelation in the Hebrew Scriptures *and* was therefore extremely challenging to the religious and political establishment of his day. Likewise, anyone who wants to truly follow Jesus would not be content to be called a "Moderate" because it is those who are *zealous* for Christ, not *moderate* for him, who will love God with all their heart, soul, mind and strength and their neighbours as themselves. They will be the ones who will be honest, gracious, pure, humble, peace-making, courageous, forgiving, compassionate, patient, kind, good, gentle, joyful and faithful.

However, in relation to *any* belief system which denies the truth of Jesus as God-incarnate, crucified, risen and ascended, being radical, fundamentalist or zealous is rightly to be regarded as a dangerous threat because it inevitably means taking up some degree of falsehood to its logically extreme, evil conclusion.

Some who first used the term "Fundamentalist" in the early twentieth century were referring to people who simply felt that many Christians had lost their way, and that the church needed to return to the "fundamentals" of the Gospel such as the cross of Christ, the virgin birth and bodily resurrection of Christ and other miraculous events in Scripture, and general biblical inspiration and reliability. Those so described did not necessarily believe in any or all the things listed above which are now associated with "Fundamentalists" and they could be described as mainstream "Evangelicals."

However, it must be said that many liberals and those outside the church do not see much or any difference between Fundamentalists and Evangelicals then or now, particularly in America, where the distinction does tend to be more blurred. In the USA, the word "Evangelical" is often associated with "the religious Right" as a political constituency. In the UK, among Christians at any rate, the word still refers primarily to theological emphasis (such as stressing active, personal faith in Christ, biblical authority over church tradition and worldly ideas, and missional discipleship) rather than political views, but the way the word is used politically in America has complicated things for some in the UK, given the prominence of American news in British media.

So are there ways in which we *should* "take the Bible literally"? I would suggest we should indeed, if "taking it literally" means:

1. Believing that the writers' presentation of God's commands, actions and character are trustworthy and reliable.

2. Believing that, in the light of the particular literary genre the writer is using, Scripture conveys the degree of focussed precision the writer intends, and in particular, having a readiness to read material that the writer purports to be theologically trustworthy historical narrative, as such.

3. Believing that it is possible to say "the Bible says" when addressing a matter of pastoral exhortation, a doctrinal issue or ethical situation (although not necessarily by simple quoting of individual verses as "proof texts")

4. Believing the accounts of the miraculous and the supernatural in Scripture.

5. Believing that the Bible speaks to matters crucial to our salvation and is the uniquely definitive revelation of God, Father, Son and Holy Spirit, on which we can stake our lives and our eternal futures.

I rejoice to say along with the Psalmist that "the word of the Lord is flawless"[35] and to believe the apostle Paul's scriptural witness that

> "All Scripture is God-breathed and is useful for teaching, rebuking, correcting and training in righteousness so that the man of God may be thoroughly equipped for every good work."[36]

Jesus gave his stamp to the authority of the Hebrew Scriptures and to the message his disciples were to prophesy in the power of the Holy Spirit.[37] The apostle Peter, who recognized Paul's prophetic writing as Holy Scripture,[38] said

---

35. Psalm 18:30
36. Second Timothy 3:16
37. See previous chapter
38. Second Peter 3:16

"We also have the prophetic message as something *completely reliable*, and you will do well to pay attention to it, as to a light shining in a dark place, until the day dawns and the morning star rises in your hearts. *Above all, you must understand that no prophecy of Scripture came about by the prophet's own interpretation of things. For prophecy never had its origin in the human will, but prophets, though human, spoke from God as they were carried along by the Holy Spirit.*"[39]

---

39. Ibid. 1:19–21

Chapter 30

A Final Word

"God is good, all the time. All the time, God is good."

This book has been an essentially reactive one, a response to a list of accusations about the God revealed in the Bible. There *are* passages of Scripture which are difficult and uncomfortable, but there is so much which should lead us to believe in the goodness of God and therefore trust him when the goodness of some of his commands and actions is not immediately appreciated. As the great preacher Spurgeon said, "God is too good to be unkind and too wise to be mistaken. When we cannot trace his hand, we must trust his heart."

Had the Israelites fully obeyed the commands and laws given by God, then they would have become established as an uncontestably shining light in the world, surpassing every other society in community cohesion, reverence for life, sexual purity, healthy stable families, wholesome creativity, dignified work and provision for rest and recreation for all, justice and equity, mercy, compassion for the vulnerable, and care for the environment.

In humility they would have observed the Passover festival[1] and remembered their former status as slaves and therefore shown kindness to foreigners and orphans.[2] Prisoners of war would not have been tortured or

---
1. Exodus 12:14–20
2. Deuteronomy 24:17–18

killed as they were by the pagan nations but treated fairly and with respect, subject to forced labor but given Sabbath rest like free citizens.[3] There would have been honor for the elderly, no murder, adultery, theft, lying, or envy of what others possessed.[4] All debts would have been cancelled every seven years[5] allowing indentured servants to be released from their obligations,[6] with generous gifts on their departure.[7]

Women would not have been used as objects of male lust and then discarded.[8] Widows and orphans would have been protected and looked after by the community with no-one taking advantage of them.[9] No one would have profiteered from a fellow citizen having to borrow for basic needs,[10] or kept a cloak taken in pledge after sunset.[11] No-one would have spread slander,[12] given false testimony in court no matter the pressures on them to curry favor with the powerful or look good in front of the crowd.[13] Even people who were in conflict with one another would have helped each other when in difficulty or made sure their property was safe. There would have been even-handed justice for everyone, whatever their wealth or lack of it, zero corruption, and no ill-treatment of foreigners.[14]

A generous safety net would have been provided for widows and orphans and asylum seekers,[15] and indeed there would have been no one who was poor in the sense of being deprived of things necessary for a healthy and enjoyable life.[16] Community festivals and family responsibility would have ensured there was no loneliness and social isolation, something that is at epidemic levels in Western society today. There would have been a healthy rhythm of life based around the Sabbath principle. The same principle operated to prevent over-intensive farming of land.

3. Deuteronomy 5:14–15; Exodus 23:12
4. Exodus 20:12–17
5. Deuteronomy 15:1
6. Exodus 21:2
7. Deuteronomy 15:12–15
8. Exodus 22:16
9. Ibid. 22:22–27
10. Ibid. 22:25
11. Ibid. 22:26–27
12. Leviticus 19:16
13. Exodus 23:1–3
14. Exodus 23:4–9
15. Leviticus 19:9–10, 23:22; Deuteronomy 24:19–22
16. Deuteronomy 15:4–5

There would have been no fraud,[17] no delayed payment of wages for the poor,[18] no lack of consideration for others as regards health and safety,[19] and proper standards for the consumer would have been guaranteed.[20] If people had a problem with something someone else had done they would not have "hated them in their hearts" but shared frankly the issue so that there could be just resolution.[21] There would have been no degrading idolatry[22] or dabbling in the occult[23] There would have been no depraved sexual acts.[24] Children and young people would have grown up with a healthy and confident sexuality. There would have been no prostitution.[25] Land would have reverted to the original owners and their descendants every fifty years at the Jubilee, limiting any growth of wealth inequality and preventing divisions in society between haves and have-nots.[26]

When Jesus was asked what the greatest commandment was and what must be done to inherit eternal life, he affirmed that there could be nothing more important than "loving God with all our heart, soul, mind and strength" and "loving our neighbor as ourselves," on which all ethical conduct depends.[27] These commands were taken from Deuteronomy 6:5 and Leviticus19:18. A society where the most fundamental of its laws involved loving other people as yourself and where this command was consistently obeyed would be the most wonderful of societies. Yes, the people failed to keep this command necessitating the coming of Christ to enable people to be born again of the Spirit, but the command reflected the goodness of God in his desire for human flourishing.

So, in contrast to the direct slurs thrown against him by Dawkins and Barker, and the doubts of some within the church, the God of the Old Testament revelation is the most marvelously *good* character in the universe. He created a wonderful world. All his laws were just and in keeping them there would have been great reward for the Israelites. He is faithful to his

17. Leviticus 19:13
18. Ibid.
19. Ibid. 19:16b
20. Ibid. 19:35–36
21. Ibid. 19:17
22. Exodus 20:4
23. Leviticus 19:31
24. Ibid. 18
25. Ibid. 19:29
26. Ibid. 25
27. Matthew 22:36–40; Luke 10:25–28

promises, longsuffering and gracious, forgiving and merciful. The New Testament announces the fulfillment of everything promised in the Old, through its witness to the Son of God who died for our sins, rose from the dead, ascended to heaven and will return to judge the world and bring his kingdom rule to completion. Both testaments reveal how amazingly good this God is, who has led us, as his children by faith in Christ, into the glorious freedom of his kingdom. Citing Psalm 145 is a fitting way to close this book. Like everything else in the Old Testament, it truly and authentically speaks of the character of the God Christians worship.

> [1] I will exalt you, my God the King;
> I will praise your name for ever and ever.
> [2] Every day I will praise you
> and extol your name for ever and ever.
> [3] Great is the Lord and most worthy of praise;
> his greatness no one can fathom.
> [4] One generation commends your works to another;
> they tell of your mighty acts.
> [5] They speak of the glorious splendor of your majesty—
> and I will meditate on your wonderful works.
> [6] They tell of the power of your awesome works—
> and I will proclaim your great deeds.
> [7] They celebrate your abundant goodness
> and joyfully sing of your righteousness.
> [8] The Lord is gracious and compassionate,
> slow to anger and rich in love.
> [9] The Lord is good to all;
> he has compassion on all he has made.
> [10] All your works praise you, Lord;
> your faithful people extol you.
> [11] They tell of the glory of your kingdom
> and speak of your might,
> [12] so that all people may know of your mighty acts
> and the glorious splendor of your kingdom.
> [13] Your kingdom is an everlasting kingdom,
> and your dominion endures through all generations.
> The Lord is trustworthy in all he promises
> and faithful in all he does.
> [14] The Lord upholds all who fall
> and lifts up all who are bowed down.
> [15] The eyes of all look to you,
> and you give them their food at the proper time.
> [16] You open your hand

and satisfy the desires of every living thing.
[17] The Lord is righteous in all his ways
and faithful in all he does.
[18] The Lord is near to all who call on him,
to all who call on him in truth.
[19] He fulfills the desires of those who fear him;
he hears their cry and saves them.
[20] The Lord watches over all who love him,
but all the wicked he will destroy.
[21] My mouth will speak in praise of the Lord.
Let every creature praise his holy name
for ever and ever.
Amen!

Bibliography

Allberry, Sam. *Is God Anti-Gay?* Epsom: The Good Book Company, 2013.
Barker, Dan. *God: The Most Unpleasant Character in all Fiction*, New York: Sterling, 2014.
Blanchard. John: *Does God believe in Atheists?* Darlington: Evangelical, 2000.
Bergner, Mario. *Setting Love in Order. Hope and Healing for the Homosexual*, Grand Rapids: Baker, 1995.
Boyd, Gregory A; Green, Joel B; Reichenbach, Bruce R; and Schreiner, Thomas R, *The Nature of the Atonement, Four Views*, Downers Grove: Inter Varsity Press, 2006.
Burnhope, Stephen. *Atonement and the New Perspective*, Eugene: Wipf and Stock (Pickwick), 2018.
Chalke, Steve and Mann, Alan. *The Lost Message of Jesus,* Grand Rapids: Zondervan, 2003.
Copan, Paul. *Is God a Moral Monster? Making Sense of the Old Testament God*, Grand Rapids: Baker, 2011.
Copan, Paul and Flannagan, Matthew. *Did God Really Command Genocide? Coming to Terms with the Justice of God*, Grand Rapids: Baker, 2014.
Cowles, C.S; Gard, Daniel L; Longman III, Tremper; Merrill, Eugene H *Show No Mercy, Four Views on God and Canaanite Genocide*, Grand Rapids: Zondervan, 2003.
Dawkins, Richard. *The God Delusion,* London: Black Swan (Tenth Anniversary Edition), 2016.
———. *Outgrowing God, A Beginner's Guide*, London: Bantam, 2019.
Edwards David L, Stott J.R.W. *Evangelical Essentials, A Liberal–Evangelical Dialogue*, Inter Varsity Press, 1989.
Gagnon, Robert. *The Bible and Homosexual Practice, Texts and Hermeneutics*, Nashville: Abingdon, 2001.
Golding, William. *Lord of the Flies*, London: Faber, 1954.
Goldingay, John. *Do We Need the New Testament?* Downers Grove: Inter Varsity Press, 2015.
Gregory, Ian Stuart, *No Sex Please We're Single, The Search for a Marriage Partner*, Eastbourne: 1997.
Guinness, Michele. *Is God Good for Women?* London: Hodder and Stoughton, 1997.
———. *Woman, The Full Story*, Grand Rapids: Zondervan, 2003.
Holland, Tom. *Dominion, The Making of the Western Mind*, Little, Brown, 2019.
Jacob, Alex. *Enlargement Theology*, Saffron Walden: Glory to God, 2010.
Jeffery, Steve; Ovey, Mike; and Sach, Andrew, *Pierced For Our Transgressions, Recovering the Glory of Penal Substitution*, Nottingham: IVP, 2007.
Jones, Clay. *We Don't Hate Sin So We Don't Understand What Happened to the Canaanites*, Philosophia Christi vol 11, no.1, 2009.

Kandiah, Krish. *Paradoxology*, London: Hodder and Stoughton, 2014.
Kirkby, John. *Nevertheless*, Bradford: Christians Against Poverty, 2003.
Kuhrt, Gordon. *Life's Not Always Easy*, Morse-Brown, 2011.
Lamb, David T. *God Behaving Badly: Is the Old Testament Angry, Sexist and Racist?* Downers Grove: Inter Varsity Press, 2011.
Lennox, John C. *Where is God in a Coronavirus World?* Epsom: The Good Book Company, 2020.
Lewis CS. *Reflections on the Psalms*, London: Collins, 1958.
Lopez, Robert Oscar and Klein, Brittany. *Jephthah's Children, The Innocent Casualties of Same-Sex Parenting*, London: Wilberforce, 2016.
Mangalwadi, Vishal. *The Book That Made Your World, How the Bible Created the Soul of Western Civilization*, Nashville: Thomas Nelson, 2011.
Marshall, Eric & Hample, Stuart. *Children's Letters to God*, New York: Simon & Schuster, 1975.
McGrath, Alister & Joanna Collicutt. *The Dawkins Delusion, Atheist fundamentalism and the denial of the divine*, London: SPCK, 2007.
Miller, Glenn. *Shouldn't the butchering of the Amalekite children be considered a war crime?* http://christianthinktank.com/rbutcher1.html.
———. *What about God's cruelty to the Midianites?* http://christianthinktank.com/midian.html
Morris, Leon. *I believe in Revelation*, London: Hodder and Stoughton, 1976.
Murray, Douglas. *The Madness of Crowds, Gender, Race and Identity*, London: Bloomsbury, 2019.
Orr-Ewing, Amy. *Why Trust the Bible? Answers to 10 Tough Questions*, Nottingham, Inter Varsity Press, 2005.
Payne, Leanne. *Crisis in Masculinity*, Westchester: Crossway, 1985.
Paynter, Helen. *God of Violence Yesterday, God of Love Today?*, Abingdon: Bible Reading Fellowship, 2019.
Pollock, John. *The Poor Man's Earl, Lord Shaftesbury*, London: Lion, 1990.
Shortt, Rupert. *Outgrowing Dawkins*, London: SPCK, 2019.
Spencer, Nick. *Darwin and God*, London: SPCK, 2009.
Spufford, Francis. *Unapologetic: Why Despite Everything Christianity Still Makes Surprisingly Good Sense*, London: Faber, 2012.
Storkey, Elaine. *The Search for Intimacy*, London: Hodder and Stoughton, 1995.
Stott, John R.W. *The Cross of Christ*, Leicester: Inter Varsity Press, 1986.
Vonholdt, Christl Ruth. *Striving for Gender Identity, Homosexuality and Christian Counselling*, Reichelsheim: German Society for Youth and Society, 1996.
Ward, Keith. *Is Religion Dangerous?* Oxford: Lion Hudson, 2006.
Wenham, John. *Christ and the Bible*, London: Baker, 1972.
———. *The Enigma of Evil, Can We Trust in the Goodness of God?* Guildford: Eagle, 1985.
Wilson, Alan. *More Perfect Union*, London: Dartman, Longman and Todd, 2014.
Wilson, Andrew. *Deluded By Dawkins*, London: Kingsway, 2007.
Wright, Christopher J.H. *The God I Don't Understand*, Grand Rapids: Zondervan, 2008.
———. *Old Testament Ethics for the People of God*, Nottingham: Inter Varsity Press, 2004.
Wright, N.T. *Jesus and the Victory of God*, London: SPCK, 1996.
———. *Scripture and the Authority of God*, London: SPCK, 2005.
Yancey, Philip. *The Bible Jesus Read*, Grand Rapids: Zondervan, 1999.

Lightning Source UK Ltd.
Milton Keynes UK
UKHW021631160920
370012UK00007B/158